Growing Up in Maine

Growing Up in Maine

Recollections of Childhood from the 1780s to the 1920s

Edited by Charles and Samuella Shain

Samuella Shain

Charles Shain

Down East Books

Contents

Acknowledgments

A number of people have contributed their time, expertise, and encouragement to us as we searched the state for these childhood reminiscences. We would like to express our gratitude to John Ladley and Leanne Pander, reference librarians at the Hawthorne-Longfellow Library at Bowdoin College; Steve Podgajny and Virginia Hopcroft at the Curtis Memorial Library in Brunswick; and the staffs of the Maine State Library, the Maine State Archives, and the Maine State Museum. Also to Elizabeth Maule at the Maine Historical Society; Earle Shettleworth, director of the Maine Historic Preservation Commission; and the staffs at the Portland Room of the Portland Public Library, the Corinna Library, the Sangerville Historical Society, the Pejepscot Historical Society, and the Northeast Folklore Archives. Our thanks also to Nathan Lipfert at the Maine Maritime Museum; Eleanor Richardson; June Coffin, daughter-in-law of Robert P.T. Coffin; Jane Radcliffe, curator of the "Maine-ly Children" exhibit at the Maine State Museum; Laura Dunham, daughter of Hazel Hall; and Virginia Halonen, Virginia Perkins's granddaughter, who all have been generous in sharing their knowledge.

Girl with Flowers, Kingfield, Maine, c. 1905. *Photograph by Chansonetta Stanley Emmons. Collection of Marius and Mildred Peladeau.*

General Introduction

This collection of twenty-two autobiographies of young Mainers growing up over the past 150 years is offered as a contribution to the social history of Maine. It will also introduce the reader to an interesting group of Maine people. Our first story concerns a boy born on Martha's Vineyard in 1785 whose migrating family brought him to Brooksville in the District of Maine when he was just a year old. Our last reporters of Maine childhood days are still living. Nearly half of our contributors are men and women who have written other books besides the memoirs from which their contributions are taken. The others are obscure, one-book writers. Five of our contributors are people who are remembering their early years and dictating to a collaborator. One entry is a poem. None is fictional. Or, to refine that last statement, we trust that our storytellers are telling the truth, even though they are reporting as adults and using the same selective memory that we all use when we recall for the record our younger days. In part we base our confidence that we are getting the truth on Robert Burns's warning to all family gatherings: "A chield's amang you takin' notes."

We arbitrarily have defined childhood as ending at fifteen. However, as the reader will discover, some Maine children at that age had been on their own for half a dozen years. In a recent history of Paris Hill, Martin Dibner, has included this item from The *Oxford Democrat* in 1908:

Harold, 8 years and Robert, age 7, sons of Gilbert E. Shaw, have cut one-and-one-half cords of wood and drawn it to the

1

house on their hand sleds since school closed last winter. If you know of any smarter boys, let us hear from them.

If we read this editorial voice as a typical local boast, we must conclude that earlier Maine families expected more of their children than modern families do. Our stories report that Maine's children responded. A boy aboard a coastal vessel was often asked to do a man's work before he was ten. In Maine farm families, boys and girls of nine and ten, willingly or unwillingly, produced like hired hands.

The family unit, often composed of three generations, makes up the larger cast of each of these histories. The two predominant settings are seacoast villages or inland farms. Two different kinds of rural childhoods are represented: those which display idyllic family scenes on established second- or third-generation farms, and the other kind that display the slender fortunes of families stuck on subsistence farms. Cyrus Hamlin, in Oxford County during the 1820s, and Hazel Hall, ninety years later near Sebec, have loving remembrances of their farm worlds. But Levi Leighton, Hamlin's contemporary, on a pioneer farm in Washington County, and Hudson Maxim, a generation younger on a "lonely farm" in Piscataquis County, never forgot the meanness of their daily lives.

The greatest number of our contributors were members of the generations who came of age between the arrival of statehood in 1820 and the beginning of the First World War in 1914. Maine's slow entry into modern times is the grand design of the state's history that lies behind these individual histories. During this span of time Maine became increasingly a bypassed rural commonwealth as the industrial revolution changed the destinies of the other New England states to the south. The great waves of transatlantic immigrants swept by Maine. Between 1850 and 1900 Maine's population grew by only 11 percent and remained in a collection of slowly changing villages and rural landscapes spotted with abandoned farms. Maine's census figures tell us that the state became narrowly urban, by 51 percent, only in 1950. For many ambitious young men and women the only way to get ahead was to get out. Hudson Maxim was one of these: "I was away out there in the woods trying to beat my way out." For many of our family historians,

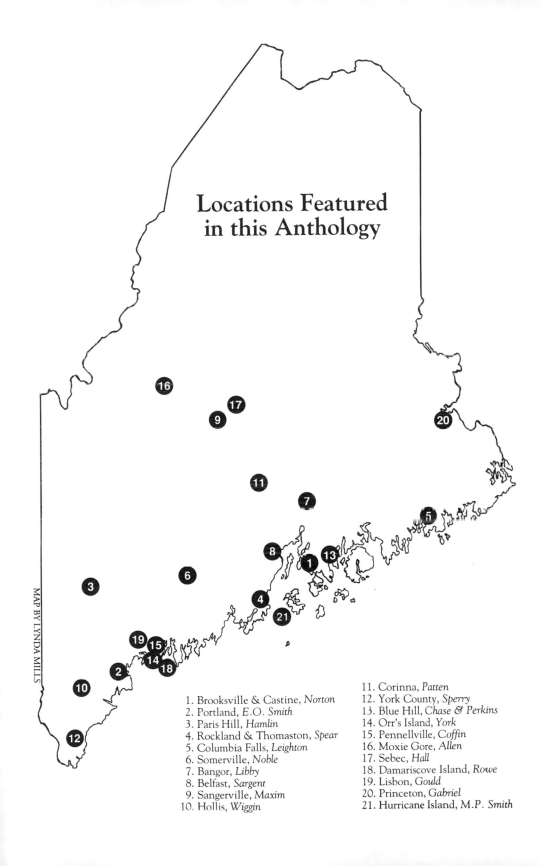

Locations Featured
in this Anthology

MAP BY LYNDA MILLS

1. Brooksville & Castine, *Norton*
2. Portland, *E.O. Smith*
3. Paris Hill, *Hamlin*
4. Rockland & Thomaston, *Spear*
5. Columbia Falls, *Leighton*
6. Somerville, *Noble*
7. Bangor, *Libby*
8. Belfast, *Sargent*
9. Sangerville, *Maxim*
10. Hollis, *Wiggin*

11. Corinna, *Patten*
12. York County, *Sperry*
13. Blue Hill, *Chase & Perkins*
14. Orr's Island, *York*
15. Pennellville, *Coffin*
16. Moxie Gore, *Allen*
17. Sebec, *Hall*
18. Damariscove Island, *Rowe*
19. Lisbon, *Gould*
20. Princeton, *Gabriel*
21. Hurricane Island, M.P. *Smith*

Old lobster traps offer a site for games in an otherwise bare dooryard on Cape Newagen. *Courtesy of the Maine Historic Preservation Commission.*

Maine's moderate rate of change between generations offered settled patterns of household order and hierarchy that modern families may envy.

Half of our writers left their native Maine to seek elsewhere their fame and fortunes, with varying results. Some stayed at home and became famous. In our introductions to each personal history we have tried to satisfy a reader's curiosity about what happened to these children when they grew up. Was the child the father to the man, as the poet Wordsworth believed? When we ask ourselves what was the single common factor that these children remembered as being influential in enriching their early lives, the answer seems to be their access to books. But then, most of these children turned out to be writers.

Charles and Samuella Shain,
Georgetown, Maine, January, 1991

Lemuel Norton
1785–?

In 1786 Lemuel Norton, just one year old, was moved by his family from their old home on Martha's Vineyard to their new one in the District of Maine. He can be reckoned as one of the youngest of the immigrants who made up a great population wave, the first peopling of Maine, at the end of the American Revolution. In 1790 the District of Maine held fewer than one hundred thousand people. Thirty years later when the State of Maine entered the Union, the population had grown to three hundred thousand. Norton explains in his autobiography that his father, a carpenter, found plenty of work in Maine. He "took oversight in building more than fifty dwellings, taking them from the stump and seeing them finished. In this way he reared a family of seven sons and three daughters."

The opening chapter of Norton's memoir brings him swiftly into his fourteenth year, when he was old enough to be apprenticed to the printer and publisher of the first newspaper east of Wiscasset, in Castine. He liked his work and his master, but the sight of glamorous vessels moving in and out of Castine's harbor was more than his "roving propensities" could bear. After two years in the printing office he asked his oldest brother to buy him out of his apprenticeship, and he signed on as a cook for a voyage to the West Indies. He remarks of his first port of call in the Caribbean that he was looking at the first village he had ever seen "except for my own beloved Castine."

For the next ten years Lemuel Norton sailed the Atlantic on voyages north and south, east and west, weathered two fierce shipwrecks, and made one long passage around the Cape of Good Hope to Java. These were the years of the Napoleonic wars, the American embargo of 1807, and the impressing of American sailors by the English navy. Norton shared in many of these national confrontations, and once, he admits, just for the prize money, he joined an English privateer in the Caribbean, manned by a crew of seventy-five, of whom sixty were slaves owned by the captain. He left the sea in 1811.

The second half of Norton's story, which displays little moral continuity with the first, tells of his religious conversion and his long career as a traveling evangelist among the coastal islands and mainland villages of Maine. When he wrote his memoirs he was in his seventies and still traveling as far south as Philadelphia preaching to sailors in their waterfront chapels.

An Account of His Early Life

I was born in Edgarton, Martha's Vineyard, Mass., June 2, 1785. My parents were Noah Norton and Jerusha Dunham. They were of English descent, though both were natives of the beautiful isle above named. My parents in 1786 moved from Massachusetts to what was then called the District of Maine. I was at that time the youngest of six children. . . .

The first event of my life that I can now call to mind, of any special interest, is that of hearing a sermon preached by the Rev. Daniel Merrill, of Sedgwick, (Orthodox,) when I was about twelve years of age. This was in the town of Brooksville, then a district in Castine, county of Hancock. This discourse affected me exceedingly, young as I was—so much that as soon as I returned home I retired by myself and wept profusely; and although that sermon was preached sixty-three years ago, and is so far back in the dim distance, I can distinctly remember this day, June 12, 1862, with what awful solemnity he portrayed the miseries of the lost in hell.

This, however, soon wore off, and I became as mirthful as ever, and used to take delight in showing to other boys of my age how much I could excel them in running, jumping, wrestling, and such like sports, which I now consider to be perfectly innocent, and, indeed, indispensable to the growth and development of children; but, however, should never be indulged to excess, or at too great an expense for their parents, as is frequently the case.

At the age of fourteen I was smart and healthy, and could do as much work as my next older brother, who was about three years the oldest. At this time my father sent me into the field with my scythe one morning to mow, and on coming out where I was at work, observed that what I had done was well done, only I had not done enough to make it profitable either to him or to myself, and in this I perfectly agreed with him; and what was a little singular, this was the first and last time I ever attempted to mow a single clip till after I was twenty-four years of age. A few days after this little affair took place, an accident befell me which I now think changed the whole future course of my life.

While chopping wood at the door, I scored a stick which required to be chopped off twice to fit it for the four-feet fireplace in the kitchen . . . and then stepped over it to stick my axe into one of the scores I had made in order more readily to turn it over, and being a little careless of how I struck, I extended the axe so far as to hit the off corner of it, which caused the axe to glance off a little—just enough to light upon my foot nearest the log . . . it made its terrible way through shoe and stocking, flesh and bone, directly down through the great toe joint of my left foot. It being very warm my blood, much heated by chopping, flowed freely from the wound, and caused me to drop my axe and make for the house as fast as possible, on entering which, my poor mother became alarmed and cried out: "Have you killed yourself?" I told her no, but I had spoiled my foot, which indeed to some extent proved true. . . . It did indeed heal up, but not sound; and after fifteen days' suffering, and my foot having become as thick as two feet, I had to call in a physician and have it opened from my ankle joint to the second joint of my great toe. . . . I was carried five miles to Dr. Mann's house in Castine village.

At the end of twenty days at the doctor's, my wound being about healed and my health being otherwise pretty good, the doctor thought it would be safe for me to return home, though not exactly as I went, he having the desire to have the villagers see that he had made a cure of me . . . insisted on my walking with crutches to the boat at the end of Main Street, in which I was received and returned joyfully to my father's house.

About this time a newspaper had just been started in the village of Castine—the only village of any considerable importance east of Wiscasset, in the district of Maine. This paper was then called the *Castine Gazette and Eastern Advertiser*, David Jones Waters, Editor, and was at this time the only paper printed east of Wiscasset in Maine. In it was an advertisement for an apprentice, and I being about fourteen years of age, and in other respects answering the description given in the advertisement tolerably well, and the physician saying I could never walk over five miles in a day, it was agreed on all sides that I should be a printer. And accordingly in the Autumn of 1799 I went into the printing office and commenced type-setting. A little before this, some young gentlemen and ladies had called in to see this new establishment in their neighborhood, and how it was that newspapers are printed, and in their passing round among the cases of type, or in some of their movements, they managed to upset a case of type so that they were piled all up together topsy-turvy, making what printers denominate "pi." It was my first work to set these on end, so that they could the more readily be distributed into their proper places in the case.

In a very few months I became quite proficient in type-setting, which business I liked very much, because it learned me rapidly how to read and how to spell. And here let me just say, that printers are the best spellers of any class of people in the world, lawyers themselves not excepted.

Here I am now in my new relation, the youngest of two apprentices, the other, Ebenezer Whitney, being about nineteen. And being the youngest, I had every week, on the day on which the paper was published, to take some seventy-five or a hundred under my arm and pass through every street, leaving a paper at every subscriber's door, or throwing it in at the door. Nothing worthy of note took place with us—everything moved on harmoniously until toward the last of December, when the sad tidings of the death of General George Washington came to our village. This seemed to make every one sad; the whole nation was clad in mourning; we all wore black crape on the right arm for thirty days, as expressive of our grief for the loss of the Father of our Country, who died December 14, 1799, aged sixty-seven years.

Our district of country was so thinly settled in those times, and readers were so scarce, that notwithstanding our paper circulated in quite a number of counties, our subscription list never rose higher, while I was in the office, than from seven hundred and fifty to eight hundred.

In the winter of 1800, my master being short of funds to meet the demands made upon him for paper, ink, &c. sent me up the Penobscot River with bills against subscribers to the amount of about one hundred and fifty dollars. Taking my journey on horseback, the roads being very bad in those days, I passed up the river as far as Coulliard's Ferry, so called, and crossed over on to the west side of the river into Frankfort, and made my way up the river, finding about one house to every one hundred acres. In crossing what is now called Kenduskeag stream, my horse broke through the ice just as I was making the opposite shore, which came very near costing me my life, and the life of my beast, too, and would no doubt have done so had he not been a very powerful beast, and by much effort rearing up his fore feet on to the ice and breaking it down, we made our way on to terra firma, having been thoroughly drenched in the waters of the Penobscot. At night I arrived safe at the house of General Crosby, where I found an excellent family and pleasant home, right about where the center of the city of Bangor now stands. In this neighborhood there might have been a house to every fifty acres—not more, certain, perhaps not that. I went up as far as Sunkhaze and crossed over on the ice to Eddington, and returned through Orrington, Bucksport, Orland, and Penobscot, to Castine, having been absent about five days and collected about one hundred dollars, which was considerable in those days. And here I would remark that there were many excellent farms on the margin of this beautiful river. About this time Mr. Waters was appointed Deputy

Sheriff of the County of Hancock, and moved into the jail, hired a housekeeper, and kept house in that part assigned for the turnkey. This brought me into close connection with the prisoners, as I had to carry them their food and pass it in through a square place in the door made for that purpose.

Among the prisoners was one by the name of James Budge, a man forty-five years of age, who was brought down the river from Bangor, who owned a large part of the land on which the city now stands. This Major Budge, as he was called, was a notorious drunkard and danger-ous man, so much so that his wife swore her life against him, and had him put in prison.

This man, by the help of a knife and a file, had taken off the sheet iron of the door and dug a hole almost through large enough for him to pass out; this I happened to discover by seeing a few of his scattered chips on the floor of his cell, which led me to pass round outside of the prison, where I discovered the whole work, where this man had labored for weeks till he had got a pile of hacks or small chips, as large as a winrow of hay, as much as ten or twelve feet long, which he had taken from the cavity above named, and would no doubt have effected his escape that night had it not been for the two or three pieces of frag-ments discovered on the floor which led to his detection. When the sheriff went in, sword in hand, he was dreadful loth to give up and lose all his labor; but it was no use; the glittering steel seemed to alarm him, and he finally yielded, to take lodgings in a more secure abode for the future, though he looked fearfully at me as he passed by, supposing that I was his detector. Some weeks after this, having greatly improved and become humble and penitent, his friends came and carried him home to Bangor, where I suppose he has long since paid the debt of nature and gone to his final resting-place. He was a man of strong in-tellectual powers, rather a good scholar, and something of a poet; wrote a great deal,—made some excellent poetry,—but rum, that demon rum, which destroys its thousands every year, destroyed him, got the mastery over him, and entirely ruined him for this world, and probably for that which is to come.

Being rather of an intellectual turn of mind, I enjoyed the business of printing very much, became strongly attached to the man with whom I lived, and should no doubt have continued with him, had it not been that I had an unconquerable desire to see more of the world than I possibly could while confined within the walls of a printing office. Ships, brigs, and schooners, coming in from different parts of the world and anchoring in the harbor, within hailing distance of our office, from time to time, greatly attracted my attention, and their splendid appearance with the men and boys on the yards and at the mast-head, furling and sometimes loosening their sails, drew my affections quite away from all other pursuits, and I longed to be a sailor. My roving propensities overcame me, and I finally came to the conclusion that I would leave the indoor work of setting type, and go and see what was to be seen in other climes and in other kingdoms.

In order to gratify this insatiate desire, which at times became almost unendurable, the first thing to be accomplished was to obtain my freedom, for I was bound as strong as my indentures could bind me to serve till I was twenty-one years of age, being now but sixteen, and five years still ahead to serve. This, however, I accomplished, by getting my oldest brother to settle up with Mr. Waters, paying him all the cash down for my time, and taking my notes, young as I was, for his security.

After settling up in the above described manner with my master, for his sake, whom I so much esteemed, and whom I so well loved, I consented to stay a few months with him and set type, till he could procure help in this emergency, for emergency it was; for type-setters in those days were hardly to be found east of the Kennebec. This business being all amicably adjusted, I packed what little I had of clothing, together with a Bible and Watt's Hymns, and leaving my father's house, went on board the good schooner "Polly" of Castine, belonging to Capt. Joseph Perkins of said place, where a berth had been provided for me to go as cook to the West Indies.

From: Lemuel Norton, *Autobiography of Lemuel Norton*. Concord: Fogg, Hadley & Company, Printers, 1864.

Elizabeth Oakes Smith, from a painting in the collections of the Maine Historical Society. *Courtesy of the Maine Historical Society.*

Elizabeth Oakes Smith
1806–1893

Elizabeth Oakes Smith was born Elizabeth Prince in Yarmouth in 1806 and at an early age moved to Cape Elizabeth. The world she was born into was a more privileged one than Lemuel Norton ever knew. Both of her grandfathers were Maine aristocrats, one with ships in the East India trade, the other a prosperous farmer with many hired hands. Elizabeth was raised to be an obedient Puritan child, but she was nevertheless a questioning, precocious one. Here in the first chapter of her autobiography she boasts, "I cannot remember a time when I could not read." As she wrote about being a child in an adult society on the edge of the eighteenth century, she was a woman in her late seventies seeking to understand how those years influenced her long and productive life as a leading American intellectual during four decades of the nineteenth century. She is forgotten now as a writer and a social reformer, but her contributions do not deserve to remain unnoticed, especially during the modern interest in woman's role in our national history. She was Maine's first professional literary woman. Her writings touched all the literary forms and tastes of her time as well as many important public issues. She was a journalist, poet, playwright, lecturer, and for one year the elected minister of an independent church in New York State.

In 1851 Elizabeth Oakes Smith was the first woman to break the sex barrier and be offered speaking engagements by the association of lyceums, a national lecture circuit. She was an imaginative advocate of women's rights. An 1852 lecture in Brooklyn was entitled "Dress, Its Social and Aesthetic Relations." At the first national women's rights convention in Seneca Falls, New York, she shocked the Quaker president, Lucy Stone, by appearing in a white gown that exposed her neck and arms. About the right of women to vote she announced, "The fact of dropping a ticket into a receptacle . . . does not look hazardous to her femininity." One male critic of the midcentury suffragist movement remembers being rendered defenseless by her stage presence: "That calm pleasant face, those soft and kindly luminous brown eyes, and that wealth of waved dark hair, drawn low over her white forehead, in the fashion of the time, won many a heart, the homage of which was kept by the always kind and tender words flowing from the faultless lips, seldom opened but to emit a sparkle. . . . She looked, acted and moved the born patrician."

At seventeen Elizabeth Prince had married Seba Smith, age thirty-one, a Bowdoin graduate who had recently founded Portland's first daily newspaper, the Portland Courier. *The marriage united two kindred literary spirits. Smith was shortly to create for his paper America's first national political satire centered on a rural philosopher: Jack Downing, of Downingville, Maine, the forerunner of Artemus Ward, Will Rogers, and Doonesbury. For the next sixteen years the Smiths lived the literary life and prospered along with Portland, which became a city in 1831. Elizabeth contributed to the* Portland Courier *essays, poems, and stories; gave birth to four sons; and, unlike her conservative husband, became an anti-slavery partisan and a follower of other current humanitarian causes.*

The good times in Portland ended when the wrong land speculation took their savings. Their next move, to Brooklyn, New York, was decisive for their careers. Seba Smith described in a letter the means by which they lived.

I have been obliged to relinquish the house we kept in Murray Street to accommodate boarders, which proved to be both an irksome and unprofitable business. I am now thrown back upon my pen for support—rather a precarious business for main dependence; it will do for a staff but not for a crutch. However since Mrs Smith and myself have each a staff, if we walk together I hope we may be able to keep from falling.

They both wrote for the many new magazines of the 1840s. Elizabeth wrote novels that satisfied the romantic and sentimental tastes of the times, also children's stories and even dime novels, one of these, The Western

Captive, *popular enough to be translated into German. Her social protest novel,* The Newsboy, *went into twelve editions in one year. Seba's* Way Down East, *a collection of Maine stories, went through six editions. Elizabeth's* Woman and Her Needs *argued that women as well as men want an abundant life. (The book has been called a forerunner of Ibsen's* A Doll's House.*) The Smith house became the center of a literary circle that included Edgar Allen Poe, William Cullen Bryant, and Horace Greeley.*

Seba Smith died in 1868. Elizabeth lived twenty-five years longer and continued her literary and public careers into her eighties. She had courageously disobeyed the Puritan wishes of her eighteenth-century mother and succeeded in combining motherhood with a professional writer's and lecturer's career, thus serving as a model for any twentieth-century granddaughters to come.

A Portland Childhood

My Grandfather on my mother's side was commonly called Esquire Blanchard or Captain Seth. He showed his French Huguenot blood by a mercurial temperament, was quick, irascible, withal generous, hospitable, and brave. He owned houses, land, and ships; and had our Congress honorably redeemed the pledges given at the purchase of Louisiana to indemnify citizens whose vessels had been seized by French cruisers, we could have been millionaires. Captain Seth was not popular with his Puritan neighbors, for whom he had no little contempt, believing them to be full of hypocrisy and cant. He was a Universalist at a time when to be one was to be ostracized by his pious neighbors.

As a child I was often puzzled between my two grandfathers, the Free-thinker and the Puritan, and could not fail to hear criticisms of them which distressed me; but my miniature judgment inclined to the Pilgrim side of the family as more in accordance with my turn of mind, though the clever, handsome Huguenot ancestor quite captivated my taste. My mind and heart found a nest, as it were, with him, and he praised me more than my other ancestor, for Puritans are chary of commendation. He read much and had a good library for that period, embracing history, poetry, and polemics. He talked rapidly, convincingly, and to the point, being full of ideas, fluent, and dogmatic.

Grandfather Blanchard was a tall, handsome man, a trifle fond of showing his person to advantage; he always wore ruffles and white-topped boots with dangling tassels. He was rather ostentatious about two granaries and fine horses, and kept a pony for me. His sideboards were well supplied with silver and cut glass bearing the family cypher. He liked a large family and had many dependents. Before meat he said a brief grace, but did not return thanks afterwards as was the custom of the Puritans. He had family prayers Sunday night only, while the former prayed morning and evening daily in their households. He was a rigid disciplinarian with his dependents, and his premises were a model of neatness and order. Altogether he blended the enterprise of a commander of the sea with the courtesy of an old cavalier.

Captain Seth and his brother were long engaged in the East India trade, which at that time involved the aristocracy of commerce. Consequently the house was stored with rare and beautiful china, lacquers, and cabinets, and in the attic were long rows of tea chests and jars of preserved ginger and bamboo chairs.

My grandfather was especially deferential to his wife, a stately woman, sedate in manner, and with a wider knowledge of books than women about her. She was able to discuss theological points like a veritable Anne Hutchinson. She was of full size and perfect poise as a mother of ten children need be. With regular punctuality she went the rounds of the household each day, inspecting larder, clothes press, pantry, and cellar, holding in her white hand a basket of keys. Afterwards she seated herself in a high-backed chair, a small table beside her, on which rested her knitting and needle-work, some book of choice reading, and the family account book. These were the days of stately decorum, order, and good housekeeping.

I have heard my mother say that she never seated herself unbidden in the presence of her mother. She used to stand, reading aloud to her, until Madam said, "You may sit down, Sophia." In the households of both grandparents the system was similar. At that time no child or dependent presumed to address parent or superior in the second person, as, "Will you please do thus and so?" but in the third person, as, "Will Father and Mother do thus and so?"

Grandmother Blanchard was supposed to have a leaning to Episcopacy, then quite as unpopular in that section of the country as the liberal views of her husband; but she kept her own council in this as in other matters.

I was bred with thoroughly Calvinistic opinion, which I questioned when a child of five years, taking my stand that if God never loved all the creatures he made, he was not a good God.

The Princes were staunch Independents and Cromwellians, radical in their aversion to Episcopacy. While Squire Blanchard's sideboard presented silver and crystal with the choicest wines and brandies, Squire Prince tolerated nothing of the kind. An austere plainness pervaded the household. For common use fine linens were made, checked and striped ginghams, broadcloths, and jeans. All these, as well as woolen blankets and carpets, were of home manufacture. There was no lack of anything, but there was a homeliness in all.

These were primitive days when the farm was sufficient to itself; the flax was raised, spun, and woven on the premises. My grandmother's brocades and grandfather's velvets were put away in lavender; high-heeled shoes and wonderful stays made of whalebone were taken out for airing. The wool that made the yearly new suit was dyed, spun, and woven upon the farm. Once a year a cheery shoemaker appeared, hammering at his last, and singing songs; and the tailoress, also, brought her "goose," [a tailor's smoothing iron] and cut and snipped and pressed. Then there was soap to be made yearly; and daily the great churn had its cream, and the great white tub its curds for cheese; and there was the screen full of cheeses, the heaps of apples in the autumn, and the stone cellar with its "bins" of vegetables and barrels of beef and pork. I went from place to place with a child's delight.

It was a cheerful household, a large number of men and women being employed in the various kinds of industry pertaining to a large family. When milking was to be done, men and women repaired with white pails to a large yard around the great barns, and in fine weather it was a pleasant sound to hear their voices in concert singing old ballads or the lyrics current at the time.

I delighted to go into the weaving room, where the whirr of the wheels and the bang of the loom was always relieved by the singing of the women. I learned to "quill;" that is, to wind the yarn upon the spools for the weaver, so that I might be the better tolerated in the room, where I was sometimes painfully conscious at hearing the workers say, "Little pitchers have big ears." Here I heard the "Nut-brown Maid," "Cruel Barbara Allen," "Fair Rosamond," "Queen Eleanor," "Braes of Yarrow," and other ballads, which I afterward found in "Percy's Reliques of English Poetry."

The ordering of a Puritan family was not unlike that of a Baron of feudal times in England, where there was constant intercourse of all the members but no familiarity. A long table down the empty hall or "eating room" received all dependents and "help" of every grade. The members of the family were "above the salt," and others were seated according to their rank. The small girl who did the chores of the household, and the boy who kindled the fires, served the tea and coffee and passed the plates.

The head of the family generally commenced some topic of interest in which those qualified were privileged to join. Otherwise, no word was spoken. One of my uncles had built himself a new handsome house, but had no family dining room, the servants being consigned to the kitchen. My grandfather was aggrieved at this innovation, and I heard him say, "I do not see how you can reconcile this to your conscience. You debar your people from all improvement of mind when you deprive them of the benefit of your example and conversation."

The household, including dependents and help of every kind, were gathered night and morning in the large "eating room" for prayers. My grandfather stood over the back of a chair as they all did, and his fine, round voice was very impressive in his fervent utterances, partaking largely of a scriptural phraseology. "Be pitiful to those that are in bonds; let the oppressed go free," was a daily portion of his prayer; and when a child of half a dozen years, I used inwardly to resolve that at sometime I would help the slaves and visit the prisoners. . . .

When I was between two years and a half old, my father perished at sea. I have a distinct memory of feeling miserable in black, and of seeing my mother's face all tears.

Later my mother married a widower with a boy and a girl. The stepfather was a kind-hearted, generous, hospitable man, who used to say playfully, "I am King of the ship and my wife is Queen of the house;" so there was harmony in the household. He was fond of me from the first and instinctively penetrated my extreme sensitiveness and habit of trying to find out the meanings of things, which greatly amused him. When his vessels came into port they brought us something from foreign parts so that our store room was not only filled with the common necessities of a household, but with all the fruits and luxuries of every climate.

I cannot remember a time when I could not read. I had a sister two years older than myself, who was sent to a school in the neighborhood, where she was regarded as a phenomenon. I missed her so much at home that an arrangement was made for me at two years to go with her.

The good teacher let me lie upon her bed for my daily nap. When my sister stood up for her lesson, I used to stand beside her and listen with amazed interest to the mystery of A B C. I never opened my mouth to pronounce a word, but with my two little hands tucked under my arm-pits, stood with intent and solemn eyes fixed upon the book until the lesson was done. No one supposed I was learning anything; but one day when my mother was exulting over the proficiency of my sister, I quite astonished the family by saying, "I can do that, too;" and all laughed. I took the book and read with perfect ease.

At first it was thought mere imitation, but on further trial it was found I could read as well as my sister. I do not think this altogether pleased my mother, who had a natural love and pride in her first-born and did not like to see her eclipsed. I saw this, and had a feeling of shame, as if I had surreptitiously obtained book knowledge. . . .

I learned very early to doubt the opinions of others. The old Pilgrim theology, when I was no more than six years old, gave me a sense of horror. That little children could be such terrible creatures "in hell only a span long," born with nothing good in them, I instantly denied, declaring that I was good, and always was, and always meant to be. At this people laughed, of course, or warned mother that I needed looking after. Others exclaimed, "Oh, what a strange child! Don't talk in this way; don't bother your little head about what is beyond you." My mother would tell me it was an improper way to talk, and bade me be silent. In these dilemmas I used to go to the Bible, and when I found the message "If any man lack wisdom, let him ask of God, who giveth bountifully and upbraideth not," the words "upbraideth not" were a sweet balm to me.

My mother was a little proud or vain of her two children by her first marriage, and seeing me, I suppose with a weird, abstract face, sometimes would say to me, "Now don't be wool gathering, Elizabeth. Keep your thoughts upon what is about you. Pay attention. You really look as if you were not bright sometimes." She did not say this unkindly, but it gave rise to painful misgivings on my part and I used to reply, "Mamma I do not think I am bright." At this she would give a quick laugh and say, "Nonsense," but never endorse my mental capacity.

I used hence to compare my mental stature with that of other school children; this led me to conclude that they were even worse off in this respect than I. The religious biographies, also, of pious children, which I read with contempt at what seemed silliness, helped to reinstate my self-respect.

Puritan children were held to a rigid routine of occupation, differing little from day to day. First, every child was expected to be out of bed-room after sunrise at all seasons of the year. Ablutions many and often were in order, for my mother believed in plenty of water and most especially in the shower bath. Every child was carefully inspected by the mother, who tolerated no rips or tears or untidiness in any form. We all knelt by the bedside and repeated "Our Father" with the greatest reverence. After breakfast we girls appeared before my mother and took our daily stent in knitting or sewing, to be done through the day whether we went to school or not. This stent was expected from the time I was three years old till I was in my teens.

Later in life I found what this unvarying toil had done for me, as I became afflicted with a busy devil that gave me no rest. I could not be idle even when I would, I must work, read, write when others did nothing. In this way, having never suffered from any organic disability, I have done a vast amount of work in philanthropy, reform, and literature. . . .

Mrs. Smith remembers these incidents from the War of 1812:

Only the families of the officers remained at Fort Preble [Portland] with an insufficient guard, when one night warning was given that a barge from the Boxer, known to be in the offing, had been detected approaching. Though the oars were muffled, there was no mistaking the design of an attack upon the ungarrisoned fortification. All the men in the village made haste to the scene of danger; we children were tumbled three or four in a bed, and all the rooms of the house were filled with the wives and children of the officers, who were away on duty elsewhere.

In the meanwhile all the men and big boys ran helter-skelter down to the fort, where the drums beat, and men manned the parapet, and lanterns went here and there. This apparently deceived the enemy, and the barge disappeared; but for several days the citizens were on guard and the utmost anxiety prevailed.

From our house on Cape Elizabeth [on the day after the battle between the *Boxer* and the *Enterprise*] could be seen all that transpired in the harbor, which was now filled by the returning boats. Men came to embrace their families, but though the word went forth, "We have conquered," there was no exultation, for both commanders of the belligerent ships lay cold in death. They had nailed their colors to the mast, and now all was over.

At length the silence was broken by the minute guns, and slowly, solemnly the two vessels rounded the point, and were brought directly in front of our house—so near that every movement could be seen by the naked eye. I watched the blackened hulls, the shattered masts, the burnt and riven canvas, and saw the glittering lines where blood had streamed over the sides. I saw a row of objects upon the back over which were folds of canvas and shattered flags. These were the bodies of the noble dead.

During this period of distress there were some things vividly comprehended by us children, as when the troops were marched away from Fort Preble, Portland Harbor, and the cavalry were exercised in the rear of our premises. It was a grand and imposing sight—the rapid evolutions—the commands of the officers—the movements of a thousand or more horses—all splendidly caparisoned. . . .

One incident of this period is graved deeply on my mind. The village school was kept by a Miss Mary Jewett, a fair-complexioned, very small-handed girl, who let us all have pretty much our own way. It was a lovely day, and we not a little disorderly, when the stirring sound of fife and drum made us all rush to the window and look out. The marching soldiery was no uncommon event, but these were different.

"There go the Porter boys." was shouted on every side—"the six Porter boys, hurra, hurra."

These six young men so filled up the scene that I do not distinctly remember whether these were all. The young men wore white duck trousers and blue jackets with anchors on them, jaunty tarpaulins with blue bands, on each of which was printed in plain letters the one word "Dash." The school children burst into an involuntary shout, but I, impressed by the music and the sight of these handsome young men on their way to battle on the great waters, was silent.

The brothers never returned. The Dash sailed out, but never came to land. Her fate was never known. Aye, the mother of those stalwart Porter boys was indeed a bereaved mother. . . .

At length these terrible events came to an end, and were followed by a general joy. I awoke to a sweeter existence. By this period only the sense of an incubus remained. I do not recall any particulars, but I was awakened at midnight by the ringing of bells, and people hurrying along the street crying in loud voices, "Peace—peace—peace." People hurried out to listen, and shook hands with each other. Women wept and the children screamed and shouted. The boys kicked up their heels and turned somersaults.

All night all the houses were illuminated. Portland bells rang loud and clear. All the ships in the harbor carried long strings of lights, and flags fluttered all day in the breeze. . . .

The Embargo, as the War of 1812 was called, ruined the shipping interests of Maine and reduced a great many fine old sea captains to absolute want; their ships were rotting at the wharves, and themselves left without the means of earning bread for their households.

Mrs. Smith on the Sabbath:

We were not allowed to call this day Sunday. Though the utmost rest was insisted upon, I rather enjoyed the day as I was more left to my little theories and abstractions. Saturday night all playthings were nicely housed, dolls no more to be looked at till Monday. Sunday morning the daily ablution was followed by the donning of the Sunday clothes, and every child over three years of age was on the way to church promptly at bell-ringing time.

My grandfather's house was something over two miles from the meeting-house, and there was on the Sabbath morning the general aroma of fresh linen through the rooms, and a staid aspect of preparation. The carriage was brought to the door, in which the fine representative Puritan pair went their way to meeting, preceded by the boy-of-all-work to open both gates through the wooded lawn to the public road. Maids and youths and dependents of all ranks, took their way across the fields, through the woods and pastures, and over the rustic bridge in the same direction. The young maids carried a pair of white stockings and slippers in their hands, which left their white, shapely feet to gleam through the green grass; arriving at the brook, the youth proceeded onward while the girls washed their feet and donned their slippers. All the way they sang in concert pious hymns, which were responded to by similar groups from other byways all tending in the same direction.

Arriving at the meeting-house, decorous, subdued salutations were exchanged, and all took their seats in their respective pews, which were a square enclosure with seats upon three sides, surmounted with an open balustrade. The prayers and sermon were very long and such as would drive a modern congregation out of the house.

There was only an intermission of an hour at which time the elders gathered under the eaves of the house—the men to discuss the sermon, and politics of the day, and the women interchanging neighborly civilities, all indulging in a delicious lunch. I was allowed to go with aunts and uncles a little distance to the pine grove, where were assembled the youth of both sexes from miles around. Doubtless the usual coquetries, rural rivalries, and love-makings prevailed, but I was too young to understand them, and remember only the lovely voices singing holy psalms to the cadence of the whispering pines.

While living on the Cape, Elizabeth Prince made the acquaintance of Old Zeke, a town character and an old seaman of many years' experience.

He was not good or attractive in any sense, but he was fond of children, having always a pleasant word or some trinket in his pocket to please those that he liked, for he was fastidious in his likings. He told brief stories of sea life which invested Old Zeke with a peculiar interest to my mind, as my father and step-father were both of them sea-captains. He was terribly profane, using strong expletives to give force to his off-hand narratives. He treated me with more respect than other children, never ran after me or attempted to kiss me, or touch me in any way, and yet I learned early that he was not content unless he had a sight of me on my way to school.

In this way seeing him daily on his little bench on the look-out for me, Old Zeke became a feature in my child life, which could only have existed in a small maritime locality like Cape Elizabeth, and I set myself resolutely by my prayers to make a good man out of wicked Old Zeke. My haughty mother knew nothing of this incongruous interest of mine till she was told one of my feats to please my poor old ogre.

On my way to school I passed what was called a shipyard, where were vessels on the stocks owned by the family, and where I watched the building of a ship with a weird curiosity. Here in the midst of lumber, tools and chips, pervaded by the aroma of drying sap from huge oak trees sat Zeke, ready to give me a cheery "Good-day, Lady-bird," and challenging me to race over the skeleton ship a hundred feet from the ground.

Instantly I sprang into the mighty frame, up and aloft from timber to timber, over long beams and rafters, never once dreaming of danger. "God bless the ship," I used to say as I went from stem to stern, then jumped down and away to school, amidst the shouts of admiration from the workmen, but mostly of all from Old Zeke. These hazardous races came to the ears of my mother, and of course were interdicted; had she said no more than, "I forbid you to do it," I should not have failed in obedience; but she spoke with contempt for the poor old mariner, and that aggrieved me.

I studied the matter over and became convinced that Old Zeke was not a bad man, but an ignorant one. I grew to pity him in the painfulest degree, and as I was forbidden to stop on my way to school, I used the never-failing remedy of all griefs to a Puritan child, prayer. One whole summer I persisted in my efforts, morning, noon, and night, with ejaculations by the wayside, and yet I could perceive no change; rather Old Zeke grew worse instead of better.

One morning on my way to school I walked directly up to my wicked friend and laid the case before him; told him how badly I felt for him, how earnestly I prayed God to make him a good, happy man. He listened a brief space in utter silence, rolling his quid of tobacco around in his mouth, and his bloodshot eyes fixed upon my face. At length he threw up his two hands and burst piteously into tears, crying out:

"Now har her. Nobody cares for poor Old Zeke—nobody thinks about him; yet he'll steer right into heaven convoyed there by this here angel."

I was relieved and comforted and ran home to find the word "convoy" in the dictionary. . . .

I was by no means content with my acquired knowledge. What I had learned was thoroughly learned, but it was so little, and I saw boys were sent to college, while the girls of the same age in a family were married, and that was the last of them. . . .

I passed many an hour cogitating plans by which I might more fully educate myself, but hesitated to name them, as I could see my mother was planning to marry her daughters, and that, while they were very young.

"I should be ashamed to hear a daughter of mine talk about falling in love. It is time enough to talk about love when she is properly married."

I heard this more than once said by my mother to persons who commented upon the attentions which my sister and I received.

One night I slept in my mother's room, and with a timid voice told her I wanted to tell her a plan I had. She assented, and I went on as follows:

"Will you let me take some scholars and earn money? I will save it up till I get enough to pay one term in college, and then I will go down to Brunswick, and board with one of the professors, and learn all the lessons that the young men learn. I will work, and pay my own way, and when I know enough, will keep a great school for girls. I will graduate just as my cousins mean to do, and then I shall not feel so ignorant as I now do."

She listened with an ominous silence, and when I closed, simply said:

"Go to sleep, child; no daughter of mine is going to be a school-ma'am."

And thus the dreams of the Puritan child came to a close, and thus down the rapids inclined my little barque. It was no sudden, irresistible descent. With a weird feeling of "what's the use," I felt myself impelled, and yet cast longing eyes toward idealisms, vast and undefined, which I was not permitted to grasp. I was Puritan, blood, bone and soul; by long descent trained to obedience. Filial obedience was no sentiment merely to the Puritan child. A parent was in the place of God, and an implied wish had the force of a command. I, a cautious little elephant, felt the platform shake beneath me, and there was nothing for me to do but to take to the water.

From: Mary Alice Wyman ed., *The Autobiography of Elizabeth Oakes Smith*. Lewiston, Maine: *Lewiston Journal*, 1924. Reprinted courtesy of the *Lewiston Sun-Journal*.

Cyrus Hamlin
1811–1900

In the first decades of the nineteenth century Elizabeth Smith had a privileged childhood amid a polite and bookish culture centered in Portland. Another member of her generation, Cyrus Hamlin, was born with similar advantages inland, in Oxford County, with a culture centered in Paris Hill. Besides books, young Cyrus also had access to a remarkable tribal family of Hamlins—his cousins, uncles, and aunts—who in two generations had firmly established in their part of Maine what Hamlin calls in his memoirs the "Massachusetts culture."

In Massachusetts the Hamlin patriarch, Eleazor, had been a "great reader of history." He had seventeen children, and out of a love for, perhaps an obsession with, Roman history, he named his first sons after the world's continents: Africanus, Americus, Asiaticus, and Europus. After them came twin sons whom he named Cyrus and Hannibal after two conquering generals of Roman times. Son Cyrus had in his turn a son named Hannibal, who became Abraham Lincoln's vice-president. Cyrus's twin brother Hannibal had a son whom he named Hannibal and another whom he named Cyrus. It is this last Cyrus who appears here.

Soon after the American Revolution, members of the Hamlin tribe moved from Massachusetts to Oxford County, in the District of Maine. Three sons of the second generation had fought through the entire war and, like other veterans, were rewarded with grants of land on the Maine frontier. They became men of influence. Our Cyrus's father became sheriff or presiding officer of the county. Cyrus's cousin Hannibal read law in local offices, chose a political career, and moved from congressman to senator to governor of Maine and so to the vice-presidency. But Cyrus and his older brother Hannibal lost their father when they were both infants, and, as this account will show, made their narrow way as a comparatively poor branch of the extended Hamlin family. At eighteen Hannibal inherited the family farm. There being no money to educate Cyrus, at sixteen he went to Port-land to be apprenticed to a silversmith and jeweler. At nineteen he was able financially to enter Bowdoin, and after distinguishing himself there, went on to the Bangor Theological Seminary and studied to be a missionary. He hoped to be sent to China or Africa, but the missionary society sent him to Turkey. There Hamlin spent thirty-eight years and created a new kind of American institution abroad: a missionary-led, English-speaking school (and later a college) intent not only on making converts but also on the secular advancement of the ambitious poor, chiefly young Armenians in this case, in a theocratic Moslem country.

Nothing daunted Hamlin. He started his "seminary" near present-day Istanbul with two students, contesting for his recruits against French Jesuit schools and the Eastern Orthodox Church, which wanted all Protestant missionaries sent out of the country. The ruling Moslems, who killed their apostates to Christianity, were another problem. To feed and clothe his ragged Armenians, Hamlin set up a sheet metal factory in his school's basement and taught his students to make stoves and stove pipes for the Istanbul market. To these he added the "Boston rat-trap" and other prod-ucts of his "industries," which included carpentry as well as foundry work and blacksmithing. Despite objections from senior missionaries who dis-trusted his secularizing methods, he succeeded in importing from America milling and baking equipment and began to bake a bread made with a hops flavoring. "Bira" bread, it was called, and it became his greatest suc-cess. When the Crimean War started in 1854 Hamlin was ready to supply the British troops with six thousand one-pound loaves a day, but, still re-specting his Oxford County Congregationalist beginnings, never on Sun-day. Florence Nightingale, who came to the British military hospital to "sanitize" it and begin to save the lives of the sick and wounded, found in Hamlin an ally and kindred spirit. Turkish women workers refused to wash the vermin-infested bed sheets and uniforms of the soldiers. Nightin-gale asked for Hamlin's help, and he invented a washing machine made of old beer barrels that agitated the clothing without human help. His various industries brought his missionary work as much as fifty thousand dollars a month. *With the profits he built thirteen new churches, each with a school-house attached.*

In 1860 Hamlin founded Robert College, named for an American businessman who financed it after meeting Hamlin and falling under his spell. It remains the pinnacle of his achievements in Turkey, the first college of higher education of its American kind outside the United States. In its long history it has educated many Turksh and other Middle Eastern elite students. Its graduates include Turkish prime ministers, ambassadors, members of parliament, and leading professionals in all fields. In 1971 Robert College was transferred by its trustees to the Turkish government. It has a new name, Bogazici University, but it follows the Robert academic traditions.

In 1873, after a falling-out with Mr. Robert, Hamlin returned to America, taught for three years at the Bangor Seminary, and then served as president of Middlebury College between 1881 and 1885, where he straightened out the college's financial affairs by energetic fund-raising and made the institution coeducational. He died in 1900.

His ingenuity and self-confidence, which were apparent even in his childhood, are summed up in his assertion that "a Yankee's faith in himself often gets him into trouble, but it doesn't leave him there." If we add to that his remembrance that in Oxford County before the Civil War "every family was a hive of industry," we can almost believe that this remarkable product of a boyhood on a Maine farm saw himself as merely a typical specimen of the Maine Yankee abroad.

Two Young Farmers

I was born January 5, 1811. I had two sisters, Susan and Rebecca, and a brother Hannibal two years older than myself. Susan was ten years older than I, and Rebecca six. Two other children had died in infancy. . . .

I was not a promising child at the start. I was pronounced "weakly."

My "head was too big." So the wise old ladies comforted my dear mother, and told her she must "never expect to bring up that child."

I was doubtless a great care and anxiety to her. My father died of quick consumption when I was but seven months old, and neighbors often said it was my mother's devoted care of the weakly baby that kept her from sinking down in sorrow. She was left with four children, two farms, and a large unsettled business, of which the lawyers relieved her to their own profit more than to hers. She had known almost nothing of the farm, and now it was to be her main support. Being of good Puritan stock and well educated for the times, faculty and capacity came with the demand, and she conducted her affairs with great prudence and wisdom. Some of the neighbors were very kind; others were not at all considerate of her interests. . . .

We were a family in which the Bible was reverenced and daily read as the word of God, and the Sabbath was strictly kept from all unnecessary labor. The care of the cattle had its fixed duties, but nothing that could be called work was allowed; and Saturday night, although not kept strictly as holy time, was the preparation for Sunday. The children were bathed, the clothes laid out for the morning, and then there was some reading in the parlor before we retired. The meetinghouse was nearly two miles distant, but it was very bad weather indeed that could keep us all at home. The church was unwarmed, and in very cold weather our heroic sufferings were mitigated by a foot stove. One of the family always had to remain behind to see to the barn or the pasture and its occupants. . . .

As little boys are always ambitious to be big, I insisted one summer day that I would take care of things alone, and mother granted my desire. I was diligently instructed what to do, and Rebecca begged me especially to be careful not to leave the great whey tub uncovered on giving the pigs their whey at noon, for her speckled chicken might get in and be drowned. . . .

That speckled chicken was quite a character. It was Rebecca's property and pet, and was a large and beautiful chicken. It knew its mistress perfectly well and was the pride of all the broods.

Well, I dipped out the whey to the pigs. I loved to look at them and see with what eagerness they drank it and wanted more. I went off and forgot all about the whey. A long time after, I thought of it and ran to the uncovered tub. Woe, woe, was me! There was the speckled chicken, its wings spread out in the fatal fluid, dead! dead! I thought, "O, what a wicked boy I am! How Rebecca will weep and break her heart!"

I took the chicken out, pressed the whey out of its feathers, and laid it on the hot chips in the sun. I knelt down over it and called upon God to restore its life. I prayed earnestly, if ever I did, and I promised if God would only restore that chicken's life, I would never do another naughty thing as long as I should live. I would be the best boy that ever was. My soul was in too great distress to stay long in one place, and I ran into the house to find comfort there; and then I came back to the speckled beauty and knelt down by it. It moved and peeped! It came to life! My joy was delirious. Before Rebecca came home it had begun to pick up crumbs like any chicken. I told the whole story to the amusement of all.

As to my promised goodness, I fear it was like the early dew and the morning clouds that vanish away; but the chicken story never perished....

Our childhood's amusements were few and simple. Among them were pitching quoits (flat stones with us boys), and "firing" stones and snowballs at a mark, coasting on our sleds and playing blindman's buff, when there were enough together to engage in it. In the autumn berrying was a rage. It began with strawberries in July, and then, later, raspberries, blackberries, blueberries, huckleberries. The land of the farms was then new, and strawberries grew as they now grow only by cultivation. They were hardly ever sold—as least I never heard of such a thing. If children from a family brought a neighbor four or five quarts, they probably did it for something which they had not, as butter, cheese, or whatever it might be. No price was set on either side. I remember giving twenty-five cents for a large milk pail heaping full of magnificent blackberries, I suppose ten or fifteen quarts, and the children thanked me heartily.

Our childhood was not without its labors. Every family was a hive of industry, summer and winter. Clothing was chiefly of home manufacture. Every family made woolen cloth, which went to the fulling mill, where it was fulled and dressed and colored. It was fine or coarse or very coarse, according to the quality of the wool and the skill of the workers. There was no little competition and pride in these domestic manufactures. Linen cloth was also made for summer wear, and it never wore out.

We boys had various duties in the house, but out-of-doors we had one task which we disliked. In the spring, before the grass was more than an inch or two high, and in the fall, after crops were harvested, we had to pick up stones and pile them into piles equidistant and on straight lines. A free surface was absolutely necessary for the mowers, or their scythes would suddenly come to grief. Never could little boys be engaged in more useful work. We were excused from lifting all heavy stones, and were assured that the little ones did all the mischief. But we hated the work, and I never knew a boy so belated in his evolution as to like it.

We could also drop corn and beans and "punkin" seeds very early. Every other hill in every other row had five beans on the south side of the corn. The beanless rows were well provided with pumpkins. The land was new, the barnyard dressing was plentiful, ashes and ground plaster of Paris were freely used, and abundant crops were the results. We had to do the ashing and the plastering of the corn. A large tub of ashes would be drawn out to the edge of the field, and the little boys, each with his pail and wooden spoon, dealt out a certain measure of ashes to each hill before the first hoeing. If it were plaster of Paris, the fingers were used, about a heaping teaspoonful being given to each hill. . . .

Our farm was situated on the county road leading from Bridgton through Waterford and Norway to Paris, the shire town of Oxford County. It had a very pleasant western aspect of cultivated farms rising to the hilltops, and beyond were the White Hills, Mt. Washington always telling us when it put on its white cap of snow.

My father, in the phrase of our courts of that day, was the high sheriff of Oxford County. He died at the early age of forty-two as has been said; and the farm life of myself and brother was without the care and help of a father. We were early inured to toil. We took to it kindly and were ambitious to do men's work when we were mere boys. Our ever-watchful mother tried to guard us against overwork, but my brother's constitution was unquestionably injured by it. . . .

Our father left a large supply of farm implements such as were then in use; but after his death our neighbors were always ready to borrow them; and when we boys were old enough to look after them a great many things which this neighbor and that said belonged to us were not to be found. . . . At length everything seemed to give out. The potato cart and the hay cart were utter wrecks, and could no more be used. The holes of the ox-bows had worn enormously large in the yoke, and finally they split out, and the yoke came to the honorable death of old age with all the rest. Owing to some trouble in the district, there was to be no school all winter long, and we resolved to see what we could do. Out financial resources were only sufficient to buy a new plow and a pair of cart wheels. We resolved to make the rest—a resolve at which our neighbors laughed. I was then about thirteen or fourteen, and my brother two years older, with a natural gift of whittling out things.

We cut down in our wood lot a nice yellow birch and obtained two lengths for yokes. We had a board pattern from a neighbor, and began to hew the log to the pattern. For tools we had an axe, drawshave, jack-plane and an augur. The poor log was never left alone; while one was taking care of the barn, the other was at the yoke. It was soon in shape so that we could carry it into the kitchen in the evening and work upon it before the fire, until our mother would make us leave it and go to bed. It was very difficult to work the curved surface with nothing but a drawshave. We heard of a man who had a spokeshave and we borrowed it. The yoke was splendidly finished. We scraped it nicely with pieces of glass, then polished the surface with hard rubbing with a dry stick. It was at length "a thing of beauty." But the holes were not bored. We bored them the best way we could—and ruined the yoke! The holes were not parallel and the bows would not enter. When we saw there was no remedy our hearts broke. If I did not cry, it was because my grief, disappointment, and sense of loss were too deep for tears.

Major Stone came along and scolded us for trying to do what few men can do well. But he comforted us. He praised the work. He said no better yoke could be made. "Make another just like that, but leave it straight on the back, and I will bore the holes." We went at it and made it, but as he did not come the very minute we wanted him, we invented a way that would hold the augur parallel to itself all the time in making the four holes. It was a complete success and our hearts swelled with pride. We gave it the highest possible finish. It was an improvement on our first one and we were glad of our misfortunes. How often that experience reappears in human life!

Major Stone came along and seeing this one said, "Well, boys, who bored those holes?" "We bored them," was the answer. "Then you have spoiled another good yoke," said he. But trying them and finding them perfect he said, "Don't you tell me a lie; you never did that." When we showed him how he laughed and said, "When I make a yoke you shall bore it." We felt lifted up. . . .

We then proceeded to make an axle and tongue for the new cart wheels, and a potato body or box body and a hay body. These were in part arrayed in the same splendor, and we reaped a rich reward from our persevering in the aesthetic enjoyment of these works of high art.

I ought not to ridicule them, however, for there was real education in all this hard training. We derived as much hard training for the real battle of life as we should have derived from ten weeks schooling.

We generally had half a dozen cows, a yoke of oxen, fifteen to eighteen sheep, the "old mare," and two or three colts of different ages, together with the young cattle reserved to supply the wastes of time. We were on the best of terms with them all. Each one had its name and seemed to know it. We really loved our noble oxen, Star and Golding, for whose patient and powerful necks we made the magnificent yoke. Our cows were Great Red, the Great Brindle, Thief Brindle, Old Scrimp, Little Red and Little Brindle—not as being smaller but younger. Thief Brindle was wicked. There was hardly a fence that she would not jump over or break through to get at the corn or whatever else her soul lusted after. And yet she was a great coward. If she saw one of us coming with a stick, she would decamp with such haste that she rarely received any righteous penalty for her deeds. Old Scrimp was also a thief, but a sneak thief, her nose in everything, watching for a chance to steal. . . .

Boys in the country cannot live long without a dog. We went to a distant neighbor and obtained a puppy and named him Carlo. He soon became a great playmate. That was all he was good for he was so much petted. . . .

The game in our environment was composed of squirrels of all kinds—red, gray and black,—partridges, pigeons, hawks, crows, woodpeckers, foxes, rabbits and woodchucks. Carlo was death on all these; but he would tree a little red squirrel and bark all night at him. My brother and I were passionately fond of hunting. We had each of us a gun, "a fowling piece." We killed something of all the above, except "bre'r rabbit." Twice we chased a bear, but never got a shot at one. . . .

I think I can recollect every book we had in our library. We had two large Bibles, . . . one with and one without the Apocrypha, Hannah Adams' History of New England, Goldsmith's History of Greece and Rome, The Vicar of Wakefield, Rasselas, Prince of Abyssinia, Elegant Extracts, Tristram Shandy, a book on farming (and, as I believe, an excellent one), but, above all, Pilgrim's Progress and Robinson Crusoe. We took . . . by combination with three other families, minister's and doctor's, The North American Review. This my mother and sisters read, as being beyond us boys; but I used to listen with eager ears, understanding some things perfectly well, and wondering if I should ever be able to comprehend the whole of that wonderful book. Our uncle, Dr. Cyrus Hamlin of Paris Hill, had a much larger library. Paris was the shire town. Mr. Lincoln, a lawyer and a poet, who became one of the early governors of Maine, boarded with him, and my sisters made frequent drafts upon the house. It was from that source we had Las Cases' Life of Napoleon, which fired our hearts against England. In our boyhood the old spirit of the intense hatred of England still smoldered in the hearts of the people. . . .

Our family was a reading family. On winter evenings one of us always read aloud, while some of the family industries, as sewing and knitting, were going on. There is a bright glow of happiness over those evenings as they recur to me in memory. To my brother and myself the family training of reading and discussion was of more value than the common school. . . . Two or three of Scott's novels were read, Quentin Durward the first; but our reading was mainly historical and biographical. . . .

Our prospective harvest was always a subject of deep interest to us from May to October. Our garden yielded an abundance of garden vegetables. Our orchard gave us an overmeasure of apples. We made from ten to fifteen barrels of cider, and put forty bushels of selected apples into the cellar for the winter. The greenings and the russets would sell for fifty cents a bushel in the spring, the glorious blue-pearmains for a dollar. . . . Making apple sauce and drying apples and pumpkins were busy household industries in the autumn after harvest.

We cultivated from four to five acres every year with the plow. The chief divisions were one acre each of potatoes, corn and wheat. The rye, oats, flax and buckwheat claimed the rest. Nothing can exceed the beauty of the fields of flax in blossom. That glory has passed away from New England. In my day our summer clothes were of homemade linen cloth. Its worst trait was that it would not wear out; we had to outgrow it. If we harvested two hundred bushels of potatoes, twenty bushels of wheat, thirty bushels of corn (shelled), twelve to fifteen of rye, twenty of oats; and peas and beans for table use, we considered ourselves well supplied. We changed into money, at Portland chiefly, butter, cheese, a fatted hog, oats, beans, and nothing else that I can think of. Occasionally we had a colt to sell, or a pair of steers.

At length there came up the practical question, What shall the younger boy do. The farm was enough for one, but not enough for two. Our other farm had been sold for a thousand dollars, and anyhow it was too stony and wet to be thought of for the youngster. . . . It was finally agreed that I should become a silversmith and jeweler in the establishment of my brother-in-law, Mr Charles Farley of Portland. . . . I [kept] my sixteenth birthday at home, January 5, 1827 and then departed for my new sphere of preparation for life's battle. . . . Hannibal and I had never been separated. I had never slept from under the maternal roof but one night. To me the change would be great.

From: Cyrus Hamlin, *My Life and Times*. Boston: Congregational Sunday School & Publishing Society, 1893.

Pearl S. Spear
1812 –?

Pearl S. Spear, of whom we know only that he was born in Rockland in 1812 and wrote one short book, was a born writer. He seems to have been blessed with a gift for writing plain graceful sentences like this modest disclaimer in his preface to The Old Sailor's Story, Written by Himself.

> I am only sorry that the work is not better done,—and yet it is just like the old sailor's life, which might have been lived better; and would be if he could only go back where that little boy started and live it over again.

But no apologies for unworthiness are needed for the pages included here. Spear first shipped out when he was nine, and his life as a boy on shipboard was as blameless as Huck Finn's. And like Huck he was a formidable storyteller. He loved to present scenes, not describe them, and he had, or persuades us that he had, a fathomless depth of memory for times, places, and people.

The events of Spear's story are often as harsh as those that any other early-nineteenth-century seaman might relate: shipboard brutality, fevers caught in tropical ports, near-disasters in winter gales, the commonplace occurrence of men overboard and lost. Like Lemuel Norton, Spear spent time on board a privateer on the Spanish Main during the South American wars of liberation. These are times he will not write about.

> I found out when it was too late the terrible nature of a "privateer." No one can tell until he passes through the bitter experience what it is to be pressed by fraud or force on board a

Pearl Spear signed on a coastal schooner like this one at age nine. *Courtesy of the Maine Maritime Museum.*

privateer or slaver. . . . But my memory recoils from it, and my pen refuses to write the sad tale.

His longest voyage was to Canton, China. In early middle age he found a wife in Savannah. They raised two daughters and he "coasted" between ports from Virginia south. Later Spear was employed as a pilot taking shipping up the Potomac River to Georgetown. At this point there are unexplained gaps in his story, but we learn that during the Civil War he came back to New England, remarried, and worked at the Charlestown Navy Yard as a teamster, steering horses not vessels. Here he had the accident that finally put him on the beach permanently. As he describes it, a steam whistle blew too close to his team; his lead horse "broached," the second horse "luffed up" and squeezed him against a wall. Result: "ribs broken, double fracture of the right leg and used up generally." Spear was back in Portland in 1875 and as his book ends he is a partly crippled reading-room attendant in a sailor's chapel in Portland, where he supplies reading matter for seamen off on a long voyage, or writes letters for the illiterate. His cheerful, generous spirit, we can believe, was on active duty until the end. "Many [letters] have been sent that would not have been but for the earnest persuasion, and sometimes by sailors who had not written home for years. . . . And instead of growing old it appears as though Pearl is coming into a new young life."

The Old Sailor's Story of His Life

The point of reckoning of my life's voyage, I am told, is from the eightieth birthday of the Father of his country. So that Young America cannot honor George Washington without celebrating the birth of Pearl S. Spear.

When a boy is inclined seaward it is apt to begin in childhood. The boy Pip has often sat in the chimney corner of the large open fireplace and listened to father and mother, (for she had made many a passage along the coast, and had a pleasant way of telling the story), and so with Jim and Rufe and many others of our seafaring neighbors, often there to tell of their adventures with storms, pirates, privateers. British cruisers, lee shores, etc., he is determined on becoming a sailor; and to start just as soon as he can.

So when Capt. Jordan Lovett, master of a small schooner, which lay at Spear's wharf, loaded with lime, bound to Boston or a market, stops at our door to bid mother good bye, Pearl hears him say, "The Trip will float in an hour and I shall have to haul off anyhow, so I guess I will go down to Owl's Head and lay there until I get a chance. The wind is South-west, what there is of it."

Now, thought Pip, is my chance.

Father has a kiln afire at the head of the wharf where the Trip lay. So Pearl must slip by him somehow to get aboard. So as Captain Lovett is talking with father, they do not notice the boy as he scuds though the lime shed and stows himself away in the cook's locker, among the kettles, spiders and frying pans.

The skipper comes aboard with his two men, hauls out to the end of the wharf and makes sail. Father casts off the last fast and away goes the Trip.

After a while he hears the captain say to Bill Munro, "Yes, we'll anchor in Owl's Head harbor tonight, and you can take the boat and scull over home on Munro's Isand. Have a range of cable overhauled and anchor ready to go."

Now Pip thinks it's time to crawl out; and he runs out of the companion-way.

"Why, Pip, where did you come from all covered with smut!"

"I want to go."

"Yes you will go—but it will be to go home to your mother. What will Aunt Dolly think! Ready about there! Draw away the jib!"

"Now," says Bill," I shall lose my chance to go home just on account of that young scamp."

"No, I'll stand up into the cove and tack ship and lay with jib aback, and you can take the boat and scull him ashore on the Point, and he can run home from there in no time, and then we can be down time enough for you to go home yet. But I think the wind is canting round, and maybe we shan't want to anchor and perhaps we can get to Portland tomorrow; and if lime's up we'll sell there," (which he did, and made a good, quick trip.)

They run up into the cove, tack ship and lay to, till Bill sets Pearl ashore and then sculls off under the davits, hooks on the boat and away they go.

Pearl is watching every maneuver, seated on that big rock and then runs home.

"Why, where have you been," says mother as she takes the tea kettle off the crane hook, for it is most time for father to come home to supper. And before he can answer, father comes in, and pulling off his peajacket says to mother, "I don't see what made Lovett stand back into the cove and send his boat ashore; but he's gone out again."

Pip eats his supper quietly and is soon in the land, or sea of dreams.

BRIG IDDO

Now all earlier recollections of childhood aside, just past nine years,—let us go down on Spear's Wharf at the shore in Thomaston,— that part which is now called South End, in the City of Rockland. There at the wharf, with half her cargo of lime aboard, settled in the mud and waiting for the tide to come in, lays the high-decked, full rigged brig, Iddo, Capt. John Spear, master and part owner.

It is summer now, and Capt. John wants to lay by a while at home, and get rested for his Winter's work, to go to New Orleans and to Europe. Edward Crockett is going master to Richmond, Va., and Jim Spaulding is going first mate. Chas. Spear, my brother, is going second mate, and Pearl intends to go, if he has to hide away somewhere: so he is aboard and trying to do anything he can,—holding a turn here and casting off there,—and so he is on board when she comes to anchor off the Point.

He is all alive and busy with the cooking utensils: and when the "Gundelow" came along side with lime, he jumps into her and is ready to hook on, when the mate, looking down on him, says, "Look here, 'Pip' if you think of going to sea in this brig, you'll wish you hadn't, I tell you. Why, you couldn't lift a boiler, no how." "But John Barrett says he will help me," I said as I grabbed the can-hooks and hooked on a cask, and sung out "hoist away!"

Now here is the brig out past Monhegan; the sun is down, and the mate sings out, "A light in the binnacle,"—and Pip gets out his tinder-box, flint and steel, brimstone matches, etc., and soon has a light. The man at the helm can see the compass very well. The lamp is filled with oil,—but not kerosene,—no such thing known in those days,—but with whale oil; and with the smell of that, and a different motion from what I had been used to, I was very seasick; and the mate was glad of it.

The next morning at four o'clock, when the pump had been tried, the log had been thrown, the watch called, etc., the second mate came on deck to relieve the mate. Then the mate called the boy aft from the caboose house, and said he must cure his sea-sickness with the oil of tarred hemp.

So with a piece of ratline, he gave me about a dozen lashes, and told me to go into the galley, and see to it that I had breakfast ready at seven bells. John Barrett was there, and in place of going below and turning in, as it was his watch below, he was at work cooking.

The brig was pitching into it quite lively, and the boy cook was as sick as could be. We had boiled salt mackarel and potatoes for break-fast, hardbread and coffee sweetened with 'Longlick,' (molasses.) So the boy, what with getting a 'good licking,' and the smell of bilge-water, fragrant food, etc., became entirely prostrate, and didn't care if they threw him overboard, or what they did. He got into the long boat, which was stowed and lashed on the main hatch, amid-ships, and hid under an old tarpaulin and went to sleep; and John Barrett, *bless his memory*, did the cooking, and all the work that the cook ought to do.

There he lay, without food or water, all that day, and the night fol-lowing; but the next morning was roused out, and had to take some more of the oil of hemp and abuse, and go to work in the cabin, and wherever the duty of cook and cabin-boy called him.

Well, it all tended to call him to look to his Divine Commander; and to harden and fit him for the rough life he was destined to pass. The Lord gave him a taste to learn seamanship, that became useful in after life on the seas and rivers.

As I look back along my wake, it seems as if that Hand had been leading, when I little thought of it. Two or three years before this trip, I remember thinking of the Great Being that made the world and me; and how I went away by myself behind a great pine stump in the pasture, where nobody could see me, and prayed to him; and how my heart was filled with love, and how bright and happy all things were, as I ran back to the house.

"Brig, ahoy!" is hailed from a pilot off Cape Henry, one morning after a long passage. "What brig is that?" "The Iddo." "Where from?" "Maine." "What water do you draw?" "Ten and a half feet." "Want a pilot?" "No." "Half pilotage,—you'll have to pay." "Don't want a pilot, if have to pay whole."

So about noon, the brig is at anchor in Hampton Roads. The captain and second mate and three men have gone up to Norfolk in the jolly boat. Oh, how pleasant it was to the boy sailing, and towing up James River, and in passing City Point, where lay a large fleet of ships, brigs, etc., loading with tobacco for Europe, taken from lighters, brought down from Petersburg.

But whenever the boy was caught looking over the side, or standing with mouth, eyes and ears open to catch every sound, and to see every sight, he had to take a dose from Mr. Spaulding that was not pleasant.

Up at Richmond, the brig is discharged, and loaded with flour,— sails for Boston and discharges there. The boy sticks by the brig, as he has become quite a useful hand, and goes down home in her.

BILL BENTLEY

While waiting at home, Capt. Almon Bennett, in a small Portland schooner, Elizabeth, engaged me to go with him to Salem. I was only too glad to go. Just as we were casting off, I persuaded Bill Bentley, a boy who had been with me about the wharf, to go with us. We arrived in Salem, and Capt. Bennett sold his little cargo of lime, and having discharged, sent me to settle and get the money,—he could neither read nor write. The merchant asked me with a smile, "Are you the mate?" "Yes, sir." "All right." So he counted out sixty Peruvian dollars, worth a dollar and eight cents apiece, and put them in my linen jacket pockets, half in each, to keep me on an even keel; and pinned them in. I went aboard feeling quite manly, loaded down with specie. We took in freight, and got under way for home just at dark. We got along very well as far as Boon Island, when the weather thickened—wind and sea heavy. We ran for Cape Elizabeth. There were no lights on the Cape then nor fog whistle,—no such a thing thought of. But we could hear something, and so took in the jib and mainsail, and lay to under the foresail. All snug, the skipper stood lookout forward. I was at the lee becket, to be ready to right the helm. Bill Bentley skipped aft singing, "We'll be home to-morrow,—walnuts and gingerbread." The captain sung out, "Right the helm, hard up." Bill ran forward to loose the jib,—"Steady so! Hard down the helm! Swim, Bill! Swim!" shouted the captain. "Why, what's the use to swim," I answered, "let's stick by as long as we can." "No, Bill's overboard!" Well, we never saw him any more, the night was dark and rainy. We could do nothing. I shall never forget the look of anguish in Bill's mother the morning we ran into Mill Creek, Thomaston. She had just found out that her son had gone in the Elizabeth with Pearl. When I went to tell her, she was standing in her door, and hailed me, "Where's William?" "He's drowned, night before last." Oh, the agony of the mother, as she turned and went to the nearest neighbor's! I think she could never bear the sight of Capt. Bennett or me afterward. It was through me that he went away, without letting his mother know.

BRIG IDDO AGAIN

One year later, the brig Iddo is at the same place in Thomaston. Capt. John himself has been to New Orleans and to France in her. He has been successful, and wants to rest. So he puts Capt. Oliver Amsbury of Martinicus [sic] in her, and Jim Grant is going mate and Charles Spaulding second mate, and that boy, Pearl, is going too,—but not as cook. He gets six dollars per month before the mast. *Only think of that!* But the men don't like it, for that puts a light-weight boy in a man's place.

We are going to Alexandria this trip, with lime. The boy steers his regular trick, furls the royals, helps to furl the top-gallant sails, reef or furl the top-sails, jib and courses, etc., and has come to be quite a favorite with the cook, "the black doctor" in the galley, and all hands; so much so, that when we arrive home, he sticks by the brig.

John Spear comes aboard. We load up, go to New Orleans and back to Boston. Then to New Orleans again; back again; and then down home.

Now I tell you this child feels himself quite a somebody, as he stands there at the helm, as we haul up around Owl's Head, with white trowsers, blue jacket and new tarpaulin hat on, one fine May morning.

"Good morning Capt. Shaw," is hailed to the light-keeper, as he is there in the top of the tower, "Good morning, good morning, and welcome home Capt. Spear," is hailed from the keeper. "How d'e do, Pearl," but Pearl has learned to mind his helm and does not answer, yet he feels glad, I tell you.

Now this Summer the brig needs many repairs: so she is hauled up, and Old Spree, the caulker, is overhauling every seam, and the carpenters, etc., are at work, and Pearl is at home with his mother awhile.

BRIG OSPREY

Now John Sears, a relation, has a small schooner, and Wellman Spear, a cousin, is going with him. They are going down to Castine. The wind is fair and she has just floated, and Pearl has helped them hoist the sails. "Pearl, come, go with us." "Oh, my clothes are home, and you can't wait for me to get 'em." By this time the fasts were cast off on the wharf, and away we go.

Now the next morning, as we are running up to the wharf in Castine, there was a full rigged brig called the Osprey, lumber loaded, and all ready for sea. The top-sails are mastheaded and sheeted home, the courses are loosed, and all the light sails.

"There, John, there's the brig I'm goin' in." "What'll you do for clothes?" "Well, I'll do the same as I did yesterday, go without em."

Now we are at the wharf, and here is the master of the Osprey, who says, "I say, boy, don't you want to go cook with me to Jamaica?" "What wages?" "Eight dollars and the slush." "Yessir I want to go but I left my sea clothes at home yesterday." "Oh, that's where the Dutchman left his cable and anchors. Never mind, we're bound to Kingston, and then over to Cuba to load sugar, so you see we will have all warm weather." "Well, I'll run into that store and buy flint and steel." "No, you needn't, you may use mine."

John Sears made me up a little bundle of things, tied up in a handkerchief, and in ten or fifteen minutes the fine brig is off from the wharf, and Pearl is aboard as chief cook and bottle washer.

Every thing goes on very well, only that Hudson Littlefield don't like me, and takes every opportunity to have something to tell about me. Hut, as the captain calls him, is older and larger than I, and I suppose could handle me if it came to blows, but I could beat him in getting aloft, or any work about decks: and here is where the trouble comes in.

We are running in past Port Royal, Jamaica, after a thirty day's passage, and the boy cook is gazing with delight at the guard-ship, with seventy-four guns, called the Magnificent, when the attention of Capt. Collins is called, to notice that the cook is idle, when he ought to be at work. So the second mate is ordered to give the fellow a ropes-ending; which was the first he got aboard that brig.

Now Kingston is about five miles above Port Royal; and when the brig came to anchor near a lumber yard, where she was to land the long lumber, the boy had made up his mind to run away the first chance he could get. So when the cargo had been partly taken out, and Sunday came and everything was cleared up, etc., Charley, one of the crew, got over on the starboard martingale guy, and jumped in and swam ashore, to where the lumber was landed,—and the cook was soon there too, to look for a place to stow away. I found that I could get ashore some night.

Charley is swimming off,—time for me to start,—so here I go. Now when about half way off, there shone two eyes of a large fish,—I thought of a shark, and sung out, "shark!" The fish darted out of sight, and Charley tacked and swam towards me, when the eyes showed themselves the second time, I screamed and made a splash in the water. The fish went out of sight, and Charley came to the rescue just in time to save me from sinking from fright. Well it cured me of the idea of trying to swim ashore to make my escape. So I kept on with my work.

The brig had nearly discharged by the next Sunday, and when the captain got into the boat Sunday night to go ashore, he looked up at me, as I was looking at him, as he sat in the stern sheets, and said, "look here, boy, I think I saw fried pork swimming around this morning. Now I intend to look into the harness cask, and if there is any more beef or pork gone than there ought to be, I'll have you seized up and flogged." Now, knowing that I had thrown over some, I knew I would have to take some of Jim Spalding's medicine, the oil of hemp. I didn't care so much about that, but I couldn't bear the grimaces of that boy, Hudson Littlefield.

When the boat was moored for the night, I took good notice that it was by having the painter fast to jib boom end, with the end of the jib down-haul for stern rope. The oars were passed in on the forecastle. So I intended, as soon as the deck watch should be caught napping, to start. But every man kept awake, until Hut Littlefield relieved the watch. When he came on deck, he brought his monkey jacket with him, and lay down near the gangway, and was soon in the land of dreams.

Now all the clothes I had were tied up in a black silk handkerchief, and one handkerchief in my jacket pocket. All my cash was one fourpence ha'penny. The captain owed me one month's pay; but I cared for nothing only to get away. So my little bundle is thrown into the boat; an oar to scull ashore with is taken and passed into the boat noiselessly; then out on the jib-boom,—the painter is cast off, and rove over martingale stay; the boy goes down into the boat by both parts, and hauls the rope after him; casts off the stern rope, and sculls ashore at the lumber yard, just as the day is dawning. "Osprey, ahoy," is hailed by the captain who has slept ashore. He stands about five fathoms away, at the regular landing; but there is a high plank fence between him and me, and he has not seen the boat.

"Now, Pearl, how will you swing clear of this collision, or this *Collins*, which is the skipper's name? If you are caught, you will have to suffer all but death itself, for you have stolen the boat,—for it can be so called, although it is made fast to a spile, all in sight of the brig. So he runs up to a corner of the yard farthest from the captain, and hides his bundle under a pile of boards; takes a short piece of plank, stands it up against the fence, runs or crawls up about as quick as a cat, and swings himself over and drops into the street, and is in possession of six cents cash and a pocket handkerchief: he runs around to the Port Royal ferry boat, a boat pulled by two colored men. They are about to start,—"Will you carry me for a thripence?" I asked. "You go for not'ing if you pull oar." "Oh yes, I can pull." So away we go, and when the sun is about half an hour high, here am I at

PORT ROYAL

very faint, sleepy and tired. I go to a fruit stand and buy two bananas and eat them.

Now then, what shall I do? I have spent my last cent; no place to go to lay down to sleep. The Lord is ever near them that trust in him. "They that seek me early shall find me." So I go sauntering along the sandy road. There stands a loft outside the barrack gate. The loft is set on perpendicular posts to keep it clear of the drifting sand, and is set so high, that such a small boy as I could walk under it, and find a good shelter from the sun.

This loft was used by the tailors and shoemakers, that worked for the soldiers stationed in the barracks. They belonged to the "regulars," and were under the orders of a sergeant, who was also head tailor. His name was Sargent. He was a Christian in name and conduct, and was liked by his superiors and all the garrison. Now he had noticed the sailor boy; so he called to him through an open window, "Go to them steps you see there, and come up here." I was soon up there, when he said, without asking from whence I came, or any other question, "You look tired; we will fix up a bed for you, where you can get some sleep: you need it." Sandy, (bless his memory,) spread a mat, and all tried to make it comfortable for me, and I was soon fast asleep.

Now when the drum beat for dinner, Mr. Sargent woke me, and told me to go down under the shed and stay, and they would bring me some dinner. So they formed a line and marched in at the gate. When they marched out again each one had something for me; and I don't know that the richest man in Jamaica enjoyed his dinner any better than I did that day. Mr. Sargent told me I was to go in with them to supper. So at the time to march in, I was there, and fell in the rear, and tried to keep regular step, which was rather difficult for little bare feet: yet I gained the applause of some half dozen officers seated on a piazza. One of them said to Mr. Sargent, "That lad can march as well as any of you." Now at one of those long tables, all seem to give me some nice food to eat; so I had a chance to be stuffed as full as I have seen mother stuff a turkey: but I had learned that it would be unwise to do so.

After they had got through with supper, and had sung songs remindful of their homes, battles, etc., Mr. Sargent told me to come with him out to the shed or loft, as it was a part of his duty to sleep there as watch, and he was allowed to have any one of the men with him that he could trust. So he and I went to the loft, where he had two hammocks slung, and there Pearl had a good night's rest and was happy.

So it went on day after day. The men had told me not to go in swimming for there was danger of being taken by "Port Royal Tom," the big shark. Now at the end of six days, Saturday night finds me again at the oar, working my passage up to

KINGSTON

in the ferry boat. I had daily gone to a spot where I could see the Osprey, and this afternoon, when the sea breeze went down, the brig had mast headed, and sheeted home and hove short, ready to take advantage of the land breeze, to get out of the harbor. So, without even bidding good bye to the kind soldiers, for I knew I could not go to their place and save my passage in the boat, away I went.

Well, we got up to the landing at Kingston, just after sunset. It was still calm. The brig's top-sails were lowered on the cap, and the reef tackles were hauled out.

So I was again in a quandary what to do. Now there was a long string of old hulks, that had been captured and taken into Kingston, and stripped of everything below and aloft, laying moored head on. The most of them had filled to bearings. The center one had a plank running from the bank, or landing, to the bows; and aboard that old hulk, alone, sitting on the pall bits, is Pearl, and about as lonesome a boy as ever was,—till after dark he is there.

Now as soon as all daylight had disappeared, I went up along the head of the wharves, to find some chance to pass the night. I met a colored man who knew me; he had been at work discharging our brig. He said, "Come with me, don't be afraid; I will show you how you can keep clear of Capt. Collins. Him bad man." I followed him at once to his cabin, in the outskirts of the city, where the poor slave lived alone. He knew I could read, and I had a small book of the New Testament and Psalms; and he was glad to have me read while he fried some plantains for our supper. After we had prayers, he showed me a little "cuddy," where I could crawl in and sleep, which I was glad to accept. Next morning, which was Sunday, he gave me some boiled yam, and fried fish, after which he told me the brig was gone, and I could go where I pleased; and I could make his cabin my home whether he was there or not. So I went aboard the

BRIGANTINE HUNTER

Capt. Daniel Armstrong of Baltimore, where they were washing decks. A boy, larger and older than I, was at work at the whip, drawing water. I went to work to help the boy, Jim Armstrong. He was brother to the skipper; but had to knock about as though he was a stranger: so I gained his friendship at once, and when it was eight bells, M., I was at the mess kid with him. I saw that his brother, the master, had his eye on me sidewise.

When two merchants were seated on one of the hen coops, "Armstrong," said one of them, "stand perfectly still, and don't move for your life." And still he did stand, for he was a man of quick decision. There on his shoulder was the largest tarantula that I ever saw anywhere. It had crawled up his back from a bale of some kind of Jamaica produce, and was on his shoulder, near his bare neck. Then it crawled down on deck, and was soon captured and put into a glass jar, in some kind of liquor, where it could be seen, and was brought with us to Baltimore, and kept as a curiosity.

When Capt. Armstrong had passed the danger, I thought he would "remember the Sabbath day," and dismiss his business; but, instead I heard the arrangements made for the long boat to go around to another wharf, the next morning, and there to load with pimento [Jamaican peppers],—that was taken as freight for Baltimore, and rates agreed upon, etc.

I slept under the awning on deck that night.

Monday morning came—all hands called. Here is the strange boy, getting his breakfast with the men, and when the boat is hauled along side, he is the first one in her, to bail the water out. "Bail her out dry, every drop," is ordered by the captain. The oars are passed in and the boat is pushed off. The boy has an oar and pulls away.

At the wharf, whither we went, there was a negro slave, lashed around a barrel in such a manner that he could not rise up, and there he lay stripped naked, and a black driver, also a slave, was laying on the lashes with a large cow hide whip. Pearl stands there looking at it with horror, when the captain said to me, "You see what they are doing to that darkey,—now if you don't handle yourself lively, you'll get the same." You may believe that I did. Why, I could lift a bag and place it in the boat, as well as a man.

So when we got the cargo all aboard the vessel, and some passengers, we got under way for Mob Town, as the sailors call Baltimore.

You may ask, "Why did you go in that vessel, with such a man for master?" Well, I meant to try to get home somehow. When I was loosing the main top-sail, top-gallant-sail, etc., the skipper was eyeing me; for one of the passengers had called his attention to that boy, to see what a "smart little fellow" that is in the main cross-trees, overhauling the gear, and when we were past Port Royal, and well outside, I was called to take the helm, and course given by the skipper; and when he saw that I could steer, and that I knew the compass, I became a favorite with all hands and the cook.

So after a passage of some sixteen days to the Cape, and four or five up the Chesapeake, we were safe at Fell's Point in Baltimore. The captain told me that I could stay by the brig if I chose; but Mr. Frazer, a man who had been boatswain, last war with England, and had been in privateers and saved his money, and was now an owner of a sailor's boarding house, came to see me, and asked me if the captain gave me any pay. "No, sir." "Well now, you come with me to my house." And I did so.

The next day, Captain Allen of

came to the house, and as soon as he saw me, he said, "Boy, do you want to ship?" "What pay?" was asked by Frazer. "Ten dollars, and a months advance. I said at once "I will go."

Frazer soon had me rigged out first rate, besides some silver in my pocket. This was on a Sunday, and everything was ready, and schooner at the end of the wharf, when we went down to go aboard. She was a clipper,—carried a top-sail and square sail. She had no cross-trees; only two shrouds of a side, and one top-mast back-stay on each side.

The mate, Mr. Jennings, was ropes-ending a young Scotchman, (that had shipped for an able seaman,) to force him to shin up to loose the top-sail; but he was drunk and could not do it. "Here comes the boy that can do it." said Captain Allen, our skipper. Hove my clothes bag on the forecastle, jumped into the rigging from the wharf, shinned up, loosed top-sail, then slid down on deck and helped to sheet home and hoist up. The vessel was cast off, and away we go down the Patuxent, bound to St. Jago de Cuba.

The next Sunday, we were scudding before the sea under bare poles, when it became necessary to heave to. The top-sail yard must be sent down. So Jack, the young Scotch sailor, was sent up to do it. It was seven bells, and the cook had taken the duff bags and beef out of the boiler, which were all in sight of Jack, when he said to me, "It's well that I am sent aloft before I eat any of that duff, or I couldn't get aloft with that in me, It's hard as a rock." So he shinned up, cast off top-sail sheets, cleared away the peril-lashing and sung out, "sway away!" when down he came by the run. He struck on two barrels of apples, that were lashed near the galleys and stove them all to pieces and knocked the beef and duff into the scupper.

I started aloft as soon as Jack fell, and got the yard down. While I was aloft, Jack had been carried aft, and was on the starboard side of the quarter deck. When all was ready,—"Watch a smooth chance! Look out for yourselves! Hard to port!" is ordered, and the vessel is brought to, without shipping a sea; else Jack would have been washed overboard. We lay under balanced main-sail.

When all was snug, we went to work on Jack. His starboard leg was broken, also some of his ribs. There was a French surgeon with us, who understood all about it. Some of us were set to work making splints, etc. The skipper put him in his own bunk, with leg set, and everything as comfortable as possible.

We were busy after that trying to secure things,—no dinner or supper, only hard bread, that was hard enough; and at eight bells, the captain sent me down to see how Jack came on, or to see if he was alive. Yes, he was alive and knew me; but he had managed to get at his leg with the left hand, and had the splints off, and it was hanging over the side of the berth by the skin, and a piece of the bone sticking out. I ran on deck and told the captain; so he and the passenger went down and lashed his hands to a hook over his head, and fixed his leg again.

So about four bells, A.M., I went down, and Jack, when he saw me, said, it was hard to be in irons. It was hard, sure enough.

At eight bells, the wind and sea had gone down, and we squared away again, and got the yards up, and were going off at the rate of knots, when the day dawned. The boat was stove, cook's galley gone, part of the deck-load washed off, and all was in confusion as is commonly the case after a gale, in such a long, rakish clipper.

Well, we arrived in Cuba the next week, and Jack was taken ashore and put in the hospital, and when heard from six or seven months later was hobbling about the streets on crutches.

We were at St. Jago a long time; for all hands took the yellow fever—myself included—and when we reached the capes of Virginia again, it was the last of January, and very cold, with a northerly wind; and being short handed, could not make a harbor. So we kept to work beating up the Chesapeake.

I was kept at the helm, being the weakest of the crew. I had no rest or sleep for two nights and one day. And when we came to anchor, at sunset, I was soon fast asleep in my bunk—pea-jacket, shoes, and all, on. The ice had become so thick, four miles below Fell's Point, that there was a track cut for vessels. Next morning, Sunday, as soon as it was light, all hands were called;—there were four of us all told, mate included. We must warp up to port.

Holes had been cut at suitable distances alongside the open path in the ice, a line was made fast to the middle of a four foot stick, which was shoved into the hole, and held by the ends cross-wise. We hove up the anchor and ran the line to the first hole, and warped up, when the mate told me to get on the ice, and run the toggle. I told him my feet were swollen so I could not get my shoes on, and I was in my stockings. "Then blast you, go in your stockings." So I went on to the ice as I was, and dragged myself with the toggle to the next hole, which was skimmed over with ice. I had to clear the ice out with my hands, to get the toggle to take, and waved to them to haul away. So they did, while I stood, feet and hands getting more frozen; I could do no more. So the mate jumped on the ice, picked me up and threw me in on deck, and there I lay till the boat reached the wharf.

BALTIMORE

The captain, meanwhile, had been up town and sent help to get her up. Frazer was there with a hack and took me to his house, where they did all they could for me; and next day, Monday, at ten A.M., I was carried to the hospital.

Tuesday, in the forenoon, the head surgeon told me I would lose my feet and right hand. I sent word to Mr. Frazer what they intended to do. He came with a hack immediately, and said to me, "My boy, are they going to cut your feet off?" "Yes sir, they say the bone is all black, and must be taken off," I whispered, for I was too weak to speak loud. "Can you stand?" he asked me. "No, sir."

Then he took me up, put my clothes on, wrapped the feet and hands up, when the doctor came in and said. "What are you doing?" Which query was answered by a brush of the right foot, as he carried me down, put me into the hack, wrapped me up, and told the hackman to make all sail for home.

There Mrs. Frazer, kind soul, had everything ready. They poulticed me from knees to end of toes, and from elbow to tip of fingers with fresh cow manure. Now that poultice worked like a charm, and I lost only one joint on the big, starboard toe, and one joint on next toe to it.

When I was up and around, it was spring. Mr. Frazer told me to stay with him, and keep his books, as neither he nor his wife could read or write, for he wanted to go to Scotland, and bring his mother over. So in a few days he took Ann Jane, his little daughter, in the good ship,

Consolation, for Glasgow, and left me with Mrs. Frazer, in charge of the house.

A Bethel church had been built, and was opened for seamen in June. I was glad, and went to it, and was benefited thereby. It was the first in Baltimore. The chaplain, when he found that "I cared for these things," called to see me, and was very kind, and thanked me for trying to get the sailors to go to meeting.

I would here mention what occurred while I was sick. Mr. Jennings, the mate of the Elizabeth, was still on board, when Mr. Frazer went to him and asked him to come up and see me. When he came, Frazer took him by the ear and led him to the bed, and said, "that is all your doing." Jennings said he did not know that I was frozen, and as he was beat out himself, and weak from the effects of fever, he hardly knew what he did. "Yes, but you were strong enough to throw him in on deck." Then he led him to the door, and kicked him into the street.

He afterwards became a different man; and when he had been another voyage, came to see me, and sitting under the awning at the door, gave me a Spanish Dollar, and asked my pardon.

HOME AGAIN

Now when the Consolation returned, and brought back Mr. Frazer, with Ann Jane and his mother, I told him I wanted to go home and see *my* mother. So, after arguments pro and con, he gave me a few dollars and said, "you may go." I went aboard the packet brigantine, Calo, Capt. Percival, bound to Boston, and from there down home.

From: Pearl S. Spear, *The Old Sailor's Story, Written by Himself.* Portland, Maine: Southworth Press, 1888.

This class at the Davidson School was photographed several decades after
Levi Leighton's school days had ended, but he would have recognized these
serious-faced pupils as fellow Maine farm children. *Courtesy of the Maine Historic
Preservation Commission.*

Levi Leighton
1818–1912

Levi Leighton was the quintessential self-made man of Maine's early years. He was born in 1818, two years before Maine became a state, and grew up in extreme poverty in the town of Columbia, thirty-five miles east of Ellsworth on the Pleasant River in Washington County. His recollections of his childhood are of stern parents, of an ever-expanding family, of little to eat or wear, and of virtually no education.

Leighton, writing his memoirs from the vantage point of seventy-two years, was uncritical of his harsh childhood. Rather, he saw it as character-building. He must have been right, because from the start he was in firm control of his ambitions and his goals, seizing every chance to learn and to do things that later would be useful to him.

After an accident with an axe (a common occupational hazard of early life in the woods) permanently damaged his right hand, Leighton decided to educate himself and prepare for a teaching career. He earned a certificate and opened his own school in Addison in 1846. Not content with the limitations of the academic life, Leighton soon turned to the world of commerce. He sailed to Boston to buy goods at wholesale and sold them back home in Columbia at retail prices. A foray into local politics led to a term in the state legislature in 1854, but the mercantile world was his main interest, and before long he was building his own ships to bring cargo to his own stores. L. Leighton and Son prospered during the Civil War, and by 1871 had expanded to include investments in real estate, a granite quarry, blueberry fields, a hotel, a saw mill, and a lumber business. Levi Leighton was an example of one of Maine's earliest entrepreneurs. He gradually turned his enterprises over to his son Horace (named for Horace Mann) and died in 1912 a truly successful self-made man.

Levi Leighton's town of Columbia, which was formed by combining two "plantations," was incorporated in 1796. In 1896 the town officials appropriated $75 to celebrate the town's centennial. Levi Leighton was appointed historian and wrote the "Centennial Historical Sketch." His pride in his small town is evident. His report includes the program for the big day—commencing with a sunrise salute and a parade at 7 a.m. and ending with fireworks and a dance. His history also offers genealogical summaries, a roster of the young men who represented the town in the Civil War, a descriptive list of the vessels built in Columbia, and a record of "Citizens of Columbia who have gone out from us to seek their fortunes in other lands": doctors, ship captains, ministers, lawyers, and "the nearest we came in sending out a vice president—Hannibal Hamlin studied law a short time with his brother Elijah L. in Columbia."

Levi Leighton concludes his report:

Thus ends our first Centennial history, and the next has begun. We can hardly realize the important position we now occupy; standing as it were with one foot on the retiring edge of the last century and the other on the verge of the new. We know some of the past, but what will be the new? It will be what we make it—noble or ignoble, happy or unhappy. Remember this and start right.

Early Life of Levi Leighton

I was my parents' second child, and was born in the town of Columbia, September 18, 1818, in the eastern part of Maine, then a part or province of Massachusetts. This town was then large in territory, twelve miles east and west and six miles north and south, and very sparsely settled. The spot where I first breathed the breath of life was on the west bank of a beautiful little stream, some six miles from the village, and some two miles from the nearest neighbor. In the little log house, . . . and almost in one room, my mother had the spinning wheel, the loom, and a round table which served as a chair between meals. One bed, which accommodated us all, was turned up against the wall in the day-time. As we were too poor to have a clock or a watch, we got our morning meal by the rising of the morning star or the crowing of chanticleer, and our dinners, in clear weather, by the sun's meridian line. Our suppers were served up by the evening star or the going down of the sun. The birch torch served for a lantern to feed the cattle by, and cut fire-wood in the dooryard in the evening, after a hard day's work.

The third child was born May 14, 1820, who was named Jason C. for a Jason Clapp, quite a prominent merchant at Addison Point. He died in Columbia, July 21, 1881. . . . The fourth child was a boy, who was named Warren, and died in his infancy. The date of his birth and death is not known.

. . . [M]y father's name was Moses, the oldest son of Isaac Leighton. My mother's name was Prudence Allen, the daughter of Gideon Allen. The Bible and Watt's hymn-book made up the family library, and when children were born, one of these books was consulted for names, consequently my grandfathers' names were Moses and Gideon, and my uncles, Samuel, Levi and Aaron Leighton, and Abraham, Isaac and Jacob Allen. As my parents and grandparents were born in the country where there always may be found a plenty of fresh and pure air, and an abundance of physical exercise, they secured to themselves robust constitutions. This inestimable blessing was handed down to their children.

When about four years old I was sent four miles to a town school. This is about as far back as my memory will carry me. The first two miles of this distance was through a secluded wilderness, in solitary paths, over mud holes, only bridged with a few small poles. The other two miles was in a traveled cart road, accompanied by other children, schoolmates, many of them older than myself. Over this road my sister and I traveled daily through the long summer months, carrying our dinner with us. Very few of our schoolmates in that school survive us. I well remember the old-fashioned schoolhouse, which was used Sunday to hold meetings in. It sat in an isolated place, near a small stagnant pond. I well remember the female teacher, a Miss Waterhouse, the inside inconvenient arrangement of the schoolroom, and the old-fashioned way of instructing youth. Could youth only know how all of their transactions in an early life will return to them in age, how all of their acts, good or bad, will continually be passing before their mind's-eye, how in old age the panorama of youth is continually before them, we think they would endeavor to make life's early years innocent, pleasant and instructive.

We carried our dinners with us, which consisted of a piece of Indian bread and a bottle of milk. As our parents were poor, we went poorly clad and poorly fed. Our little feet became sore at times, traveling so far every day over that rough road with bare feet. The bruises on the bottom of them would often produce "stone galls," and the mud and water on the top of them would cause them to chap very badly. Our little feet were washed at night before retiring, and if very sore a little urine was administered, which was a severe remedy. Our whole family subsisted on food obtained from the virgin soil. Our bread and vegetables grew on burnt land. Pudding and milk was our diet as often as once a day, and our children today would be more healthy if they were obliged to subsist more on this kind of diet. I believe that milk is a natural diet for children.

A Mr. Holmes Nash of Addison, built a saw mill on the falls just below, and quite a large boarding-house near it, which opened up a road out from the secluded place, and brought us in some neighbors. I well remember that at the raising of that mill, rum sweetened with molasses was carried around among the men and boys in a pail, with a dipper to drink out of. Here at the age of eight years I had my first drink. No building could be raised without rum, and no raising crew could separate without a wrestle first, and then a fight. At husking and general musters it was the same. Who will favor free rum today knowing the consequences of it before we had any prohibitory law? I visit this romantic place once in a while, and while standing almost upon the identical spot where I was born, I live over again my early boyhood days.

As soon as my parents had made an opening in this secluded wilderness and got things comfortable around them, they sold their little homestead to one John Puffer, who, with his family, had come from Massachusetts, anxious to become a pioneer in the wild woods of Maine, and we moved back some two miles into the woods, away from roads and schools and all the social privileges. A little clearing had been made here, and the walls of a log house were put up by one Brown, who married a sister to my mother, Polly Allen. His nearest neighbor was a Peter Magee, who married another sister to my mother, Hannah Allen. Brown pretended to be very pious, and was often seen wending his way to some poor cottage in the woods, with Bible and hymn-book under his arm to hold a prayer-meeting. These meetings were held oftentimes in the only room in the house, and the reading and singing were by firelight. The seats were of the rudest form—hewn timber resting on bricks. A large part of the audience could not read or write, and sang by rote. I remember a few verses sung at these meetings. One was, "Stop."

> Stop poor sinner, stop and think,
>   Before you further go;
> Will you sport upon the brink
>   Of everlasting woe;

And another was,

> The day is past and gone,
>   The evening shades appear,
> O may we all remember well
>   The night of death draws near.

And at the funerals you would hear sung,

> Hark from the tomb a doleful sound,
>   Mine ear attend the cry;
> Ye living men, come view the ground
>   Where you must shortly lie.

And another, a little more encouraging to saints,

> When we've been there ten thousand years,
>   Bright shining as the sun,
> We've no less days to sing God's praise
>   Than when we first begun.

These simple pioneers of the wilderness were told that to save their souls they must attend these meetings, and sacrifice what little rural comforts could be obtained, and feed and lodge all of the itinerant ministers who came along. I remember the names of some of them. Elder Isaac Case, Elder Samuel Allen and Elder John Billings. Many conversions were made, my father and mother among the rest, and a Baptist church was organized; Moses Worster for deacon, and my father for church clerk. Early one morning after a prayer-meeting in the evening, this Brown, before mentioned, could not be found, having sometime in the night, with the hired girl, taken his departure to parts unknown. It was afterward ascertained that they walked some seventy-five miles to reach the British Provinces, where they intended to live together as husband and wife. No one pursued such religious hypocrites, as no one should, for they are always a pest to any community.

About this time another member of our family was born, who was named Asa G. Leighton; born in 1825 and died January 6, 1872. . . . My father covered about one half of these log walls, and built in one end a stone fireplace and a cat chimney. All of the cracks between the logs were chincked with moss. It had only one entrance and that was through the front door, where the latch string was always hanging out. My father about this time commenced to pray in his family morning and evening. These prayers were only repetitions made mostly in the same language; one or two sentences I still remember. "O Lord, keep us in the paths of rectitude for we are prone to stray as the sparks which fly upward." To understand this you had to stand outside of the house in a cold winter evening, while one is punching a spruce fire inside, and see the sparks rise out of a cat chimney. If the wind blew they would all go astray. As there were no Sunday-schools for the children a copy of the Orthodox catechism was placed in every house for the children to learn. I was an early graduate in that and can repeat it now. I think it did me no harm, for in later days I hunted up the origin of the questions it contained, and formulated answers for myself. . . .

We lived here on this place, only as squatters, known as the "Brown place," for about two years. Then we made our third and last move, which was on to the farm where my mother was born, and on this farm I worked hard until I was twenty-one years old. I forgot to mention, however, that before we made this last move, another member of our family was born, who as named Otis M. Leighton; born July 7, 1827, and died February 21, 1881. We had just settled down in an old, dilapidated framed house when another member was added to our family, who was born March 30, 1830, and is now living on the same farm, having married one William H. Ingersoll. She was named Cyrene B. Leighton. My father bought the betterments of this farm when I was about twelve years old, conditions of payment being seventy bushels of potatoes and ten tons of hay per year, for six years. We had the soil to buy after this.

About this time my father secured the services of a young man by the name of Daniel Sinclair, a very prudent and industrious person, who afterward married my oldest sister, Lovicy Leighton. This farm was void of comfortable buildings and any good, substantial fencing; but by constant labor and frugal living, in the course of six years we supplied all of these necessities, and paid for the betterments of the farm. I worked hard on this farm summers and in the logging woods winters until I was twenty-one years old, a period in life, when, according to the laws of our state, a young man is free. I worked for my parents up to this time with increasing interest, believing that I honestly owed all my service to them for careful nurture from infancy up. Boys and girls nowadays are but little help to their parents, and often squander away the hard earnings of their parents after they attain to their majority. They are not self-supporting before they are twenty-one years old, and of course fail to be afterward. Parents should bear much of the blame for this.

At this time I was very ignorant. I had no school privileges in my pioneer homes. I could read plain English quite intelligently, write a simple letter, and had pursued the study of arithmetic through the fundamental rules. I seemed to have an idea that every man should keep his own account, consequently I procured a small memorandum or account book, making in it a daily entrance after I was of age and at work for myself. This was but the simple beginning of my subsequent financial attainments. This little book I keep sacred as the starting-point of a business life. I had no access to books or newspapers. I knew but little of the world outside of our humble home and rural district or neighborhood. I had looked forward to this period of life with feelings of anxiety, when I would be at liberty to do business for myself. The future then looked to me all pleasure and happiness. I was in robust health, and possessed a good degree of ambition to spur me on. My chief ambition though was to earn money enough to buy a small farm and stock it with sheep and cattle, and secure a good and agreeable partner to help carry it on. Of course this was all I knew of the world. I had hardly traveled over my native town. I had no trade or profession but farming, and that in its most simple and rudest manner. My teachers had told me who made me and set me a-going and that I was born in Columbia, county of Washington, and state of Maine; that the sun rose in the east and set in the west. I had never studied geography, and thought that the hills and dales within the limits of my vision comprehended the whole world. I knew that we never failed to have spring, summer, autumn and winter, and must prepare for them. I could see the sun, moon and stars in the blue firmament above our heads. I knew nothing of the laws of nature, of science, of government, of politics or religion. Although in that uncultivated state I loved to listen to the singing of the birds, which sometimes would at evening linger around our cottage door, of the frogs in springtime in a pond near by, holding their evening concerts. I loved to inhale the sweet odors of the clover and the roses. I loved to listen to the crickets in a summer evening, which would chirp from their hiding places in the large stone or brick hearths, while resting from a hard day's work.

We had no mosquito bars or screen doors in those days; the only protection we had against the numerous invaders, black flies, mosquitoes and midges, was a smoke, made in an iron kettle, which was filled with chips and door dirt and set to the windward of the house, so that the smoke could enter our sleeping-rooms. We chose to endure the smoke rather than the frequent biting of these insects. I was ignorant of the great field of knowledge I was soon to enter. I labored hard, enjoyed a good appetite, and slept soundly every night. I did not then realize that the best of my years had passed into oblivion. My parents had taught me my catechism, but I did not comprehend its meaning. Lot's wife turned into a pillar of salt just for looking around, and that small ark, holding so many animals, with such poor ventilation, were then, and are now, fearful mysteries to me.

There were no Sunday-schools in our district at this time and all the Bible history we got was found in the catechism. My parents were both Christian people and I believe honest in their profession, and no doubt gave me early impressions of truth and honesty. Parents by example and precept should never tire in making these early impressions upon the minds of their children. Teach them in simple, childlike language which they can understand. It is better than to teach them of imaginary things, which they cannot see and cannot comprehend. Teach them that they cannot buy a good character after the purchase time has passed. My father with a large family was in no condition to give me anything, not even a decent suit of clothes, which might be denominated my freedom suit, so that I realized I must leave my old home, the home I had labored so hard to make comfortable and happy, the dearest spot on earth to most every one, around which all through life cluster most pleasant memories. One half of a century has elapsed since I was twenty-one years old, yet I can vividly remember all of the incidents of that period of my life. I must not only leave my dear old home with all its pleasant surroundings, but my kind parents and brothers and sisters, all younger than myself. I resolved to cut my own fodder, and sometime in the near future, make for myself a pleasant and happy home by practicing a good degree of industry and economy, as most any one can do who will make an effort.

From: Levi Leighton, *Autobiography of Levi Leighton, Written at the Age of 72 Years*. Portland, Maine: Brown Thurston, 1890.

This photograph of "Buckskin Sam" in full regalia appeared in his autobiography, *The Life and Adventures of Buckskin Sam.*

Samuel H. Noble
1838–?

We know nothing of Samuel H. Noble, a.k.a. "Buckskin Sam," save what he tells us in his autobiography, which was published in Rumford Falls in 1900. Reading this colorful saga soon informs us that there was nothing shy nor modest about Buckskin Sam. He was a showman and something of a braggart, and, if his book is to be believed, his life was one long adventure story of which he was inevitably the hero.

After leaving home to seek his fortune, Sam predictably signed on board a coasting schooner; he picked the Elizabeth *because that was his mother's name. Terrible storms at sea and near drowning were his lot. He jumped ship in Buenos Aires, worked on a sheep farm, and was kidnapped by Pintes Indians with whom he lived for six years before he was able to escape. Then it was off to England and a stint in the British Army, a war in India, wild animal hunts, back to the British Isles, to America and, in 1864, two years in the 1st Regiment of Connecticut Cavalry. Sam seemed to have been present at most of the major battles and events of the Civil War. He parlayed all this excitement into a lecture tour. His stories would end with a Maine woods scene pitting himself against not one but five bears. He emerged victorious, of course.*

The part of Sam's narrative that is pertinent for our purposes is the chapter "From Boyhood to Manhood." In just three pages he tells us of his poor and surely joyless childhood. He was born in 1838, semi-orphaned and bound out before he was seven. He rose above this impoverished background, enlivened his schoolmates with his antics, became a sure-shot hunter, and at eleven was on his way to the amazing rest of his life.

From Boyhood to Manhood

I was born in the town of Kennebunk in the state of Maine on the 16th of June, 1838. At that time my father was the landlord of the village hotel. In 1841 my father died, leaving my mother with three children, an older sister, a younger brother and myself. After my father's death my mother disposed of the property and then moved to her father's in the town of New Sharon, Maine, where my younger brother was adopted by his grand-mother. My sister stopped at home.

After my father's death I lived with my mother until 1844, when I was six years of age. I was then bound out to a man by the name of Nathaniel True of Fayette, Maine, where I lived for three years. At the age of nine I left Fayette and lived with my uncle in Readfield, Maine. Two years later, in 1849, I again lived with my mother in the town of Somerville, Maine, which is eighteen miles east of Augusta.

In the fall of 1849 I began to attend the district school; and lived as country boys do. The school house was of wood about 30 feet square, with the door on the front side. As you passed through the outer door you came to a long entry with a door at each end leading into the school room. The stove sat in the center of the room and the schoolmaster's desk was at the back of the room. The boys occupied the left side of the room and the girls the right, facing the boys, so the boys could not cut up any of their pranks unless the girls saw them. As for myself I was always up to some prank to make the girls or boys laugh.

After a while the snow covered the ground, and the little ponds of water began to freeze over and there was some skating. I took my skates to school for the noon time sport. At this school there were about twenty-five boys and about the same number of girls.

After I had been going to school a short time my parents bought me a slate, so I took the slate to school and the master asked me why I brought it. I told him that my parents sent me with it. Then said the master, "You shall not use the slate." But this was not the end of the slate question. I made a profile of the school-master upon it and turned it around so that the girls could see it, at which they began to laugh for it looked so comical. And no wonder, for it had a big nose and the hair stood right up on end. The school-master brought the girls to account for laughing and as I did not want the girls to get punished for my "shines" I told the school-master that it was my slate that caused the disturbance. Then to punish me, he made me go over and sit between two of the largest girls. That suited me pretty well, but I was there not long before the girls jumped up with a shriek; then over comes the master to bring the girls to account again.

"What is the trouble now?" said the master.

"Why, Sam is sticking a pin into us."

"Sam, come out into the floor, sir."

"All right, sir."

"Go out and cut me a bundle of sticks, and I'll tan your jacket for your conduct."

"All right, sir."

About three hundred yards back of the school-house was an alder swamp. So I put on my skates and away I went; it being a cold day the alders were all frozen and brittle. As I thought I was to have a sound thrashing, I prepared the sticks for the battle. I took my knife and cut about half way through each of the sticks so that when the master struck me with them they would all break. I cut about one hundred of them and took them into the school-room, and throwing them down on the floor took my seat.

I had no more than taken my seat when he called me back.

"Take off your jacket, sir."

"It's too cold, sir."

"Stand up here and I'll warm you, sir."

So he commenced the "Battle cry of freedom" upon my poor back, but I did not forget to laugh. After he had disposed of all the sticks the school-room looked as if there had been a squall or cyclone, for the floor was covered with sticks. When he had wreaked his vengeance upon me he said,

"I guess you are warm enough now, ain't you?"

I said, "If you had another hundred I should have frozen to death."

After I went back to my seat I thought "Oh how I love to go to school." The reason I did not like to go to school was that I had bought me a dog and gun and they took up all my attention.

When I went to school I sat with some of the larger boys in the back seat near one of the windows. One day I heard the bark of a fox-hound and knew from his voice that he was on a fox track. I could stand it no longer, so got one of the larger boys to raise the window and out I went. I started home for my gun, to which I had given the name of "Old Kill-duel" for the stock was painted red. After running one or two miles the fox took off in another direction around the mountain and I came back without the fox.

A few days after, a black bear was seen to cross the road near the schoolhouse, and I was on the war-path again with my dog and gun. I chased the bear over the hill and down into a swamp where the snow was so deep I could hardly make my way. In plunging about in the snow, sometimes head down and sometimes heels up, I got my gun wet. At last the hound drove the bear in sight, I up with my gun, the cap snapped but the gun did not go off, so I lost the bear. Soon it began to grow dark and I made tracks for home, tired and hungry as a bear. That finished the bear hunt.

One morning mother woke me from my slumber and said there were three partridges in a birch tree. So I took my gun and went up to the edge of the woods, right in sight of the house, When I got there I saw two sitting about two feet apart and one above the other two, so I took aim between the two and at the one at the top of the tree, then I blazed away and one fell dead at the foot of the tree, one near where I stood and the third one went over my head and almost out of sight in the snow. So I was like the man who killed three birds with one stone for I killed three partridges at one shot. I once shot at a partridge on the wing. The one I shot at kept right on, but there was one on a log in the same direction and I shot her.

Well, this page is the last one of my boyhood at home.

From: Samuel H. Noble, *Life and Adventures of Buckskin Sam, Written by Himself.* Rumford, Maine: Rumford Falls Publishing Co., 1900.

Thomas Libby
1848 – ?

In the spring of 1862, fourteen-year-old Thomas G. Libby, of Lincoln, claiming to be sixteen, enlisted in Company A of the First Maine Infantry Regiment, later to be called the First Maine Heavy Artillery. He weighed 103 pounds and stood five feet three inches. The First Maine was being recruited in Penobscot, Hancock, Piscataquis, and Washington counties, and there was no lack of volunteers. The news from Virginia had been very bad. The Union forces had suffered a string of defeats and taken heavy losses during the spring campaign to take Richmond. More volunteers were badly needed, and Maine responded. Libby's accommodating recruiter, Captain Clark, even upped Tom's age to eighteen, presumably in the spirit of the occasion.

Tom's description of his two years' soldiering reads like a boy's account, with all the horrors left out. (It seems to have been written years later by an older Thomas Libby who became "a prominent business man on Vinalhaven.") The First Maine saw horrors aplenty. After a year and a half of guard duty and artillery training at Fort Sumner, a fortification built to defend Washington, the First Maine joined the Army of the Potomac and reverted again to an infantry regiment. At the bloody battle of Spotsylvania Courthouse, out of 1600 men the regiment suffered 155 killed and 374 wounded. At the Union attempt to break through Lee's strong defenses at Petersburg, the First Maine was designated as the "storming column" in a charge that was made along the whole Union front. Somewhat fewer than 900 Maine men participated in the charge; 632 were either killed, wounded, or missing. The First Maine's battlefield loss that day, according to its official history, "far exceeds that in any other regiment in the Union

THOMAS G. LIBBY, Recruit.

Thomas G. Libby, fourteen-year-old recruit in the First Maine Infantry Regiment. *Courtesy of the Maine State Museum.*

armies during the Civil War." The First Maine Monument now stands on the spot.

Young Tom Libby was comparatively lucky. He was one of those only wounded in the Petersburg charge. The record reads, "gun shot, left hand, two fingers amputated."

A Sketch from the Ranks

I enlisted in the spring of 1862, Company A, at the age of fourteen years, weighed 102 pounds, height 5 feet 3 inches, being one inch less than the required height, secured mother's consent, father, Thomas S. Libby, having enlisted in the spring of 1861, Company C, 7th Maine. After receiving advice and assurance from Dr. Wilson, our family physician, that I would not be accepted, mother gave her consent. After having her sign her name to the Government papers I put my age down as sixteen years. I had never been away from home, had never seen a sailing vessel, steamboat, or train of cars. Having an understanding with Capt. W.C. Clark, the time soon arrived when he took me to Bangor with the Company, where we went into camp, waiting for the Regiment to be finally made up and mustered in. Imagine my surprise and wonderment on reaching Bangor to behold such a large city with its vast fleet of vessels, steamers, and cars; everything that my eyes beheld was a continual panorama of a new life. The day soon arrived for us to be examined and mustered into the United States service. In the meantime Captain Clark had new papers made out with my age down at eighteen with mother's name signed by myself. In the afternoon, about 2 P.M., on the day our Company was examined, my name was called. With face aglow I marched into the doctor's tent, where I found Captain Clark who was to intercede for me and try and get me through. In order to make my height good I secured from mother's quilt a large quantity of cotton batting to put in the heels of my boots. I had all that I could get in when I entered the tent. Imagine my surprise when I was asked to remove my boots, then coat and vest, until I was revealed in Nature's garb; a match could have been lit on any part of my body. All fear vanished and my heart beat with joy when I soon learned that I had been accepted. Soon I received my first suit of blue and equipments. The suit, although the smallest made, was large enough for two boys, but proud I was as I marched to the daguerreotype saloon, then on wheels near the camp, and had my picture taken and sent it home to mother, that she might see how her young soldier boy looked. This was found long years after among her treasures, when she had passed beyond to her haven of rest. I had taken in well the wonderful sights about Bangor and was anxious to move on to see the more glorious scenes yet to be revealed, and to meet my father, where at Washington I thought the soldiers all met together, where they went out and fought the rebels and back at night. Last of August our Regiment was off for Washington. I shall never forget the reception received in Boston and Philadelphia. The ladies made us feel more than proud of ourselves as Lincoln soldiers. Many was the time I was grabbed and kissed and asked if mother knew I was out, and where her apron string was; if I were going to drive the cows home; grease well the upper lip (the fuzz was starting); how I would like to take you home. What wonder that I was overjoyed to be a soldier with the continual changing of the scenes of a new life.

Arriving in Washington we soon commenced a soldier's life in earnest. Drilling, building forts, falling trees, picket and guard duty was our daily life. Spring and summer of 1863 I was with the Company on Mason's Island guarding conscripts. Returned to Fort Sumner and remained there fall and winter of 1863 and 1864. With five other comrades we built a small log hut where we lived until ordered to the front, spring of 1864,—a band of boys who were ever on the lookout for all the good things that might come within our grasp. We made a false cellar, the trapdoor of which came under our lower bunk. It was here we stored all of our drawings, which together or separately we were expected to keep a surplus on hand: milk taken from the cows early in the morning, eggs, potatoes, apples, and cabbage, all from Lodge [a nearby farmer] and his neighbors about camp; pies, cakes, fruit, etc., from our sutlers; supplies of beef, sugar, molasses, pork, hard-bread, and candies at Commissary Department, whenever one of our number was on guard at the Department. While we were never caught in our work, we never missed bringing in what we went after but once. This occurred upon one dark night in February, 1864. Four of us started for a plantation about two miles from camp to secure a beehive with its contents of bees and honey, having located the place and laid our plans the day before. Arriving at the place we selected our hive, plugged up the holes and started across the field for a ravine a mile away. We had not proceeded more than a dozen rods when the planter's dogs sent up a terrible howl; but on we went until we found the owner with two others with more dogs in hot pursuit, closing on us as we neared the ravine. Feeling there was no chance to get away with the hive we finally gave it a toss in a clump of shrubbery and put for camp. No one ever knew who tried to get away with the beehive.

The order May, 1864, to join the Army of the Potomac for active service was gladly received. Camp and fatigue life had become monotonous. We had not up to this time realized what actual war was. But soon after passing through Washington on review we found ourselves at Spottsylvania, where upon the altar of Liberty many of our comrades' lives were sacrificed, one of whom was of our camp number, who was by my side when he fell. On, on, I went with my Company and Regiment to do what I could to help weld together in the fiery furnace of war a crown of glory for the old First Maine. During our campaign we often foraged on our own account; whenever pigs, hens, cattle, or smoked hams came within our reach they were appropriated to our wants. While at Cold Harbor I was out on picket; inside of our lines and not far away a large plantation was located, and while inspecting the place for water to fill our canteens I heard the welcome sound of a squeal from pits. Soon locating the pits, I went in with the others to secure one. Imagine the broad smile on the faces of the boys of my post when I walked in with a small pig under the breast of my coat. What a feast! After skinning, we cooked the pig in an old coffee-pot, without salt.

Leaving Cold Harbor we finally brought up before Petersburg, where I was wounded. Finally reaching our division hospital, located near a large plantation about six miles in the rear of where our boys made the fearful charge, a few days over one month found our little band of six who left Washington with such high hopes with only one still left in the ranks; five had been killed, wounded or fallen by the wayside on the long, weary marches. The second day after arriving at division hospital my wounds were dressed. During the five days I was detained there, thousands of wounded soldiers were brought from the field every day, among whom were hundreds of the Regiment, many of my Company, including boys of my happy schooldays. Every day found me administering to the wants of my comrades who were more severely wounded, a number of whom gave up their lives and were consigned to the soldier's grave. On June 23d arrived at City Point, there waited a week for a transport, from there was taken to New York, thence to Portsmouth Grove, R.I. Hospital, which was carried on by contract, prisoners of war faring better than our sick and wounded soldiers who were there. On July 28th a favorable opportunity was given me to get beyond the guard and escape, which I improved. Finally getting aboard of the 3 P.M. train for Boston, with a hospital pair of drawers and shirt received at City Point, with a long gray gown given me by the visiting ladies of the Sanitary Commission, with no shoes or cap, and weighing but ninety pounds, without a cent, I was overjoyed to get started for nearer home. Arrived in Bangor the second day, found that I could not report there. Started for Augusta, where I reported at Coney Hospital. Our boys were well taken care of here and I soon received a full suit of blue. When upon the following day I called upon the Governor, who kindly received me and listened with pleasure to my story of escape from the Portsmouth Grove Hospital, with many kind wishes he pressed in my hand a five-dollar note and stated I should receive a thirty days' furlough, which I did, and for home to see the loved ones. I was glad to go. At the expiration of the thirty days returned to Augusta, where I remained until April, 1865, when I received my discharge on account of my wounds.

From: Thomas A. Libby, "A Sketch from the Ranks," in *The First Maine Heavy Artillery 1862–1865*. Portland, Maine: Horace H. Shaw, 1903.

Dudley Allen Sargent
1849–1924

Dudley Allen Sargent was a man with a mission: to devote "much of my time and all of my energy to the development of physical education in America."

Sargent, who was born in Belfast, Maine, in 1849, took several false steps before embarking on a career in physical education. In 1864, following the tradition of a coastal Maine boy, he shipped out on a coasting schooner, the Moses Eddy, *a stolid, cumbersome vessel carrying a load of barrel staves from Belfast up the Hudson to West Point. The return cargo was eight hundred finished barrels filled with cement to be used for the fortifications along the Maine coast. The pay was fourteen dollars a month, the work was hard, and he was desperately homesick. He came ashore at the end of the voyage determined never to go to sea again.*

Dudley Sargent also briefly considered the law and the ministry as professions, but his interest in physical fitness prevailed, and following a brief career as a gymnast with several traveling circuses, he accepted the post of Director of the Gymnasium at Bowdoin College. He was twenty years old and had never finished high school, but his sense of mission led him not only to develop a pioneering program at Bowdoin but also to be tutored at Brunswick High School in order to enroll in Bowdoin as a freshman in 1871. At Bowdoin, as elsewhere, he found opposition to a physical education program. It was considered effete and extraneous. There were no organized sports in place at the time, and attendance at gym classes was voluntary. Sargent changed all that.

After his graduation from Bowdoin, Sargent, who by now was something of a specialist in physical education techniques and equipment, went to Yale, where he ran a similar program while simultaneously attending

Dr. Sargent's 1927 autobiography included this photograph.

Yale Medical School, from which he graduated in 1878. Sargent found no takers for his plan for a course in education that would teach according to his principles and his curriculum, so he went to New York and opened the Hygienic Institute of Physical Culture. The institute offered specialized physical education programs for people of all ages, abilities, and disabilities. It was a success, but he did not renew his rent on the building and instead took off for a summer of lecturing and teaching at Chautauqua. In the fall of 1879 he began what was to be a forty-year career at Harvard when he was appointed director of the Gymnasium and associate professor of Physical Training.

During these years at Harvard, Dudley Sargent continued to expand on the physical education curriculum, initiating detailed physical examinations of the students as a basis for designing a program planned for the whole person and inventing and improving the apparatus used for these programs. He ventured into the commercial end of the field, marketing his own designs for Indian clubs, parallel bars, etc., but found the world of business too difficult and distracting. Sargent was importuned by "The Society For The Collegiate Instruction of Women," now Radcliffe College, to organize a department of physical culture. In 1881 he opened the Sanatory Gymnasium, later to become the Sargent School for Physical Education, in the realization that properly trained physical education teachers were essential to well-run programs. Years later the Sargent School was to become a part of Boston University and now is known as the Sargent School of Allied Health Professions. This school now awards undergraduate and graduate degrees in such fields as occupational and physical therapy, rehabilitation counseling, and nutrition, but no longer awards degrees in the teaching of physical education. Sargent also developed for Harvard a summer program in physical education training, which he considered his major success.

Dudley Sargent liked to tell a cautionary tale of his effort to carry out two jobs at once. As a child he tried to combine a paper route with the job of walking a neighbor's cow to and from pasture. The cow, of course, was not cooperative. She wandered into his newspaper clients' gardens, and the scheme was not a success. But as Sargent said in his autobiography, "I failed to learn the lesson, that to do two things at a time means to do justice to neither. Through life I have tried to deliver papers while I drove a cow to and from pasture."

Despite this disclaimer Sargent managed to keep several balls in the air at all times while concentrating on his goal: his "50 year fight for the recognition and promotion of physical education in the schools and colleges of America...." He single-handedly brought physical fitness into the national consciousness and was successful not only in developing programs and designing the necessary equipment but also in establishing schools for the training of physical education teachers.

Dudley Allen Sargent died in July 1924. The following chapter from his autobiography tells of his early days in Belfast. It is not difficult to see the "man with a mission" in these reminiscences.

In Belfast

In 1859 I did leave Hingham to return to Belfast. My new home was with my widowed mother, who kept house for Mr. and Mrs. Cad Hayford, whose son, Axel Hayford, had married my mother's sister. Certainly in my own estimation, I was at this time travelled. I fancied that I had knocked round enough in the great outside world of Hingham, Cohasset, Nantasket, and Boston which I visited once or twice, to have acquired the air and knowledge of a man of the world. Tested from a scholastic standard, however, the situation was different. It was ignominious, indeed, to find that I was not even up to the boys of my own age in school. Much as I resented and railed against the stupidity of those in authority, I went into a grade of the grammar school with boys two or three years younger than I. My associates were, of course, boys in a class or two above me. In my own grade, unfortunately, I did not have enough to do to keep me out of mischief. The circumstances did not make for serious study.

The school in which I started was known as the Intermediate

School. I soon left that for the Select School. There was practically no chance for physical activity connected with the curriculum. At recess, in the springtime, we tumbled about in our own games of hide-and-seek and leap-frog. We competed in the usual stunts, turning hand-springs, cartwheels, running and jumping. I remember that I was the first to try back-hand springs. For want of a mat to land on, the boys obligingly lay down on the ground, and let me turn over on them. In the winter, we skated and coasted and snow-balled. Never did a town offer better opportunities for coasting than Belfast. The school building was surrounded by hills. We frequently had ice for skating. In Maine, Nature is very generous in the matter of winter weather. . . .

But in these days, we had more serious matters to consider than sports and playtime. The oncoming Civil War sobered the most irresponsible of us. National energy turned toward military training. Even with this movement came the great discovery which bore down upon us again in 1918, that a huge percentage of our young men were physically unfit. In 1861, we could not select our army with such scrupulous care as we did in the World War, and fit and unfit were thrown into squads to go through a bit of rough training and to learn the manual of arms. Long before the first bewildering newness of training wore off, those lads were rushed to the front, often to die before they had learned to shoulder arms properly.

Those early days moved so swiftly in a blinding panorama of action, that they come back to me as a hazy confusion of stirring scenes, of mad, breathless preparation, days filled with hope and agony and fear. I remember the raw recruits drilling on the common, marching and going through the elementary formations; I remember the great rallies that stirred me to the depths of my being; I remember listening to the inspiring music of the bands, as it beat the departure of our young manhood of the North to fight that of the South; I remember following the few I knew to the enlisting offices, seeing them sign up, to become one of the raw recruits on the common; I remember seeing them depart, and later some of them coming back wounded, or worse, stricken with awful diseases. The Civil War was nearer to us than the World War. We realized it because a strong censorship did not keep the public from knowing and seeing. News travelled to us more quickly when it did not have to cross an ocean. Our anxiety was never at rest for a moment. We saw the immediate results of war. Yet, in spite of its reality, there was not one of us who would not have gone gladly had we been old enough to get into the service.

In the atmosphere of wild excitement, it was impossible for the boys and girls to jog along in the commonplace rut of school. We lived and breathed nothing but the war. Returned soldiers told of their personal experiences, while extra bulletins proclaimed battles lost or won. We were not old enough to go to the front, but like all boys in their early teens, we had heard of some wonderful exception made for a mythical person, no older than we; and basing our hopes upon such phantasmal chances, we secretly watched for our opportunity to become General Grant's aide, or even General Sherman's drummer boy! In time of peace, the average number of boys and girls who go through High School is small. But in that time of war the pupils dropped out in amazing numbers. Discontent was the touchstone. Everyone craved action. We lacked all interest in our educations. Such lack of interest is not uncommon in the young; for, with the glowing vitality of youth, all knowledge which is not directly applicable to needs, is superfluous. Before young people reach the stage where they see actual constructiveness in their school work, they are likely to be discontented, and very likely to be disinterested. There is nothing gripping in Algebra and Latin for the large majority.

I imagine that it was this lack of interest, increased by the restlessness inherent in the war, that caused me to leave school when I was thirteen years old, in 1862. I went to work on the government battery, which was being constructed near Patterson's Ledge in East Belfast. My uncle, Mr. Hayford, had the contract for this construction, and through him I stepped into a man's job. I worked with a pick, shovel, wheel-barrow, and a heavy wooden maul. I was paid $1.50 a day, man's wages, for my efforts, and I tried with all my might to do a man's work. The tools which I handled were used in rotation. This scheme kept one man from tiring of any one kind of labor. A man who was weary of shovelling exchanged his shovel with a man who was tired of his pick. This system accomplished a great deal of work, and seemed to eliminate much fatigue.

One foreman in charge of the pounders or maulers devised a scheme, consistent with the times. He lined up his fifteen or twenty men, and put them through a regular drill, in which each man pounded in perfect rhythm with his neighbor. When one stopped, all stopped to rest. After a few minutes, the work would commence again, all in perfect unison. It was an enviable lesson in efficiency, applicable to modern times. Would such a scheme not work effectively in our municipal street service?

The batteries were completed in 1863, and I returned to the Select School. I was under women teachers again, but now, at the age of fourteen, for the first time, I took school seriously, and began vaguely to understand what a school was for. Probably the manual labor which occupied my spare time sobered me to a realization of the necessity of a good education.

At this time of my life my diary records what a typical young fellow I was by such remarks as "Had a cigar," "Down street in the evening," or "Played cards up in Moses' room." I also reflect the spirit of the young blood by a note of having had the gloves on with Murphy, and later, of walking round the square. How I found time for these trivialities puzzles me: but I find few youngsters who do not make time for their fancies and fads.

My smoking and card playing began and ended that year, but my boxing was destined to be a more permanent fixture. Perhaps its permanency had some connection with my giving up smoking. Another amusing entry in my diary was that of the day when I "Shaved with a razor." What I had shaved with previously, I cannot say. I balanced this occasion with an item of note the next day. I lifted 300 pounds of nails. I was indeed a man! I weighed 140 pounds; more than the average weight for my age.

At this time I began practising more or less systematically with dumb-bells and Indian clubs. I found a book entitled "The Family Gymnasium" which interested me greatly. There was a picture of an Englishman, named Harrison, so well do I remember the book, who was swinging a pair of Indian clubs, each of which weighed 37 pounds. I regarded this man Harrison's physique with envy; Indian clubs became immediately necessary to my happiness. Out of a piece of cord wood, I sawed two clubs and finished the handles with a hatchet and draw-shave. Completed, my toys weighed about 20 pounds each. At fourteen years I began to use these monstrosities regularly. Of course there were only one or two movements which I could achieve with such unwieldy weapons. Although these clubs were much too heavy for general use, they gave me unusual strength in my shoulders and chest. The other extreme, to which people have gone today, of using 1 or 2 pound clubs for school and college gymnastics, is equally undesirable.

Speaking of gymnastics, one of our favorite school stunts was to see who could jump the farthest after swinging back and forth on a rope. But the great test of courage and strength was of still more aërial nature. The Unitarian Church, opposite the school, had a lofty steeple; we used to try climbing it. One schoolmate, Justus Lewis, was the only boy whom I ever saw accomplish the feat. Later he lost his life on the Pacific coast, while trying to save the life of another. I remember that as a boy he was a born athlete.

Since school occupies only a few hours each day of the boys' and girls' time, and since the school term allowing for weekends and holidays is in all little more than half the year, the influences outside of school hours play a large part in moulding the lives of young people. The natural conditions of a town, and even those which are accidental, shape the activities of the youth of a community more than any other factors. Belfast, spread over a series of low hills, sloped up or down at every angle, from the gentlest to the steepest. Even if they realized it, few of its inhabitants would have acknowledged the constantly enforced climbing as the matchless if wearisome agent which maintained a town full of healthy citizens. But in winter, the young people, at least, keenly appreciated the rolling landscape. I have never known better coasting than we had over those white hills, nor better coasters than we were. Night after night, with a starry sky overhead, we plodded up the inclines to fly down again on our sleds. The ascents, which might have been tiresome had we stopped to consider them, were chances to harangue one another on the respective merits of our sleds. No race-horse owners ever backed their studs more steadily or vigorously than we did ours. We picked our favorites; there was "Old Ironsides," and "Dreadnought," and "Speedwell," and a dozen others. There were always interesting problems to be considered. Some insisted upon a full-round or half-round shoe, while others recognized only a flat runner. Then the question arose in regard to the desirability of a narrow or broad seat on a stiff or rickety frame sled. Great were the battles that ensued! And, as today, it was always difficult to make the defeated boy realize, and more difficult to make him acknowledge, that the victor was the more skilful in the race. The old alibi of luck always loomed portentous.

Speedy coasting was, however, a science, not a chance. A method, just as scientific as the rules of any sport, appertained to this game. The coaster grasped his sled with the right hand on the right side of the front bar, and the left hand on the rear bar near the left side. With the sled held in this manner before him, he ran at top speed, and threw himself and the sled forcibly forward. He lay on his right thigh while his left leg trailed behind as a rudder. The right hand, changed to the left side of the front bar, brought the weight of the body full on the right forearm and elbow. Everything depended upon the skill with which the racer threw himself, and the speed at which he could run to get a flying start. . . .

The moral aspects of these natural sports are of grave significance. I mentioned the girls coasting, and I remember them dancing and skating. Otherwise I can think of no sports in which girls took part. As for the dancing, it was the usual conventional school type, conducted more to teach social dances and ball-room etiquette, than to allow any motor outlet for pent-up vigor and feelings in which young people in their early teens abound. Small boys and smaller girls, dressed up to look like little men and women, schooled with all the airs and graces of grown-ups, and sent to smirk and simper at dancing school, are not being prepared, at least consciously, for the best sort of manhood and womanhood. This hot-house physical education only wakens and stimulates a sex consciousness at a time when boys and girls should be unaffected and free. The generally accepted and socially sponsored card parties and church sociables, with their kissing games and so-called dancing, perniciously weaken the moral fiber of strong, healthy, clean boys and girls. And the next morning, the sight of the same object of feminine loveliness, to be sure not quite so lovely in longlegged gingham and pig-tails as she was in fluffy party muslin and curls, but alluring still, is not conducive to lightning calculations in arithmetic, nor to faultless spelling. It puts an undeniable "crimp" in the three R's. Yet the elders approved and applauded; and the girl who had the effrontery to engage in any form of athletics more strenuous than the polka or the schottische, or an occasional coast, was a hoyden or a tomboy. No one seemed to realize that there is a time in the life of a girl when it is better for her and for the community to be something of a boy rather than too much of a girl.

From this paradox of boyhood many of us emerged, as I have hinted, and with the progress of the war grew to men before our time. We skated and danced, but life threatened us increasingly with new problems and graver responsibilities. We were ready to undertake more serious contests than coasting.

From: Ledyard W. Sargent ed., *Dudley Allen Sargent: An Autobiography*. Philadelphia: Lea & Febiger, 1927.

Hudson Maxim
1853–1927

Hudson Maxim and his more famous brother, Sir Hiram, were raised in circumstances in back-country Maine that seem least likely to have produced two of nineteenth-century Maine's most gifted sons. Their father, Isaac, was a farmer and mechanic who moved from one bare-bones new settlement to another in Piscataquis County without ever seeming to improve his family's fortunes. He would move his wife and eight children to a site near a mill dam and run off its power a grist mill, a turning lathe, and a buzz saw, but, as Hudson will point out, the Maxims seemed to live without ready money and often with little food. Even allowing for a rich man's dramatizing for posterity his rise from lowly beginnings, Hudson's reported facts about their poverty seem persuasive.

Hiram, the oldest child, after a remarkable self-education in mathematics, physics, and chemistry not begun until his twenties, arrived in New York in the 1870s ready to compete with Edison as an inventor of electric lights, dynamos, and motors. His inventive genius moved in all directions; he registered 119 American patents between 1866 and 1891. In 1881 he was sent to Europe by his firm, the United States Electric Lighting Company, under an extraordinary arrangement. The company, frustrated by the speed with which his inventive mind worked (he was constantly upsetting their plans for the commercial exploitation of their earlier products), made a bargain with him. It was this: to go to Europe for ten years on a retainer of twenty thousand dollars a year, stay in close touch with all European inventions in the field of electricity for the company's sake, but pledge that he would not make any new inventions in electricity of his own. Undeterred by that limitation, Maxim turned to ordnance, to the invention of the first fully automatic machine gun. In three years he

Hudson Maxim (left) and his famous older brother Hiram shared a hardscrabble childhood in Piscataquis County. Hudson wrote the manual for his brother's best-known invention, the machine gun. *Courtesy of the Sangerville Historical Society.*

had it perfected. *His gun fired at the rate of six hundred shots a minute when the trigger was engaged just once. His design remains the basis of all the automatic guns that have followed. It has been called by a modern expert "the most remarkably innovative engineering accomplishment in the history of firearms." Hiram became a British subject in 1900, and he was knighted by Queen Victoria in 1901 in gratitude for his service to the British empire. His gun had proved to be the perfect weapon for mowing down the natives who stood in the way of the spread of British dominion, especially in South Africa and the Sudan.*

Hudson Maxim was the only member of the family to get a formal education beyond the lowest grades of grammar school. He had a less brilliant scientific career than his thirteen-year-older brother. It did not begin until his thirties, when Hiram asked him to come to England and bring with him some talented American mechanics to help improve the British technology of gun production. Hudson ended up writing the manual for Hiram's first machine gun. Up to that point Hudson's effort to get an education had kept him busy and poor. He finally graduated from Kents Hill School at the age of twenty-five, having supported himself by jobs in stone quarries, on farms, as a school teacher, and as a traveling salesman of books and patent medicines. As he put it, "I was away off there in the woods, trying to beat my way out." His chance came when he began to put his experience in his brother's gun factory to his own use. Under his brother's tutelage he had become an expert in ordnance and explosives, and he made his own inventions in this field the basis of his success when he returned to America.

Hiram never forgave him. He stole it all from me, was Hiram's charge, and a lifelong feud and estrangement followed. In America Hudson took out a patent on a smokeless powder that he had first analyzed in England with Hiram. Du Pont bought his patent and made him a rich man and a consultant to the company. He made another explosive for a shell that would pierce armor plate, and called it Maximite. The United States government bought the formula for fifty thousand dollars. It is a wonderful irony that from origins as obscure and unpromising as those hamlets in Piscataquis County these two men should have become millionaires during the greatest armaments race the world had ever seen, as the leading nations of the West got ready for the First World War. The du Ponts received a check for sixty million dollars from the Russian government for a "multi-perforated cannon powder" invented by Hudson Maxim.

Hudson's remembrances of his childhood were told to a journalist who took down his story in a series of meetings. This method may raise questions of second-handedness and accuracy during an age before tape recorders. But we believe that it soon becomes apparent to a reader that Hudson was a gifted storyteller. He is ready with particulars and has an instinctive sense of how details can shape a family scene, how sensual rembrances of tastes and smells can persuade a reader of an authentic whole.

Life on a Lonely Farm

While we were living at Grandfather Stevens's house Father was looking about for a farm. As he had only fifty dollars to pay down, he didn't have a very large choice of farms that he could buy on his terms. One of our neighbours was Deacon Bartlett, a fine old gentleman of the sterling sort that does honour to the human race, and he owned an unoccupied farm only a half mile from my grandfather's. He offered it to my father for two hundred and fifty dollars—house, barn, and some thirty acres of land. The farm wasn't much of a farm, nor the house much of a house, nor the barn much of a barn, but the deal was made, and the farm became our home.

A man named Dutton lived there before we did, and we called it Duttonville, though it was only an outlying farm in a little bit of a clearing in the woods. The house was in the middle of the clearing far back from the highway, and no other house was in sight. This home, where I lived between the ages of ten and thirteen, and one at North Guilford where we moved next, are the two most closely associated with my boyhood life. I was in them a comparatively long time, at the most impressionable period of my youth.

About half of the Duttonville clearing was a pasture. No brush or trees to amount to anything grew in the pasture, and it furnished enough grazing for a cow and a horse and a few sheep. It was fenced with split cedar rails laid up zigzag, except on one side, where there was a stone wall. We had grassland to provide hay for our stock, and we had a garden patch.

Beyond our place a new road went on through the woods—I don't know where. We had no neighbours in that direction, and you wouldn't see anybody go along that road once in a dog's age. Our nearest neighbour was my grandfather Stevens, and somewhat farther on lived old Deacon Bartlett. Next came the schoolhouse at a cross-roads, two miles from Duttonville, and a half mile more brought you to the village of Upper Abbot, where there were a church, a black-smith's shop, a gristmill, and a combined store and post office.

Our house was a clapboarded, unpainted little building a story and a half high. In front of the old shack of a barn was a small barnyard surrounded by a post and rail fence. There was a set of bars at the entrance to this barnyard, and when we wanted to go in or out we either let down a middle bar and crawled through, or let down the two upper bars and stepped over. We drove the cow home from the pasture each night in summer, and Mother milked her in the barnyard in warm, pleasant weather. The barnyard served in winter as a place where the cow could sun herself and run around. Mother always wanted to milk her cow rather than have any one else do the milking. She thought a milker had to be in sympathy with the cow or the cow would dry up.

There wasn't a fruit tree of any kind on the place, and there were no shade trees near the buildings. The vicinity of the house was absolutely bald-headed so far as trees were concerned.

On the ground floor of the house was the kitchen in a small ell. Next to the kitchen was a sitting room, and beyond that were two bedrooms. Upstairs was one big room, with the chimney running up through the middle of it. Sam and I had our bed at one end, and a curtain partitioned off another bedroom, which Sister Eliza sometimes occupied.

The roof leaked more or less, but wasn't as bad as the sides of the house, in which were great cracks right through to the outer elements. These let the winter storms beat in, and we'd wake up in the morning and find our heads covered with snow. When a window pane was broken and we had no glass to replace it, Father put in a piece of board or stuffed in a cloth.

There was plaster on the walls of some of the rooms, but others were just rough boards. Mother stuck on newspapers and brown wrapping paper when the cracks between the rooms were too conspicuous.

The kitchen floor was bare, but some of the rooms had rag carpets or rag rugs which Mother made. Our old clothes furnished the material. After we wore them out, she would cut them up into narrow strips and braid the strips to use for rugs, or weave the strips into carpets.

The chairs were primitive wooden ones that Father probably picked up in his peddling, and no two were alike. Mother had a rocking-chair, which she sat in when she was sewing or knitting. She did her spinning and weaving in the sitting room, and there she kept her flax wheel, which she called "the little wheel," and one for spinning wool, which she called "the big wheel," and her loom. We didn't have much space left for seating purposes, and we used to sit round wherever we could find a place.

My father peddled pictures that he bought from a New York publisher; and he made and sold frames for the pictures. Some of those pictures were hung in our rooms. On a kitchen shelf was a large clock with wooden gearing.

We used to have corded beds. Sometimes, when you had nothing but a feather bed under you, the feathers would work one way and the other, until you almost lay on the cord. You had the pattern of the bed-cord on your back the next morning and could play checkers on it if you wanted to.

Mother wove blankets for the beds, and she bought calico and cotton batting and made comforters. During the Civil War cotton got to be so expensive that people took the cotton out of their comforters and sold it. Now and then Mother would make a patchwork quilt—a crazy quilt, we called it. She'd swap pieces of calico with the neighbours to get variety in colour and figure.

I don't recall having sheets on the beds in my early youth. Anyhow, we didn't have them during the war. Sheets were worth nigh their weight in gold then, and we slept between the coarse woollen blankets of home manufacture. We had pillows, and the pillow cases were of blue drilling. The pillows were stuffed with feathers—oh, my! all kinds of feathers—of geese, ducks, and hens. Those pillows were fine. We had mattresses—sometimes of corn husks, sometimes of straw. I've helped to fill them. A feather bed would be put on top of the mattress. You'd sink down into it, and it would come up around you and keep you warm.

Of course, there couldn't but one of us boys sleep comfortably in a bed. Any more than that, and we'd kick each other. But beds were scarce, and we had to double up.

During fly-time—the latter part of August and the first part of September—the flies often were just like a swarm of bees in the house. When we gathered round the table to eat, the flies gathered there, too, but we could eat faster'n they could. If you went out in the woods fishing, the black flies would get after you in a regular cloud, and every one of them would bite. The blood would run right off you

And the mosquitoes—why! they'd simply eat you up. If they got too bad, when they were flying round the house and into it on summer evenings, we protected ourselves by building a smudge in the dooryard, using chip-dirt from the woodpile mainly. Then came the question which could stand the most of the smoke—we or the mosquitoes. We placed the fire so that the smoke would drift across where we were sitting outdoors or in the house.. Sometimes we had several smudges going, and the smoke was pretty bad, but, Lord bless your heart! not so bad as the mosquitoes would have been without it. Mother had a big cooking utensil, eighteen inches across and four or five deep, which she called the "iron basin." Often we made our smudge in that. Then we could shift it from one spot to another if we wanted to.

I've always had the habit of eating rapidly—far too rapidly. I suppose that the way we children ate when we were at home there in the back country of Maine had a good deal to do with my getting the habit. Whatever food happened to be the most substantial portion of a meal was put in a big dish and placed in the centre of the table. Near this was a platter of bread cut into slices, or, more likely, johnnycake cut into hunks. Whenever we had baked beans, which was every Saturday night, Mother made a loaf of brown bread. About once a week she stewed a beef shank, and after thickening the stew she put in big crusts of bread. It was wonderfully delicious the way she used to make it.

As soon as the table was set, Mother gave the signal for us to come. She often called us as she called the pigs to their repast—"Chug, chug, chug!" And then we all went for the food. Mother usually dished out the stew, or whatever it might be, for us, but unless she was on hand we would dip into the dish for ourselves. There was no delay worth mentioning at any time. You see, it frequently happened that the food was insufficient for our many appetites, and each of us lost no time in getting his or her part of it. Short rations was one of the hardest things we children had to bear. If only there was a plenty we had no complaint to make. How coarse the fare might be didn't matter.

Our table was just a bench which Father had made of smooth pine boards. Mother had a white tablecloth somewhat disfigured by stains, and she would darn it when holes appeared. She used it only on special occasions. I don't remember having any napkins.

We didn't use much flour. Corn meal served instead. When some neighbour killed a pig or a cow, we generally got a piece of it at a very low price. Mother made hulled corn, and after she'd boiled it we ate it with milk. We filled up on it, and, in a little while, we'd be hungry again and would eat some more. It tasted amazingly good. We seldom had bleached sugar, but my father used to go to a grocery store and buy a molasses hogshead from which the groceryman had sold the molasses. In that there always was a lot of wet, soggy brown sugar. We called it "hogshead sweetening." It was very palatable. We ate it on bread and on flapjacks.

Our staple diet was mainly corn bread and mush and molasses. We had fried fat pork and boiled potatoes frequently; and when we kept a cow, we had milk with our corn-meal dishes—a combination that is hard to beat. Whatever Mother cooked tasted good, and her stewed fruits were delicious. Sometimes she let us have skim milk to drink if the pigs didn't need it more than we did. She used the cream for butter, and we children did the churning in an up-and-down wooden churn.

She made two kinds of cheese—a full milk cheese that was wonderful, and a skim-milk cheese that wasn't bad to taste, but was the toughest blamed thing you ever saw. You could break a brick on it, or make a sole for your shoe out of it. However, cheese of any kind was a rarity and a luxury in our house. One old cow wouldn't supply us with much, and we were a hungry family. Mother allowanced us on butter. Mostly we had molasses instead of butter on our bread, and we used fried pork fat on both bread and potatoes.

We always had quite a garden in which we raised potatoes, beets, carrots, sweet corn, and other vegetables. But we didn't do real farming to amount to anything, and never grew a surplus to sell.

Mother was a great one for making apple and pumpkin pies. She made custard pies, too, but not often, because they took eggs, and eggs could be sold. She used to dry apples and pumpkins. After the apples had been peeled, cored, and sliced she'd run a cotton string through the pieces and hang them up to dry. The pumpkins had to be pared and sliced and strung, too, and the scallops of drying apples and pumpkins were hung one below another in the kitchen all round the room. Of course, the flies would light on them, but that didn't matter. They were washed before they were made into sauce and pies.

Tea was a necessity to my mother, but she made it go as far as possible. She'd steep it two or three times, then take the tea leaves and dry them, and afterward boil them to get out the last bit of flavour. Father also drank tea. It wasn't supposed to be good for young folks, and we children never drank it unless we had a headache. Wherever we moved, there was always a cider mill in the neighbourhood, and when sweet cider was available we'd fill up on that.

Blackberries were wonderfully plentiful, and there were lots of red raspberries and wild strawberries. The place that excelled all others for blackberries centred round a ledge on a pasture hill and covered a tract about two hundred feet wide and a quarter of a mile long. It was a neighbourhood resort, and the berries were particularly big and soft and luscious. Both blackberries and raspberries seemed to thrive among the rocks and along the waysides and fences. Strawberries grew everywhere. There were two kinds, one was round in shape and grew only in the open. The other was long or pear-shaped and preferred the seclusion of the tall grass.

We used to tap the sugar-maple trees in the early spring when the thawing weather came. A forehanded farmer would carry a kettle to the woods and boil down the sap there. We were not forehanded. We just tapped a few trees, and brought the sap home and boiled it on the stove.

I didn't have a pair of shoes until I was thirteen years old. In winter I sometimes tied old bags around my feet when I was going out to help in the barn. If the weather was very cold I had to stay in the house. But because my feet never had any covering they got so accustomed to the cold that they could endure a good deal of frost without great inconvenience.

Lack of shoes didn't prevent my going to school, except in the very severest weather; and my two younger brothers went with me, no better shod. We could go on the hard snow and ice much better than we could through a light snow, because the light snow would get up inside our trousers on our bare legs, which couldn't stand it so well as our feet. The way we managed was to run with all our might as long as our feet could endure the cold, and then climb up on a fence, or sit down on a boulder or a stump, and rub our feet and ankles with our hands; and then we'd rush on again.

One winter we had a big thaw that was followed by a sudden freeze; and the snow, which still lay deep over the fields, was covered with a sheet of glare ice firm enough to bear a person up. While things were in this condition, my brother Sam and I, after we had gone to bed on a bright moonlight evening, looked out of the window, and were greatly tempted by that slippery crust. So we crawled out and ran around in our shirttails for a while, sliding on our bare feet. But we soon got our fill of joy and had started to return to the house, when, lo and behold, there was Ma'am standing at the window with a switch in her hand. We hesitated between staying out and shivering, or going in to be warmed up by that switch. We decided that we preferred a thrashing, and we got it.

The only hat I ever had until I was quite a big boy was a little fancy straw one with a ribbon on it that my brother Hiram gave me when I was about seven years old. I was tickled to death and treasured it as a choice possession.

Mother made cloth caps for us—made them out of any old thing she might have—and she put flaps on the caps to come down over our ears. The flaps had wool or fur on the under side, and they had strings on them that we tied under our chins. Occasionally she made us a cap of muskrat skins lined with cloth. She used to knit woollen mufflers for us, but we didn't have them often.

I wore a heavy flannel shirt in winter. Mother spun the wool, wove the cloth, and made the shirt. It usually was dyed a gray colour with a dye she made from copperas and white maple bark stewed in a big kettle. In summer I wore a cotton shirt of blue drilling, and the rest of my summer clothing was trousers with sometimes a jacket.

Now and then my mother or my sisters knit us boys a pair of mittens. But for the most part we had cloth mittens, the material for which Mother cut from an old pair of trousers or other worn-out garment. She often lined them with woolly sheepskin.

We used to get pretty dirty and grimy with grubbing into the ground in our play; and, in spite of an occasional washup with soap and water, we quickly were grimy again, and we stayed grimy most of the time. But in my mother's dictionary there were two kinds of dirt — clean dirt and dirty dirt. The kind we used to get on us from delving in the ground she considered clean and healthful dirt. Mother was a great chaser of the dirty dirt in her housekeeping. Few persons are aware of the kindliness of dirt. Soap and water, applied too often, may do a lot of harm to a growing child. Soap neutralizes the acid secretions of the skin and is weakening, but, of course, it's a good thing once in a while. . . .

Soon after we moved to Duttonville my grandmother died. That left Grandfather alone, and it became my task to go up and spend the night in the house, to be with him in case anything should happen to him. One morning he brought me an auger, a short, round pine stick of the same diameter as the auger, a hammer and a saw, and a little packet of something done up snugly in a paper. He told me to go into the woods and bore a hole in a white maple tree, put the packet in the hole, drive the pine stick in hard, and saw it off. Then I was to bring back the tools to him, and never under any circumstances tell where the tree was located.

My curiosity was aroused. What that commission meant was more than I could compass. On recounting the affair to the home folks they said: "Oh! Grandpa's got the toothache"; and I learned there was an old superstition that if a person who has a toothache pares his finger-nails and toenails, and wraps the parings in a piece of paper and gets someone to bore a hole in a white maple tree and plug them in, the toothache will be cured.

Superstitions never die. Lots of folks still believe that if they want their beans to grow they must plant them at the right time of the moon. We had a horseshoe nailed up over the door of our house. It was supposed to bring luck, or keep away the witches, or something of that sort. We didn't believe in such superstitions. Still, we felt there might be wisdom we'd missed in our philosophy, and that the safer course was to have a horseshoe in place. . . .

The principal attraction I remember in connection with Dutton-ville was a large trout brook that ran through our pasture. It broke the monotony of our surroundings and was a source of keen interest and pleasure to us children. A strip of alder bushes and trees of various kinds grew along it and some of the trees were quite large. Boulders strewed much of its course, and there was one picturesque fall. When the brook was in flood it raised the devil going through there. A deep pot-hole in the rock below the fall used to have a mysterious interest for me. At last I puzzled out the secret of its origin. I found inside of it a lot of stones, which had been smoothed and rounded by the churning action of the water; and the stones, in turn, had ground the hole in the rock.

Sam and I and some of the other boys used to fish in the stream al-most every day. Our uncle Amos, who was a devout Methodist, told us it was wrong to fish on Sunday, and that if we persisted in doing so some awful calamity might befall us, just as likely as not. However, we weren't much impressed by his warning.

One Sunday, when we were out fishing some distance from home and had been quite successful in catching a good string of fish, the sky became overcast. It had been a bright, sunny day with no weather clouds in sight and no thunderheads in the west; and the strange, ominous gloom brought to mind the admonitions of Uncle Amos. Perhaps he was right after all, and our Sunday fishing was about to bring some dire catastrophe on us.

The darkness increased, and the sun became a great red ball of a constantly deepening hue until it was obscured altogether. We hurried home with all speed, and while on the way we noticed ashes falling from the sky and examined some of them. They were charred leaves, and we were more terrified than ever. We thought the world was burning up and that we'd done it!

After we reached home, the darkness got so dense that the chickens went to roost in mid-afternoon. Father said the darkness was caused by a cloud of smoke from some great forest fire to the north of us. Later we learned that thousands of acres had been burned over in Canada. We felt relieved that we hadn't done it, and concluded we could still safely fish on Sunday. . . .

One time, two boy neighbours of ours went fishing with Sam and me. They had beautiful fish-hooks—regular "boughten" ones, and the hooks weren't ordinary "boughten" ones either, but were bent sideways so as to give the fish a better chance to bite them. Sam and I had nothing but pin-hooks, and the contrast disturbed me. Somehow, I mustered up ten cents and went to Upper Abbot on a shopping tour with that ten cents.

I bought several little articles that I much needed, and then blew in what remained of my money on sticks of candy—red-striped sticks of candy. But I forgot the fish-hook, which was what I had especially come for, and only thought of it after I had been sucking the last stick of candy until the red stripes on it had become pale. Back I went to the store to trade that stick of candy for the fish-hook. The storekeeper looked at the candy, and accused me of having sucked it. I protested that I had not. He gave a side look at me, handed me a fishhook, and took the stick of candy and threw it under the counter. I have always felt guilty and mean when I recalled that transaction.

Once, several of us boys were making an excursion along the trout brook, and somebody suggested that we see who could swallow the largest number of small pebbles that were scattered along the waterside. I succeeded in swallowing more than any of the rest, but my sense of triumph was dulled by the uncomfortable weight of those pebbles in my stomach.

There was a little hill on our farm where wintergreens grew plentifully, and one day while Lucy and Hiram and I were picking wintergreen berries there I caught three black crickets. Hiram said he would give me five cents apiece if I would swallow them. So I swallowed the three crickets, but I never got the fifteen cents. I found those crickets very scratchy fellows for a while after I'd gulped them. I wonder how much it would take now to get me to swallow three of those crickets. Money was a great inducement then. But I wouldn't repeat that performance for gold enough to sink a ship.

We boys sometimes did the swallowing stunt with little newly hatched trout. We'd drink them down in water, just out of bravado, and we could feel them swimming about in our stomachs. . . .

I never wanted anything on earth so much as I wanted a gun when I was from ten to thirteen years of age. One day my sister Lucy got a letter from Hiram, who was working in Uncle Levi Stevens's machine shop in Fitchburg, Massachusetts. He said he would send me a gun as soon as I could read the Second Reader through and pronounce and spell correctly every word in it.

I immediately set myself to that task in dead earnest, and I worried all the members of the family with the book to get them to pronounce the hard words and hear me read and spell. In a couple of months I had mastered the book, but Hiram didn't send me the gun. He told me afterward that Uncle Levi said it would be very foolish to put a gun in the hands of so young a boy. I guess Uncle Levi was right.

However, about a year later, my father traded some of his wares for a little old fowling-piece, and he gave it to me. I cleaned and polished the gun until it looked like burnished silver; and in all my love affairs that gun never has been outrivalled in its appeal to my affections, except by Mrs. Maxim, sometimes, when she is at her best. I worshiped that gun. It was, however, only a small muzzle-loading shotgun, and its mainspring was so weak that the hammer often failed to explode the percussion cap, and I would miss getting the rabbit or partridge I aimed at. I decided that something must be done to remedy the defect, and I resorted to the expedient of putting the head of a match in the percussion cap. This always could be fired by the fall of the hammer, notwithstanding the weakness of the mainspring.

One day I was sitting in the kitchen with the gun, which I had loaded with an extra charge of gunpowder and a double charge of what we called cut shot—shot we made by cutting a flat piece of lead into small squares. I was going out to get a woodchuck, and I wanted to be sure not to lose him. I had just put a match head in position, and was letting the hammer down gently on the cap, when to my amazement and horror that match head took a notion to act prematurely. Off went the old gun with such a bang in the confined space of the room that it seemed to me the most infernal noise I'd ever heard. A hole as big as my arm was blown through the ceiling.

My mother was near me spinning. In fact, the room was so small that no one could get far from anybody else in it. She threw up both hands, thinking that the world itself had exploded. I had the greatest difficulty in accounting to her for the misbehaviour of my gun, and I didn't use the head of a match any more. It was too risky.

One day, while running along beside my father's wagon, I caught the barrel of my fowling-piece in a wagon-wheel and it was badly bent. I was in great trouble, and I hastened to the blacksmith to see if he could straighten it, but I couldn't get him to take my trouble seriously. He looked at the injured gun and asked if it was loaded. I told him that it was, and with a bullet.

"Well," he said, "take it home and fire it, and as the bullet moves down the barrel it will straighten out your gun."

I went home and consulted my father. "The blacksmith is mistaken," he said. "Firing the gun won't straighten it. Besides, you don't want the gun straightened. Leave it as it is, and you can shoot round stumps with it."

But he wouldn't let me fire the gun in the usual way. He rigged it up on a box so I could stand behind the house and fire it with a string and be perfectly safe if the gun should explode—and it did explode! When I took the fragments to the blacksmith to show him that his advice had been bad, he laughed and told me to go and buy a new lock, stock, and barrel for the gun, and it would be all right.

My brothers and I all cooked in our early youth—every kid for himself. We used to cook at any time and eat at any time. Each of us had a little garden of our own, and these gardens provided us with many a tasty morsel in addition to what we ate at the common table.

Sometimes Ma'am would help us in our cooking. If fact, she generally lent a hand.

The trout brook was a great source of supply for our irregular cooking, and our bow-guns would bring down an occasional bird. After I got my small fowling-piece, we secured more birds. We used to set deadfalls and box traps for rabbits and squirrels, and caught a good many in that way. Now and then we'd get a woodchuck and eat him.

There was one time when diphtheria was epidemic all about us, and people died like flies. Mother got a little anxious. The water in our well didn't smell quite right, and she and Father decided that the well must be cleaned out. It had an old-fashioned box curb, and we drew the water with a well-sweep and oaken bucket. Round the base of the curb were holes where the rains had worn the earth so that surface water ran into the well, and through which indiscreet animals might enter and fall down. My father got Charles Jackson, a farmer neighbour, to come and bucket out the water and clean out the well. We children watched him at his task, and when he got near the bottom of the well the water had a horrible odour, and he baled up innumerable remains of rats and mice, and toads and frogs, and snakes and rabbits, and about every other animal known. After the water was all out he let fresh water run in and repeated the operation several times until the well was clean. It was a wonder that we children didn't get diphtheria, but we didn't. . . .

One time Pa and Ma'am primped up and drove over to spend the day visiting Charles Jackson's folks. I had made a four-wheeled go-cart, and for months I had been looking longingly at our idle calf. My eagerness to hitch that calf to my cart was a perfect passion. Now the opportunity had come! Sister Eliza and my brothers Sam and Frank all harboured the same desire and shared the same enthusiasm.

That moon-faced calf looked so genial, mild, and gentle that we had no thought of any hazard in the enterprise. But as soon as we hitched him up and he found himself a part of the rigging, he kicked and jumped and bellowed to beat creation.

We all piled on the cart for the ride, but the calf left the main travelled road and struck out across the field toward his mooing ma, who answered his calls from the pasture. One hind wheel broke, and

Eliza and Frank fell off. Then the other hind wheel went and Sam with it. I alone remained, holding on to the reins and the cart for dear life. Then the two front wheels went, the cart became a drag, and I, too, fell by the wayside, while the calf, with the remnants of the vehicle, went hurtling along to the pasture. He didn't seem to see the fence; straight at it he went with such violence that it was levelled, and there was a family reunion between the cow and the calf.

We spent the rest of the day in mending the fence and in trying to convince the calf that we didn't mean anything after all, in order to get near enough to detach the tell-tale equipment which was still adhering to him. But that calf was wilder than any deer, and our blandishments didn't succeed. We held a conference to devise some explanation to offer Mother; but none of us could suggest anything that looked reasonable. We gave it up, and with the unanimous concurrence of opinion that the situation was bad.

When Ma'am came home and went to milk the cow she was astonished to see the attachment to the calf, and she asked lots of embarrassing questions. We made the best we could of a bad situation, but it was bad!

Once we got a young crow out of a nest and raised him. By George! he was a wonderfully intelligent creature. One day while my grandfather was hoeing potatoes in a field his son, my uncle Amos, came along and saw a crow fly down out of the sky and light on Grandfather's shoulder and begin to "talk" to him. When the crow had anything to say to you he'd put his beak right up close to your ear. Grandfather talked back, and meanwhile kept on working, with the crow riding along on his shoulder. It was a miracle to Uncle Amos, who didn't know about our having a pet crow.

The crow would eat anything on earth. He'd fly down where the chickens were feeding, and he'd get his part—you needn't worry about that! If the chickens attacked him, he'd throw himself on his back and clutch at them with his claws. Oh! he was wicked with his claws.

I was fishing in the pasture brook one day, and caught an unusually large trout. After putting it on a crotched stick I continued my fishing, but pretty soon I heard a little rustle behind me and there was that damned crow. He'd got my trout, and he flew away with it to the roof of the house and began eating it. I threw stones and sticks at him and scared him away, and then I climbed up and got the trout.

The worst fault of the crow was stealing. He'd sneak everything from the house that he could carry, just out of deviltry. He liked bright things best, and he'd throw them down the well. By accident we saw him doing it. He'd stand on the curb of the well, drop something in, and cock his head on one side to see it strike the water. When Jackson cleaned out the well he found down there in the bottom nails, spoons, knives, and forks that the crow had thrown in, and a watch chain we'd missed, and a brooch that belonged to one of my sisters.

From: Clifton Johnson, ed., *Hudson Maxim: Reminiscences and Comments*. New York: Doubleday Page & Co., 1924. Reprinted by permission of Margaret Johnson Rutter.

Kate Douglas Wiggin
1856–1923

The universe had an air of having been made to order especially for my delectation, and I realized gratefully that I was a
human being with joyous opportunities of sharing the life
around me. . . . For I was a born "participator," and I fear that
from the beginning of time nothing ever occurred in my immediate vicinity in which I did not long to take a hand.
                                                    —*My Garden of Memory*

*Kate Douglas Wiggin was an exemplar of the American woman writer
of the late nineteenth and early twentieth centuries. Writing was one of the
few professions open to women at that time, and Wiggin used her strength,
intelligence, and ambition to become a notable success. By the time of her
death in 1923 (she was in England finishing up her autobiography,* My
Garden of Memory, *at the time) Wiggin had written twenty-nine novels
(nineteen of them for children), seven plays, numerous essays, and several
poetry collections, and had edited a dozen literary collections. She was a
hard worker.*

*Mrs. Wiggin's ancestors had deep roots in Maine. Her paternal grand-
father, Noah Smith, was a member of the state legislature, speaker of the
house, and secretary of state. Kate Smith (later Wiggin) was born in
Philadelphia in 1856, but after her father's death, her mother remarried
and the family moved to Hollis, where Kate and her "Small Sister" Nora
were raised. Hollis, on the Saco river, was a bucolic setting, according to
Kate and Nora, although these decorous youngsters took risks. They amused
themselves by skipping across the logs rafted up on the river and, at a nearby
sawmill, gaily rode the cut timber like bucking broncos as it was fed into*

An early portrait from *Kate Douglas Wiggin as Her Sister Knew Her,* by Nora Archibald Smith. Houghton Mifflin Co., 1925.

the circular saw, jumping off at the last minute. But their favorite activity was reading. They devoured every book in the house—reading and re-reading the family set of Dickens—and everything they could borrow from nearby friends and relatives.

Mrs. Wiggin's education was fragmented: she was taught at home, attended the Gorham Female Seminary, and boarded at several other schools in New England and elsewhere, ending up with six months' attendance at Abbott Academy in Andover, Massachusetts, before joining her family, which had just moved to California in search of a better climate for her ailing stepfather. Here the young Kate Smith searched for a career and finally got involved in the nascent kindergarten movement. She studied with a pioneer in the field and, in San Francisco in 1878, founded the first free kindergarten west of the Rockies. Her career as an educator continued as she established a training school for kindergarten teachers and administrators, and she wrote several books on the subject. But Kate Douglas Wiggin the novelist was emerging. Several of her early works, including The Birds' Christmas Carol, which was privately printed in 1888, were written to raise funds for the kindergarten cause. In 1881 Kate Smith married Samuel Bradbury Wiggin, an old friend from Boston who had come out west in hopes of establishing a legal career. The young couple moved back to New York, but Mrs. Wiggin made annual trips to San Francisco to keep tabs on her kindergarten ventures. In 1889, while she was in California, Samuel Wiggin died.

In 1890, feeling the need for a change of direction in her life and a desire for validation of the literary quality of her early books, she submitted The Birds' Christmas Carol and The Story of Patsy to Houghton Mifflin. They were accepted, were successful, and Mrs. Wiggin found herself with money in her pocket and an urge to travel. An understanding friend subsidized a trip abroad for Kate to rest and to see the world, so off she sailed to England and the Continent. After her return to New York, Kate embarked on a new career—public readings of her work. Her literary friends encouraged her, and soon she was much in demand both at home and abroad.

It was on a trip to England that she met her second husband, George Riggs. By then Mrs. Wiggin and her mother and sister had found a house to rent in Hollis that suited them to a T, and they were very excited about *fixing it up and subsequently buying it. Riggs was brought to Hollis and, fortunately, pleased all of Kate's friends and neighbors. They were married in New York in 1895, honeymooned in London and Venice, and returned to settle in New York, a part of a very full social and literary set that included W.D. Howells, Mark Twain, Rudyard Kipling, Richard Harding Davis, and Ellen Terry. The Riggses formed a pattern of spending three months in Great Britain in the spring, three or four summer months in Hollis, and the remainder of the year in New York. Mrs. Wiggin wrote wherever she found herself: her travels abroad provided the background for the* Penelope *series, but the house in Hollis, "Quillcote," was where most of her later books were written and others "polished, finished and proofread." Hollis, and Quillcote in particular, were the constant in Mrs. Wiggin's life, the place she most identified with, the place that gave her the most material for her many novels. "Quillcote began by being the most idyllic place for work ever known," she wrote. In 1904 her literary contribution to the state of Maine was recognized by Bowdoin College, which gave her an honorary doctor of letters degree. She was the second woman to receive this honor; the first was Sarah Orne Jewett.*

Mrs. Wiggin was primarily known as an author of books for children: Rebecca of Sunnybrook Farm, *and* Mother Carey's Chickens *are among the most familiar. Many of them were set in Maine and had a strong regional flavor. Although today's readers may find the style of the turn of the century overly moralistic and sentimental, Wiggin's sure sense of her Maine characters and of the social manners of the period ring true. Her prose was clear and forthright, often humorous. She was an articulate portrayer of her world and an important figure in the educational and literary scene of her time.*

When Mrs. Wiggin was ten and living in Hollis she kept a journal for a few months. Excerpts from this surprisingly mature record of a child's daily life appear in her autobiography and are reproduced here.

Diary of a Truly Little Girl

I once kept a journal when I had attained the ripe age of ten summers. I set down in a mottled-covered blank-book daily, for a portion of one season, all the doings of my life in a small New England hamlet. . . . It is an innocent, humdrum, human little document, chiefly interesting as a chronicle of a child's life in a Maine village.

1866

March 24th: I got up this morning at twenty minutes past seven; then I went downstairs and dusted the parlor, which took me until breakfast time. After breakfast we read the prayers for the day and two chapters in the Bible. Then Nora and I went out to feed the hens. We found one egg. After we got through I put on my things and went for the milk. After I got home we went up to Grandmother's to spend the day—Mother, Cousin E., and all three of us children. I read a little while in the new "Harper." The story that I read first was "My Fathers-in-Law." It was real funny, but it didn't sound true. Then Grandma said she wanted me to help her. Cousin E. went out with me; she mashed turnips, and I pounded beefsteak with a broken plate to make it tender; then I fixed the sausages for dinner, helped set the table; then we sat down. We had a real nice dinner—sausages, beefsteak, pickles, turnips, potatoes, cheese, biscuits; for dessert—pumpkin and apple pies, coffee, apple sauce. After supper I dressed and went to the Bible class. I read once, and answered three or four questions.

March 25th: Upon looking out of my window this morning I found it was raining in torrents. I was very much disappointed as Father and I expected to go to Hollis Center to buy a lamb and two more hens. Ours seemed so cold and hungry that I took hay and stuffed it in all the little holes of the hen-house and then took a nice clean board and put it in a place where the wind didn't blow, and put their food and drink on it. I caught the tame hen too, and had a little fun with her. Then helped Mother make the beds, then studied for two hours. I had California for a lesson in Geography to-day. It was easy and real interesting; I had a long Latin lesson and I suppose it seemed the harder for me because I hate it so; did four or five sums, and then practiced till dinner time. After dinner I went to see if there were any eggs, but there were not, so I went indoors, went upstairs, brushed my hair, washed my face, and went downstairs, and worked on my nightgown case. By that time it was five o'clock, time for me to make the milk toast for supper. I put the milk in the frying-pan, and then mixed the thickening, and put that in with a large piece of butter. Nora came out then and toasted the bread for me, and I dropped it in the drawn butter and let it soak a good while till it was soft, and then laid it in the dish. Afterwards I poured the rest of the milk over the toast. I guess it was nice, but you can't save butter. If you do, the gravy tastes like paste. After supper Mother played for Father and me to dance by, and then I for Father and Mother.

March 26th: I did not wake up this morning till Cousin E. called me. I was sleepy, but I had to get up, so I did. The first thing I did was to run to the window to see if it was a pleasant day. It was, so dressed quick, for if it was pleasant we were going to get the lamb. (The lamb is not for use, but for fun.) There wasn't any thing to do for breakfast, so I cleared up the parlor; then when Father and Mother came down we read the Bible. After breakfast I made the beds, and then with Father and Nora went up to Grandmother's to harness the horse. After I had been there a little while I saw Mr. F. riding up the road. I ran down to ask him if we could have the lamb if we came over for it. He said he should have to ask a dollar and a quarter for it instead of a dollar. I ran up and told Father, and he said the lamb wasn't worth it. I couldn't help crying, I wanted him so much. Mother said she was real sorry, and she didn't care anything about the extra quarter, but it was too much for a lamb. Father came down in a minute with the horse to go over to the Center for the hens, so I got a basket and we started. On our way over we called at Mrs. E.'s; she wanted to give me the quarter, so that I could have the lamb, but Father wouldn't let her. We stopped at the blacksmith's to get the horse shod; waited to get warm a minute, and started for the hens. We had such a time catching them! We had all but one, and Mr. K. said she was the "slipperiest critter he ever see." *Father stopped at Mr. F.'s after all and bought the lamb (!!)* Afterwards we had to study. Everything went wrong; had to get my lessons twice. People came in every three minutes. Fed the lamb, then ate my supper, and went to bed early.

April 1st: Rose early this morning and practiced a half-hour before breakfast. After breakfast I went for the milk, also for a dozen of eggs for one of our hens that wants to set (or sit). After I got home we read the prayers, and then I thought of some way to make an April Fool of Uncle H. I should have fried some cotton-wool doughnuts, but he was sick and couldn't have eaten them. I had to carry up some medicine to him. Father was down at the store then, but soon came and went into the house, but came out in a few minutes, and said, "Here is a little maple sugar that I bought for you; divide it among you." So I went out and sat down with Janie on the sled and opened the bundle and saw— an old hammer, a piece of bark and one of tin! I felt cheap then, I tell you! I took the bundle then and made April fools of all the people in the place with it, came home, read the Bible and practiced before dinner. After dinner dressed Phil and myself, then went down to Miss R.'s to get her to show me about my music lesson and how to make a pair of garters for Aunt J.'s baby. After supper, as it was too rainy to carry the garters in to Aunt J.; I practiced a half-hour, then went upstairs, and Mother read out loud a beautiful war story about Benjamin F. Porter, a boy only sixteen years old and a Lieutenant.

April 2nd: Practiced half an hour before breakfast; after that went on some errands for Mother, then went to the pond and saw F. and W. take the ice out. I sat on the sluice with a beanpole and poked the ice, which the boys sent down over the falls, but Nora got her feet wet as usual, and went into Grandma's to dry them. Then we had to rip my embroidered blue dress because Miss R. was going into Portland and was going to take it in to be colored. After dinner went into the kitchen to see Billy, the lamb, washed. He had a long piece of his tail frozen, and when he was washed it came right off, which was a horrible surprise.

April 3rd: Rose early and went downstairs, practiced a half-hour before breakfast. After breakfast we read the Bible, then went for the milk, and invited Miss T. and Mrs. C. over to tea, for we were going to have Grandma's family besides. Came home and went up with Cousin E. to Grandma's to borrow some milk, butterplates, and muffin rings.

Miss T. taught me a polka in the forenoon; after dinner ironed a good while, all the handkerchiefs, towels, napkins. Then went into the parlor, and read till it was time to dress. After supper Miss Jennie Usher sang; I don't know the real name of it, but I call it "Jamie," then "Maggie's Secret," "The Brook," "Too Late," "The Bridge,"— all beautiful songs. Then I played Mozart's Turkish March, and was clapped; then we had a game of "Muggins" till the company went.

Housework of all kinds seems to have been accepted in a cheerful spirit, as witnessed by the following excerpts chosen at random:

April 4th: This morning we commenced house cleaning, or at any rate we moved *down*stairs to clean *up*stairs. We carried great armfuls of clothes and threw them with feather beds and mattresses downstairs, and after we had thrown them all down we tumbled down on them, and carried them by armfuls into the bedrooms. After we got the beds made up, Mother swept and we went upstairs; while she was sweeping, we took tacks out of carpets, as many as we could, and then, when she came up, we had to clean up the playroom. Hannah was taking up her carpet, so Mother and I had to get dinner. I dressed myself and went to take my music lesson. It was a lovely thing called "Departed Days."

Before supper I went with Nora into the storeroom and got some apples for mincemeat. Mother peeled them, and Nora and I chopped to the tune of "Yankee Doodle." It makes it much easier.

April 9th: After breakfast we read the prayers as usual, then I made the beds, and there was still time though to have a play before studying, so we went over to Carll's to see them dig the cellar under the new ell. Came home and studied, which with the reciting and practicing took me till dinner. After dinner I went in to Aunt J.'s to see the baby, then came home and wrote my journal; then Nora and I went up in Dunn's woods to get some boxberries. Practiced till supper time when I fried the pancakes. Uncle H. came down, and I played for him till bedtime.

April 17th: Helped Hannah fry the cakes for breakfast. After breakfast I quilted a little and then studied. It never took me longer to get my lessons, for my head ached dreadfully. After dinner I quilted twenty-four squares, then Nora and I stripped up a lot of rags and sewed them together, and I braided a little on them to make a rag mat for our play house. Carried Mrs. C.'s book back to her, and afterwards took down a book to both Mrs. D. and Mrs. S., "Uncle Tom's Cabin" to the former, and "Yusef, or a Crusade in the East," to the latter, also borrowed two bound numbers of "Littell's." Oh, how splendid!

April 21st: After breakfast Uncle Henry came down and asked us up to dinner, so Mother said she would and bring something. Hannah and I went ahead, I with a lemon pie, and she with some parsnips. After we had given them to her we went out in the garden by the brook, and stayed there till dinner time. After dinner we all went up in the woods, and got Grandma a lot of things to make root beer of, "Linkum Piny," Liverwort, Motherwort, Ivory Leaves, etc.

April 28th: After dinner read a little out of a book of poems, "The Hidden Way," then went out in the kitchen and played jackstones for a while, after which we went to walk, came home quite early, *had perfectly splendid tarts for supper.*

May 12th: After breakfast we read the Bible, then I helped get Nora off for meeting. Then sat down and read awhile in my favorite book "Uncle Tom's Cabin" after which I wrote a letter, also my journal, then Mother read a very interesting account of the great Paris Exposition out of the "Tribune." I want to go awfully, but, of course, there is no possibility of it. Cousin F. came in just as she had finished and brought me some beautiful wild flowers, Hepaticas, Anemones, and May Flowers. Pretty soon Nora came and brought me a nice Sunday School book—"Patience, or the Sunshine of the Heart." All the children in the Sunday School books are as good as pie.

May 19th: Rose at seven this morning. After breakfast we put on our new calico dresses. They fitted nicely and I think they are beautiful. Then after waiting some time Willie came up with the horse and we started for church, had a beautiful ride up, and got there just in time. We had our Sunday School lessons good and our Commandments also. We had some very nice books; my most interesting one was "Mary Lewis, a little Orphan but a Christian girl."

I have finished the "Minister's Wooing." After supper I watered the plants. I am to do it for a cent a week. (!)

May 21st: I did not miss in school this morning and had good lessons in the afternoon. Got up two in spelling, *so I am now Number Six!!*

May 24th: Father gave me a piece of land to make me a vegetable garden, so I went right to work. First I hauled manure in Phil's little cart, and hoed and mixed it in with the earth, then Nora and I went up to Grandma's and got some Beet seeds, Corn, Potatoes, Lettuce, Tomato, Peas; it took us a great while to plant them and make a fence round it and it wasn't a very big garden either.

June 2nd: Miss R. asked me if it was pleasant if I did not want to ride up to Moderation with her the next time when she goes to give a music lesson. I said I should be delighted to. I jumped rope till bedtime. Oh, I hope it will be pleasant! I have got to be down at Miss R.'s by six, ready to start. It is eight miles. Even with her good horse we cannot make it in an hour.

June 7th: Hannah called me at five o'clock this morning. I dressed myself in a nice clean gingham dress, then ate a little breakfast and went down to Miss R.'s. It was a perfectly lovely day, and when we got on our way it was so early and everything was so fresh that we were having a beautiful ride. The birds were all singing and the apple trees all in bloom, and so many weeping elms and other splendid trees I never saw before.

June 8th: I cut up some rhubarb for pies and for sauce, then helped make cake and cream pie, after that I wrote my journal, and then practiced till dinner time. I had my pinball cut out, but could not make it because it had to be ironed. As I couldn't think of anything else to make I thought I would buy some calico at the store to make baby's bibs. Well, I got some pink calico, a quarter of a yard; it will make three and it was only four cents. I had time to bind one before supper; after it Nora and I went over the other side of the river and played hide and coop in the lumber yard.

June 11th: Nothing happened during the day, but when I got home from a drive they told me that Lambie had choked to death. Oh, how sad I did feel; it seemed as if I couldn't keep from crying, and I did when I got into my room alone. He cost a dollar and a quarter and only lived two and a half months! We are never going to have another. He wound himself up in his rope and then fell down a steep bank.

July 4th: It has been a very hot day and not much fun. I was unhappy quite a while remembering last Fourth of July when Mother was away and Aunt J. was taking care of us and she gave me five cents to spend and told me to divide it with Nora. I took three cents and gave her two because I was the oldest; and next day, and ever since, sometimes at night, I feel ashamed, for it was mean and I know I ought to have given her two and a half and been fair.

July 6th: Made Phil's cart into an ambulance and Nora and I are going to have a hospital for sick bugs and other things. I got four little willow branches and dropped them into the cart for a bed and then made a cover of white curtain lace. It is perfectly lovely and we soon hope to have it full of invalid insects, though Nora hates worms and crawling things.

July 13th: I have had some trouble with lessons this week, but none at all with behavior for a very long time. It seems quite natural to be good. (!!)

So ends the commonplace little chronicle! I could not have been a Pharisee at the age of ten, so I hope this allusion to the ease with which I attained perfection of conduct may be pardoned by the reader. The record was made on a Saturday night, and I was probably in a happy and serene state of mind, looking back upon several days of unusual virtue. . . . Father, mother, brother, sister, grandmother, uncle, cousin, playmates, all rise in their accustomed places as I turn the leaves of the journal and read the faded childish handwriting, but I see them on a background of the hills and fields of New England, with its summer heats and its drift of winter snows. I see the fast-flowing river, the sawmill on its brink, the little red-brick district school, the white-painted meeting-house. All together they make the picture I love best, that of the dearest of all my many homes.

[Two years later, when Kate was twelve, she had the great good luck of meeting her literary hero, Charles Dickens. Excitement in her family ran high when it was learned that the Great Man was coming to America to give readings and would, incredible fortune, make an appearance in Portland. Kate and her mother were to go to Boston for a visit, so a stopover in

Portland was included, but alas the price of tickets to the reading was too great to permit the youngest member to attend. Kate was crestfallen but stoic.

The next day, on board the train to Boston, she was delighted to see that Charles Dickens himself was a passenger. Mrs. Wiggin was never a retiring child, and as soon as his companion, a Mr. Osgood, left his seat...]

I never knew how it happened; I had no plan, no preparation, no intention, certainly no provocation; but invisible ropes pulled me out of my seat, and speeding up the aisle, I planted myself breathlessly and timorously down, an unbidden guest, in the seat of honor. I had a moment to recover my equanimity, for Dickens was looking out of the window, but he turned suddenly and said with justifiable surprise:

"God bless my soul, child, where did you come from?"

My heart was in my mouth, but there was still room to exercise my tongue, which was generally the case. I was frightened, but not so completely frightened as if I had been meeting a stranger. You see I knew him, even if he did not know me; so I became immediately autobiographical, although palpitating with nervousness. I had to tell him, I thought, where I came from, who I was, where I was going, or how could I account for myself and my presence beside him in Mr. Osgood's seat? So I began, stammeringly, to answer his question.

"I came from Hollis, Maine, and I'm going to Charlestown to visit my uncle. My mother and her cousin went to your reading last night, but of course three couldn't go from the same family, it was so expensive, so I stayed at home. Nora, that's my little sister, is left behind in Hollis. She's too small to go on a journey, but she wanted to go to the reading dreadfully. There was a lady there who had never heard of Betsey Trotwood, and had only read two of your books!"

"Well, upon my word!" he said; "you do not mean to say that *you* have read them!"

"Of course!" I replied; "every one of them but the two that we are going to buy in Boston, and some of them six times."

"Bless my soul!" he ejaculated again. "Those long thick books, and you such a slip of a thing."

"Of course," I explained conscientiously, "I do skip some of the very dull parts once in a while; not the short dull parts, but the long ones."

He laughed heartily. "Now, that is something that I hear very little about," he said. "I distinctly want to learn more about those very long dull parts."

And, whether to amuse himself, or to amuse me, I do not know, he took out a notebook and pencil from his pocket and proceeded to give me an exhausting and exhaustive examination on this subject; the books in which the dull parts predominated; and the characters and subjects which principally produced them. He chuckled so constantly during this operation that I could hardly help believing myself extraordinarily agreeable, so I continued dealing these infant blows, under the delusion that I was flinging him bouquets.

It was not long before one of my hands was in his, and his arm around my waist, while we talked of many things. They say, I believe, that his hands were "undistinguished" in shape, and that he wore too many rings. Well, those criticisms must come from persons who never felt the warmth of his handclasp! For my part, I am glad that Pullman chair cars had not come into fashion, else I should never have experienced the delicious joy of snuggling up to Genius, and of being distinctly encouraged in the attitude. . . .

"What book of mine do you like best?" Dickens asked, I remember; and I answered with the definite assurance of childhood, "Oh, I like 'David Copperfield' much the best. That is the one I have read six times."

"Six times—good, good!" he replied; "I am glad that you like Davy, so do I—I like it best, too!" clapping his hands; and that was the only remark he made which attracted the attention of the other passengers, who glanced in our direction now and then, I have been told, smiling at the interview, but preserving its privacy with the utmost friendliness. I had never looked behind to see how my mother was faring. There are great crises in life when even mothers must retire to the background. For the moment I had no mother, family, friends, or acquaintances, no home, no personality; I was a sort of atom floating in space, half conscious that I could not float forever, but must come to earth again.

"I almost said 'Great Expectations,'" I added presently, "because that comes next in our family. We named our little yellow dog 'Mr. Pip' out of your book. They told Father when they gave him to us that he was part rat terrier, and we were all pleased, because, if he was, he wasn't all mongrel. (That means mixed-up.) Then one day Father showed him a trap with a mouse in it. The mouse wiggled its tail just a little, and Pip was so frightened that he ran under the barn and stayed the rest of the day. That showed that there wasn't enough rat terrier in him to be right, and the neighbors made fun of him and used to call 'Rats!' when he went down the street. We loved him just the same and he had as hard a time as Pip in 'Great Expectations.'"

Here again my new friend's mirth was delightful to behold, so much so that my embarrassed mother, who had been watching me for half an hour, almost made up her mind to drag me away before the very eyes of our fellow passengers. I had never been thought an amusing child in the family circle; what, then, could I be saying to the most distinguished and popular author in the universe?. . .

"Did you want to go to my reading very much, child?" was another question. Here was a subject that had never once been touched upon in all the past days—a topic that stirred the very depths of my disappointment and sorrow, fairly choking me, and making my lip tremble by its unexpectedness, as I faltered, "Yes I did, more than tongue can tell! I know how I feel when I read one of the books, but I wanted to hear how it sounded."

I looked up a second later, when I was sure that the tears in my eyes were not going to fall, and to my astonishment saw that Dickens's eyes were in precisely the same state of moisture. That was a never-to-be-forgotten moment, although I was too young to appreciate the full significance of it.

"Do you cry when you read out loud, too?" I asked curiously. "We all do in our family. And we never read about Tiny Tim, or about Steerforth when his body is washed up on the beach, on Saturday nights, for fear our eyes will be too swollen to go to Sunday School."

"Yes, I cry when I read about Steerforth," he answered quietly, and I felt no astonishment. "I cried when I wrote it, too! That is still more foolish!"

"Where do you cry the worst?" I asked. "Our time is when it says, '*All the men who carried him had known him and gone sailing with him and seen him merry and bold;*' and here I grew tearful and reminiscent.

We were now fast approaching our destination—the station in Boston—and the passengers began to collect their wraps and bundles. Mr. Osgood had two or three times made his appearance, but had been waved away with a smile by Dickens—a smile that seemed to say, "You will excuse me, I know, but this child has the right of way."

"You are not traveling alone?" he asked, as he arose to put on his overcoat.

"Oh! my goodness!" I said, coming down to earth for the first time since I had taken my seat beside him—"certainly not; I had a mother, but I forgot all about her." Whereupon he said, "You are past-mistress of the art of flattery!". . . .

Dickens took me back to the forgotten mother, and introduced himself, and I, still clinging to his hand, left the car and walked with him down the platform until he disappeared in the carriage with Mr. Osgood, leaving me with the feeling that I must continue my existence somehow in a dull and dreary world.

Excerpts from *My Garden of Memory,* by Kate Douglas Wiggin. Copyright 1923 by Houghton Mifflin Co. Copyright renewed 1951 by Houghton Mifflin Co. Reprinted by permission of Houghton Mifflin Co.

The cover for an early Frank Merriwell adventure novel, written by Gilbert Patten under the pseudonym "Burt Standish." *Courtesy of the Corinna Public Library.*

Gilbert Patten
1866–1945

A boy lay reading in bed in a big, unfinished chamber of an old house in Corinna, Maine. He was reading by the yellow light of a kerosene lamp that stood on a wooden chair beside the bed. The lamp had been placed in that low position so that its light, shining through an uncurtained window a few feet away, would not fall upon the gable end of a lurching barn at the rear end of the house, where it could have been seen by the boy's father or mother, who occupied a bedroom on the first floor. The greater part of the chamber was in shadow and darkness. The position of the lamp compelled the boy to lie close to the edge of the bed and hold the book extended at an angle to permit the light to fall upon the fine print that covered the pages. Entranced, spellbound, the young reader followed the swift course of the sanguine tale:

> A rumbling roar of fury broke from the crew, and they hurled themselves upon their captain while shots resounded through the cabin. They were fired by the youth, and the bullets found the hearts of those they were aimed for, his two pistols spitting red in the dark.
>
> But it did not check the maddened buccaneers, and rushing forward, a dozen seized the boy and he, too, was crashed bodily to the floor.
>
> "Freelance is dead!"
>
> The cry came from the lips of the ring-leader, as he

rose to his feet, a drawn knife in his hand, the blade crimsoned to the hilt—

There were sounds in the shadow-haunted chamber, the faint rasping of an unoiled door hinge, the soft sluff of a stockinged foot, the creak of a loose floor board. Holding a candle and shading it with one hand, the boy's nightgowned mother stood in the doorway.

"Willie,"she whispered. "What are you doing, Willie, reading at this hour? It's midnight, and after. You'll ruin your eyes. If your father ever caught you— What's this?"

She had advanced quickly to the bed and taken the little book out of the boy's hand. One glance at its cover was enough.

"A dime novel!" There was reproof and sorrow in her voice and on her face. "Where did you get it? Such dreadful stuff! It'll be the ruination of the boys in this country." Little did she imagine that the boy in the bed—her own boy whom she had hoped, and still hoped, would become a minister of the gospel—was destined to follow the profession of a dime novelist. Little did she imagine that one day she herself, having read one of his stories through to the end, would lay it down and look at him with strange pride in her face and pronounce it "very good." She had hoped he would become a preacher. Well, he has been charged with preaching in his dime novels, and so, maybe, she had her way after all.

This was the way Gilbert Patten of Corinna began his autobiography in the Saturday Evening Post *of February 29, 1931. He was then sixty-five years old and ready to tell the millions of Americans who had read his books in their youth the story of the man who had written the long-running epic of Frank Merriwell and his brother Dick. The Merriwell books have been called the longest series in publishing history, 245 volumes in all, of which Patten had written or was closely concerned in the writing of 208. Between 1896 and 1913 Patten had written a twenty-thousand-word Merriwell story for each weekly issue of a nickel magazine, Street and*

Smith's Tip Top Weekly. *Shortly after their magazine publication, three or four of these stories were bound together to make a fifteen-cent book, a separate title in the Merriwell series. His working routine was to turn out five thousand words a day, a complete story every four days. His best production record, he reports, when he was trying to get ahead of schedule to look up new background for his fiction or to take a vacation, was fifty thousand words a week. He began writing in longhand, moved on to one of the early typewriters, and ended up giving dictation to a stenographer.*

George Jean Nathan, the critic and literary historian, remembered the nationwide spell the Merriwell stories had cast: "His readers numbered millions, and included all sorts of young men, rich and poor. For one who read Mark Twain's 'Huckleberry Finn' and 'Tom Sawyer' there were ten thousand who read Standish's 'Frank Merriwell's Dilemma: or, The Rescue of Inez.'   The little candy stores of that day . . . had longer lines of small boys with nickels in their hands every Friday than Barnum's circus ever could boast." Sinclair Lewis, at a party in New York during the First World War, was astonished to meet the real Burt L. Standish (Patten's pen name for the Merriwell books): "My God! Not really? Why, Burt, you old wretch, I cut my eye teeth on your trash."

Patten, christened George William, shed those names and assumed many others during his long career as a writer of cheap books for boys. He started writing very early. Born in Corinna in 1866 to parents both over forty, he was an only child and described himself in his adolescence as almost a physical freak. At fourteen he was six feet tall and weighed less than 115 pounds. His parents were Adventists, anxiously preparing for the second coming of Christ. There was much churchgoing and, in between, prayer meetings in the parlor. His father, a carpenter, was a gentle giant who had been in his youth a river-driver in the north woods but was now a pacifist who forbade his son ever to fight. His family's oddness, and perhaps his own, led him to find a more attractive world in books. He investigated every imaginative escape available, moving, he reports, from Sabbath school literature to the Bible, to something called The Prince of the House of David, *then to those blood and thunder "dime novels"—they were actually a nickel—produced in America in great numbers after the Civil War.*

He was soon writing stories himself, "even before I knew how to spell *some of the words." At sixteen he sent two stories, "A Bad Man" and "The Pride of Sandy Flat" to the Beadle and Adams publishing house in New York. To his amazement, they were accepted, and he was sent a check for six dollars. By age eighteen he had moved beyond short stories to novel-length thrillers, and he was being paid $75, and finally $150, each. He changed his mind about going to Colby College and at twenty married Alice Gardner, the brightest girl in his class at Corinna Academy. (She had always encouraged him and corrected his spelling and grammar.) At twenty-three they moved with his parents to Camden, and he continued to send to New York stories with titles like "Hustler Harry, the Cowboy Sport" and "Wild Vulcan, the Lone Range Rider." His income was now two thousand dollars a year, and Camden couldn't hold him. He and Alice moved on to New York, the center for all dime-novel publishers and their hack writers.*

But in the nineties the fashions in stories for young people were changing. Nick Carter detective stories were in, and a new kind of juvenile hero was attracting young readers. In 1895 Patten was asked by Street and Smith to invent a series that would compete with the exploits of a new "realistic" contemporary hero, Horatio Alger. Using a few of his own youthful trials in Corinna, Patten created Frank Merriwell, "the sort of fellow that the majority of American lads would like to be." In the Saturday Evening Post *autobiography he went on to explain:*

> Another decision was reached before the initial tale was written. This was that the stories should contain the gospel of health and strength—a clean mind in a sound and vigorous body. For my own weaknesses as a boy had made me a worshiper of strength of body and mind. . . . And the pacifism of my two hundred and thirty-five pound father and my timid one hundred and ten pound mother, both of whom lectured me almost daily on the shamefulness of fighting . . . converted me into a shrinking lad with a sense of inferiority. So it was natural for me to wish to make Frank a fellow such as I would have liked to have been myself.

The first episode, "Frank Merriwell; or, First Days at Farwell"—

Farwell was the prep school that prepared Frank Merriwell for Yale—was a sellout. At the end of the first year the weekly circulation of the Tip Top Weekly had grown to one hundred thousand. At their height the weekly numbers rose to two hundred and fifty thousand. It would be impossible to describe briefly the art of storytelling that Gilbert Patten brought to the Merriwell series, which gave his books such a powerful attraction to American boys for seventeen years and far beyond. (The Merriwell books were still selling on newsstand racks well into the thirties.) Perhaps Patten's least sentimental and morally suspect statement of his art was this: "When you're writing regular fiction, you draw your characters from life. But when you're writing for boys you draw your characters from the imaginary world that boys live in." But even the Merriwell saga lost readers as tastes in juvenile fiction changed. The arrival of the first nickelodeons was a heavy blow. American kids had found another exciting use for their nickel at the end of the week. In 1914 Gilbert Patten turned over the Merriwell brothers to other Street and Smith writers. But he wrote Merriwell scripts for movies, and later a comic strip and an unsuccessful attempt at a radio serial. Patten's life darkened as publishing and writing projects failed; he lost his house in Camden and his apartment in New York. His publishers had profited immensely from the Merriwell books, but Patten never owned the rights to any of his printed work, not even to his self-invented pen name. When his poor financial condition became known, New York columnist Franklin P. Adams appealed for a benefit fund to help him, but Patten returned all the money. His California daughter-in-law came east to rescue him from a hotel room in New London, Connecticut, and persuaded him to come to live with his son's family on their avocado ranch. He died there in 1945.

The Creator of Frank Merriwell

I can remember when there was no meat market in Corinna. Country butchers came along at intervals, peddling beef and pork from carts. Like my father, many villagers raised pigs to slaughter for their own consumption. Usually they were butchered after cold weather came on in November so that they could be frozen and kept in that condition while being used as required. I doubted if I ever tasted roast beef in the first fifteen years of my life. Sometimes mother bought cheap cuts of beef for stewing or to be used in the mince-meat she put up in glass jars until it was baked in pies. And pies in our house were coincidental with visitors to dine.

There was likewise, at that time, no fruit store in the town. Native apples and purple damson plums—the latter then grew plentifully in Maine—might be bought in season from the grocers who happened to have a supply, but no imported fruit was handled regularly by any merchant.

The first time I ever saw a pineapple was on a Fourth of July when the town was having a celebration. By hustling and some hard work I had earned thirty-six cents which was all mine to spend on that day, but they had slipped away so fast that I was down to my last dime when I came face to face with a great temptation.

On a temporary stand in front of his store, Ed Folsom was offering for sale slices of peeled and sugar-smeared pineapple.

Five cents would get me one of those sweet, juicy, cool-looking slices, and the sight of them made my mouth water like a boiling spring. I was drooling when I tore myself away. But I had saved my dime only to spend it shortly thereafter for a bunch of firecrackers, and long years went by before I knew what pineapple tasted like.

Before long I was tempted again—and fell. This happened one day when I'd met the afternoon train and some stingy arrivals who hung onto their hand luggage and their two-cent pieces.

Had one of them loosened up and let me carry his grip, he would have saved me from taking another step on the well-trodden downward path. I hadn't finished telling myself what I thought of the last one, who pushed me aside, when I saw something which made me forget my annoyance.

The locomotive was shifting a freight over to the siding, and the train crew was busy. At the moment, no one else happened to be on the station platform. Before me was the car that carried both express and baggage, which had been left on the main line with other cars bound through to Oxton, eight miles beyond. The big side door was wide open and there was nobody in the car.

But there were some burlap covered baskets in there, one of them having a broken slat from which protruded the blushing cheek of a rosy golden peach.

Never before had I seen a real peach, but I knew this was one because I had seen pictures of them. It was as big, almost, as my two fists and much more beautiful than the pictures. I swallowed several times, fast, and prepared to act.

I glanced cautiously around. Nobody was watching me. I moved fast. I scrambled up into the car and ripped the broken slat of that basket still wider open. Out popped the gorgeous peach right into my hand. I didn't stop to examine it there. I put in under my jacket and got out quick.

When the stream was low, one could get down onto the big rocks under the railroad bridge below the mid-town crossing. That was where I went. Securely hidden, I brought forth my plunder and admired it.

Never before had I tasted anything half as delicious as that stolen peach. I gobbled it in ecstasy, the sweet juice dripping from my chin. Never since have I tasted anything half as delicious.

Not until I devoured it all but the clean brown stone did I realize what had happened. Then it came to me that I had made myself a criminal beyond retreat. The peach was irretrievably gone. It was in my stomach and could not be returned to its rightful owner. . . .

I had been told a hundred times that the first false step was always followed by another. I had been warned that it was just by such small false steps to begin with, many a poor wretch had started on the road to prison and the gallows.

Well, maybe I was on my way; but, oddly enough, when I thought of that beautiful peach and how absolutely delicious it was, I was sorry I hadn't taken a little more time, while I was about it, and hooked at least one more. I'd often heard the saying that one might was well be hanged for stealing an old sheep as for stealing a young lamb.

Although I was an introvert, I was still too young to perceive the reasons for many of my mental attitudes and my likes and dislikes. But I did know that the boys who were called good by my elders often were lackadaisical prigs with neither the courage nor the inclination to do the things that might get them into trouble. And some were downright sneaks and tattlers who spied on other boys and carried tales to their parents or to school teachers.

On the other hand, many so-called bad boys were merely boisterous, high-spirited, fun-loving fellows who indulged in rough-and-tumble horseplay and practical jokes—just natural, healthy boys who were neither bullies nor sneaks. They were the kind I admired and wanted to be associated with, but they had called me a "goody-goody" because thus far I had heeded my father's warning about fighting, which made me seem to lack the spirit to stand up for my own rights. . . .

One evening, to my surprise, I was invited to join some of the so-called bad boys who were smoking two-cent cheroots out behind Sam Morse's store. Still more to my surprise, I was offered a comfortable seat on an empty box and given a cheroot. Up to that time I had never smoked anything stronger than rattan "cigars," made by cutting up the ribs of cast-off umbrellas. But now, not only puzzled but flattered by the attention I was receiving, I didn't back away from that tobacco cheroot. This was my opportunity to get in right with some high steppers, and I didn't propose to muff it.

I got along swimmingly for awhile, didn't choke, didn't cough—much. I knew they were watching me. I saw some of them grinning behind their hands and winking at one another. Somebody asked me how I liked my cheroot and I said it was "bully." I didn't like it much but I wasn't going to let them know. I pretended to enjoy every puff. I was showing these fellows I was no softie.

Next thing, I'd have to take up chewing tobacco. That would be the finishing touch. I felt like laughing. I took the cheroot out of my mouth, tipped my head back and blew a whiff of smoke upward. I almost fell off the box. Something had made me slightly dizzy.

I looked at my cheroot and found that I hadn't smoked quite half of it.

"What's the matter, Willie?" asked one of the grinning gang.

"Not a thing," said I, putting the cheroot back between my teeth and taking a good long drag at it.

That was the finishing touch.

The pit of my stomach squirmed and I began to feel queer all over. I tried not to show it, but in less than a minute I was convinced that I was going to be a very sick child. I said I had to be going. They sought to detain me and urged me to go on smoking.

I dropped the cheroot, reeled to my feet, clasped my hands over my uneasy stomach, and fled from their midst and the sound of their hilarity.

Somehow I avoided my mother's sharp eyes and got up to my bed in the open chamber. But I didn't shed more than half my clothes before I was compelled to lie down and hold fast to the bed while it whirled and reared and bucked like a wild bronco. Then my stomach started bucking also, and I didn't give a rap if the bed threw me off and broke my fool neck.

Mother found what was left of me in the morning, limp and weak but still breathing. She was shocked by the sight of me—and the floor beside the bed. She wondered what I had eaten that made me so ill.

I admitted that I couldn't think of anything. She kept me in bed and doctored me up while I tried to figure out some way to get even with the smarties who had made a sap of me. Not being able to conceive a plan for retaliation, I decided to show those fellows that I could smoke as well as anybody. No matter how tough the going might be, I was going to learn to smoke. But to do so I must have money to buy cheroots or smoking tobacco, and I didn't have a copper to my name.

So as soon as I could I started searching for any kind of a paying job and finally found one that nearly broke my back. I sawed and split a cord of hard and knotty wood, for which labor I received twenty-five cents. It took me three days with my father's bucksaw and ax, and I was sore and lame for a week.

And then when I tried to buy cheroots from Sam Morse, he wouldn't sell me any. "You're too young," he said. But there was another boy whose father kept a store and sold tobacco and cigars, who got them for me. I paid him, but I doubt if the money ever reached his father's till.

I had to do my smoking secretly when I could find an opportunity, and it was quite a while before I could smoke a whole cheroot without gagging. However, I worked up to that point by degrees and spent much more than twenty-five cents before I arrived there.

Eventually the evening came when I joined the gang behind Sam Morse's store with a lighted cheroot in my mouth and kept on smoking it until the cheroot was too small to hold. . . .

Nevertheless, even that did not win me full fellowship with the gang. They had been surprised and impressed, but they failed to loosen up with me. I was still Willie Patten, and somehow that meant I was still an outsider. I had to do more than smoke a cheroot to get past the barrier, but what?

I was still wondering about that, when there came a Sunday on which I made a getaway from home without being detected and called back. I did this by going up the hill away from the village. But unfortunately I ran into two boys who were coming out of the home of Amos Dunn, a farmer who lived in a white house at the top of the hill. Old Amos and his family were away, and Bert Kilson, who was living there then, had taken Tommy Wood into the cellar to treat him to some of the farmer's hard cider, which was fortified with alcohol.

Now they fell on my neck with whoops of joy, and back into the cellar they went, taking me with them. I didn't get what they were trying to do until I found myself with a brimming tumblerful of old Amos's chained lightning in my hand. I'd really begun to think they were crazy.

"It'll make hair grow on your chest, Willie," said Bert. "We've had three glasses apiece and we're feeling great."

It was terrible, but I forced myself to swallow it. Before I could get my breath my glass was filled again and coming my way. I balked. I tried to beg off. Tommy Wood got me by the neck again. He was much older and stronger than I, and I knew he could handle me with one hand tied behind him.

"Down it," he said, "or we'll hold you and pour it down your throat."

I downed it—and it downed me. I'm sure I didn't drink a third glass. Sometime later I found myself lying alone, beside a pond and watching the world spin with the movements of a dying top. At times the ground tipped until I had to clutch the grass with both hands and hold fast to keep from falling into the sky below me. It was exciting, even terrifying. I was much more upset than I had been after smoking my first cheroot. Let's let it go at that and skip further details of what happened there.

I didn't know what had become of Bert Kilson and Tommy Wood, and I didn't care. I wanted to get home, even though I expected to catch a birching by my father. I was sure it would make him quite angry to see his carefully guarded son come reeling home as drunk as a boiled owl. But I was in luck. He didn't see me. Company had arrived while I was away, and an impromptu prayer meeting was taking place. I sneaked in and crept upstairs while they were singing a hymn. I didn't have to pretend I had a bad headache when mother found me stretched over my bed after the company left.

"Why, Willie," she said, "why didn't you call me instead of lying up here and suffering all this time?"

They hadn't even missed me! That discovery helped me as much as Mother's ministrations with cold compresses and a camphor bottle. . . .

Even though many memories of my boyhood in Corinna are extremely vivid, that entire period in my life seems fantastically unreal and dreamlike. Wood-burning stoves were then in nearly universal use in cooking and heating. Railroad locomotives burned wood too, and the stoves which heated the cars sometimes roasted passengers alive in train wrecks. Homes were lighted by kerosene lamps or candles. Very poor people often used "slut candles"; such a candle was a shallow open dish containing animal fat in which burned the end of a saturated wick or woolen rag. They furnished a wretched, fluttering light, smoked horribly and were sickeningly noisome.

Some persons in our village who had been "up to Boston" and seen gaslights still thought kerosene lamps more convenient and better for interior lighting. In the meantime there was talk about a new kind of light produced by electricity, but how light could be obtained without a flame no one could seem to understand. The current opinion of the best local minds was that Tom Edison, the inventor, would never get anywhere with such a crazy scheme. . . .

The telegraph was still a great wonder and I, like several other boys in town, became ambitious to learn telegraphy. We were inspired by the advertisement of a small pocket gadget of metal with which clicking sounds similar to those made by a telegraph key could be produced.

"Become a telegraph operator and earn big pay," said the advertisement, and all of us looked forward hopefully to the time when we would be earning big pay. So we raked up dimes by hook or crook or good hard work and sent away for those pocket telegraph keys, a copy of the Morse code, and full instructions for learning telegraphy. Only one of us became a telegraph operator in later life, and he certainly earned all the pay he received for running a small town railway office, where telegraphy was a minor part of his job. . . .

Probably my first attempts to express myself in verse were inspired by the poetry in the school readers then in use. In particular I remember "The Burial of Sir John Moore" and the stirring line, "to heartbeat and drumbeat a soldier passes by." Among other poems were William Cullen Bryant's "Thanatopsis" and Poe's "The Bells," which were sometimes used as declamations by older scholars. These led me, later, to study metrical writing and to become familiar with the works of many famous poets then in vogue.

The poetic urge came upon me at a time when I had begun to take a sentimental interest in girls. Hitherto they had held small attraction for me, as associates, and sometimes they had annoyed me. I had tolerated them as playmates only when necessity compelled, but now I was growing up and changing with the passing years. Although I still read dime novels, I was beginning to take an interest in more romantic and fluffy fiction. A strange restlessness was coming over me, bringing with it a disturbing sense of shame. Sometimes it caused me to be grossly rude with girls who attracted me most, pulling their hair or pushing them around by bumping against them, as if by accident or awkwardness.

There was one exception, however; I was never rude to Addie Hutching. I was slightly younger than Addie, but she was the girl of my dreams—literally, it seemed. Imagine how dashed I was when I discovered that Addie and Frank Nutter, my best friend, were secret sweethearts. . . . I didn't let either of them know how I felt toward Addie. I hid my secret sorrow in my heart, fully expecting to carry it with me to my grave. Nor did I let them suspect that I was wise to what was going on, for I didn't want them to think that I had spied on them. But, needing a confidant, Frank eventually let me in on their secret, and I became the bearer of little notes and oral messages between them.

I dramatized the situation, becoming the noble hero who had made a mighty sacrifice for a beloved pal. By nature I was easily moved to merriment, but now I gloomed around with a long face and behaved so queerly that my mother was alarmed and attempted to doctor me up with some kind of herb brew that was bitter as gall. One dose of that cured me—when I was around home. Then I decided to be a hermit and took to the woods; but I always came back when I was hungry, and slept under the paternal roof at night. Two or three times I managed to slip away with Father's ancient muzzle-loading shotgun, with which I mercilessly slaughtered the harmless wild creatures—the birds and the squirrels that I would not have harmed had not cruel fate robbed me of the woman I loved and turned me into an unfeeling brute. It was pretty silly, but I enjoyed it.

But before school opened in September I was fed up with the hermit stuff. Play acting without an audience wasn't so good. I decided on another role for myself; I would become a devil among the little ladies, a dashing Lothario, a regular Don Juan. That was the kind of chap Bert Day was, big and handsome and a killer with the fair sex. I would be like Bert, that was what I'd do. Nothing stopped him. If anything got in his way he just laughed and kept right on going. So I spruced up as much as I could, assumed a devil-may-care air and really made myself feel like a different person. I actually winked at some of the girls right in school on the first day of the term, being careful, however, not to let the teacher catch me at it. When one of them made a face at me I grinned back at her. That was the way to carry it off, I'd been allowing myself to be squelched too easily.

At noon intermission the next day I got back early to the schoolhouse and found another boy and two girls there ahead of me. The boy, whom I'll call Dick, which wasn't his name, was older than I but much smaller. He was a snappy little chap and quite a blade with the girls. . . . He was romping and laughing with the girls when I came in, and without seeing me, one of them ran right into my arms. I gave her a smack on the mouth before she could get away. Well, she spat in my face. I wiped it off with my sleeve and started after her.

Dick grabbed me. "What do you think you're doing, Rolling Thunder?" said he, hanging on to my arm. Now Rolling Thunder was the derisive nickname that I'd been tagged with because of my dime-novel reading and story-writing habits. It annoyed me and made me very hot under the collar.

"Mind your own business, Peanut!" said I, giving him a snap and thrust that broke his hold and sent him staggering. He tripped against the teacher's raised platform and fell upon it. Up he bounced like a jumping-jack and slapped my face. Then we went to it.

He stood on the platform and I on the floor, which brought our eyes about on a level. He hit me on the chin with his fists, and I poked him in the stomach and slapped him right and left with both hands. I never saw anyone look more astonished and bewildered than he did. I was fighting mad—and fighting. It was so unexpected and incredible that he quit in less than half a minute. He backed away, staring at me in amazement.

"Come on," I said. "I haven't started yet." But he was all through and I had won my first fight. It hadn't been much of a fight, but others were to follow that wouldn't be so easy. . . .

For the first time I was invited that winter to many parties given by boys and girls in their own homes. It was customary for a visiting boy to bring a girl with him, but the only girl I would have enjoyed escorting was Addie Hutchings. That being out of the question, I arrived alone until it became embarrassing to appear that way. Finally I braced up and invited Jeanie Hamilton to accompany me. She was a big girl, red-cheeked and handsome in a way, but not at all my type. I liked them small and cuddly.

As there were not enough chairs for everybody that evening, Jeanie sat on my lap. She was in the heavyweight class and seemed to get heavier rapidly. Some of the other fellows were holding girls on their laps and were plainly enjoying it, but my spindly legs were not built for the load they were carrying. They began to ache and grow numb.

I gritted my teeth and tried to hold out until the party got under way, but lacked the staying power. When I couldn't take it any longer, I tried to make a joke by suggesting that she take my chair and let me stand up a while—if I could stand. Everybody laughed, but Jeanie turned still redder. For the rest of the evening she didn't know I was on earth. It was easy for me to put my foot in my mouth when I tried to be funny.

Later we played such games as Who's Got the Button?, Spin the Cover, The Needle's Eye, and Post Office. To play The Needle's Eye, we held hands and formed a circle around the room. Then we walked slowly beneath the clasped hands of a boy and a girl who stood on chairs, one outside the line and one inside. As the human circle moved along, everybody sang:

> The needle's eye it doth comply,
> It carries the thread so true,
> It hath caught many a smiling lass,
> And now, alas, it hath caught you.

The boy and the girl on the chairs took turns selecting somebody about whose neck they would lower their hands, and there was merriment and kidding when the one chosen tried to avoid being captured. The singing continued until a climax was reached and the couple on the chairs kissed at the end of the song.

Of all the girls present Addie Hutchings was the one most frequently caught by the Needle's Eye. Practically every fellow in the room seemed to have his eye on her, and she clearly reveled in her popularity. Some of the girls failed to hide their jealousy, and one boy was miffed; for not once did she try to catch me when it came her turn to make her choice. Also I observed with resentment that Bert Day was her favorite. He would be, the big skate! I let her trot right along by when I got a chance to make a selection.

We played Post Office after that and I was surprised when the postmistress announced, "There's a letter for Mr. William Patten." Mr. William Patten, not Willie! And I knew that Addie Hutchings was in the room that represented the Post Office. There was a general titter of laughter, and I felt my face burn as I stood up.

The shaded kerosene lamp in the Post Office was turned down just enough to make a homely girl look attractive in the dimmed light, but Addie needed no such device. When the door closed behind me I stopped and looked at Addie, who was waiting for me in the middle of the room. She laughed softly. Her chin always took on a bewitching little twist when she laughed.

"Come and get your letter, William," she said.

Now I would show her where she got off. I said, "Addie, you're a flirt. I don't want any letter from you."

She came to me swiftly. "Don't be silly," she said. She put her arms around my neck and kissed me.

Long ago! Long ago! Boys and girls together.

From *Frank Merriwell's "Father": An Autobiography* by Gilbert Patten ("Burt L. Standish"), Edited by Harriet Hinsdale, assisted by Tony London. Copyright ©1964 by the University of Oklahoma Press.

Willard Sperry
1882–1954

Willard Sperry represents an important segment of Maine's population: the summer people. His book of memories, Summer Yesterdays in Maine, *is an affectionate, sometimes sentimental, ode to his happy childhood days in a coastal summer cottage in York County. Sperry's father bought the cottage in 1885, and the family summered there for most of the next fifty years. As Sperry explained:*

There are, of course, two ways of taking a summer vacation. One kind of vacation is to be had by sloughing off civilization and going back to nature in the wilds. The other is got by stirring up the cultural subsoil of your life's setting. Happily the State of Maine recognizes both opportunities and ministers to both needs. . . .

In the early days of Maine tourism, people came and stayed for the whole summer, first in grand hotels that were built for the purpose and later, as visitors "from away" made a greater commitment to summer in Maine, in "cottages." Some of the cottages, those on Mount Desert Island for example, were large and imposing. Others, like the Sperrys', were simple and satisfying. After World War II, visitors drove through the state, stopping briefly at cabins and motels and campgrounds. The habits of tourists continued to change. The summer cottage is less common now; certainly the three-month summer vacation is a thing of the past. There are no figures for the tourist population in 1885, but a 1985 survey indicates that during that year over six million people came to visit Maine and to share the natural beauty and relaxed pace that Willard Sperry so enjoyed.

Sperry grew up to be a noted theologian. He graduated from Olivet College in Michigan (his father, also a minister, was college president) and was selected to be one of the first Rhodes Scholars. He earned the first of his two master's degrees at Oxford. As a minister he served several Congregational parishes but soon moved on to teaching and writing about the state of religion in America. He was appointed Plummer Professor of Christian Morals and dean of the Harvard Divinity School in 1925, where he remained until 1953. He published twenty-one books and a number of articles and essays, and he was a member of the committee charged with revising the Standard Version of the Bible. Sperry continued teaching and preaching and commenting on world and church affairs until his death in 1954. His summers in Maine had been an important part of his life. In writing his memoir, he said: "I have had a good deal of joy and no little help these last years in thinking back over these carefree summer days on the Maine coast."

The Cottage

My father bought the cottage in 1885 for two thousand dollars. So far as we the family were concerned it was one of the wisest things he ever did. He was not always so successful in "building up an estate." On other occasions he bought, at least on paper, some copper in the "U.P." of Michigan, and some land in Denver. There undoubtedly was copper in the Upper Peninsula, but it certainly was not where father's stock certificate said. And there indubitably was land in Denver, for after father's death we periodically had his lots located and verified. When it became clear that Denver had not developed according to the original prospectus, and that our Colorado estate bordered on the city dump, we were glad to unload for the taxes. Yes, the rocks "down to high-tide mark," as the York County deed said, with the blueberry and huckleberry bushes of that 150-foot frontage in Maine, were his best investment—not to overlook stray shy checkerberries as well. We knocked about from one official church parsonage or college residence to another, but with each passing year the cottage became more and more the family home. Our tether was sometimes a hundred miles long, sometimes a thousand, at times three thousand, but for nearly fifty years the cottage was ours—known, accepted with uncritical affection, patched, painted and reaffirmed.

Getting there was for the first year or so a heroic business. The train from Manchester did not go, in our direction, beyond Portsmouth. After that it had to be a stage coach, an honest-to-goodness Buffalo Bill, wild West affair, from which mail carriers might have fired at Indians. It is a great thing to have ridden in a stage coach, not as a decorative item in a pageant or parade on the Fourth of July, but as a paying passenger about his lawful business.

Since the stage began its journey by crossing the Piscataqua, a word as to that river will not be out of place. The Piscataqua is, for nine out of ten vacationists going through New Hampshire into Maine, the boundary line between the two states. It is one of those boundaries which seems to do something to the scenery, to work a visible change in the outer world. This impression is probably an illusion; most of the difference must be in the mind rather than the landscape. Nevertheless, the pines by the roadside in Kittery look darker, and outcropping rock is more constant than in the Hamptons ten miles back. In the late spring the snow lingers in the niches of the ledges a fortnight after it has gone in Massachusetts. Anyone who crosses that river instantly feels the difference. I suppose what the Piscataqua really means to us, whether we are young or old, is, "School's out!"

As to the river itself, it is a moving, businesslike body of water, with swirling tide rips. Down toward its mouth is the "Pull-'n-be-damned," where in the days before motorboats the fisherman labored in vain at his oars against the current. When the ebb or flood is running strongest the can buoy which marks the mid-channel is pulled almost out of sight under water. The old wooden bridge from Portsmouth to Kittery was, even in the '80s and '90s, a rather rickety affair. There were indeed two independent parallel bridges, but for all practical purposes the roadway and the railway ran side by side on the same bridge. This dual bridge was periodically inspected by divers, and in its latter years they are said to have come up and reported it in perfect condition, save that the piles all stopped three feet short of the bottom!

Once aboard the coach at the Portsmouth station, there were seats on top for more mature and favored passengers, perhaps merely for firstcomers. From that swaying eminence one could survey a wide, wide world. It is one of the remote sorrows of my life that I was in those days much too young to rate a top-side seat. A story lingered on in our family of an irreverent college boy who, on one trip, was a fellow passenger outside. The stage was trundling past one of those family graveyards, found in the corner of many a New England pasture. Most of these graveyards are neglected. This one, however, was spick and span. It had four granite posts at the corners of the lot, and heavy iron chains looped between the posts. The grass was clipped close and neat up to the edge of the hayfield round about. Only one thing was missing; no headstones were to be seen, indeed there seemed to be no graves. "Huh!" said the boy, "he isn't having much luck with his cemetery!"

Before I was five or six, the stage coach had given way to the railroad. Meanwhile, for the first year or so that we went by stage, my lot and portion in its crowded interior was a little pillar between the front and back seats. It was made of a foot of iron pipe set in a floor socket, crowned with a small square board innocent of any back and thinly topped off with a bit of red Turkey carpet. I was planted on this perch, and as the coach lurched, was propped up by hands coming from the point toward which I was being pitched. This circumambient chair back, made up of human hands, would come to life and into action as occasion required. Otherwise I was left to my own devices, rather like a weather cock, free to spin about as the winds of the spirit veered, either to stare tentatively at strange faces on one seat or with mute appeal at the family on the other seat. There was much bouncing about over granite ledges which cropped out constantly across the dusty road; there was the excitement of one or two changes of horses; until in the end ourselves and our bags were dumped out at the foot of a path through the bushes, where the road had all but ended. . . .

And so, whether by coach or train or trolley, we got to the cottage. It was small, but gay. It was painted red when first bought and stayed so in our time. Its color gave local habitation to a plaintive negro ditty we heard somewhere and as children sang with zest,

> Oh, the little red caboose,
> Oh, the little red caboose,
> Oh, the little red caboose
>> Behin' a train.
>> Choo! Choo!
>> Choo! Choo!

> Oh, the little red caboose,
> Oh, the little red caboose,
> Oh, the little red caboose
>> Behin' a train.

The carpenters and painters originally charged with its exterior decoration were, given the standards of the day, men of taste and invention. Along the ridge pole there ran the familiar scalloped sky-line board, with holes bored in its billowy bulges to give good value for the money. The roof was painted in diamond fashion, white and red. The total effect was undoubtedly arresting. The sky-line trimmings eventually blew off and were never replaced. When the time came to reshingle we saved something by omitting the diamond motif, fortified also by a subtle suspicion that the red and white period of art had passed. But since that pattern had become part of my aesthetic second nature I was prepared for the brick vagaries of Keble College in Oxford, when later they burst upon my view, and even now I can sit and look out of my office window in the University Church in the Harvard Yard to contemplate without too much concern the multi-colored roof of Memorial Hall.

Originally there was a front and side porch only. This was never screened, and much of one's life there had to be passed fighting mosquitoes. There were various types of "swatters." There were punks to burn, after a losing battle there were lotions, and finally there was the inalienable right to scratch. We can never have spent long enough there at any one time to develop the immunity to mosquitoes which the natives have. We had a local boy who did chores around the place and one day some one asked him whether the mosquitoes bit him. He replied with sober Maine caution, and with characteristic understatement, "Well, I don't know that I'd go so far as to say that they bite me, but at times they do pester me a mite." Later a screened back porch was added which got some shade from straggling oaks, and picked up what west wind there was on hot days. This was my mother's favorite place. It was less public than the front porch and more suited to her reserved nature. There were always people passing on the path which ran along the Bluff in front of the house, people who talked loudly and stared. Originally the path had run as a chain of neighborly links down the line between one front door and another. Eventually, in the interests of more privacy, we all clubbed together and built a proper rock-paved path farther out toward the sea. We never went into the matter legally, but presumably a right of way had been established which could not be closed.

Inside, the cottage boasted no intricacies. It was unashamedly forthright. A front living room used up a good half of the ground floor, a dining room the other half of the main rectangle, with the kitchen in an ell. There were four bedrooms overhead. And that was all. The bathroom, you ask? My friend, stop and think. A bathroom presupposes a water supply. There was, it is true, for some years, a huge wooden cask, as big as those you see in the tobacco ads, which was perched on stilts to catch rain water from the angle in the roof between the body of the house and the ell. It eventually rotted and fell apart, its ground space being taken over by the new back porch. So long as it was there it provided a measured amount of soft water for washing, but it was hardly a "water supply."

Drinking water was brought from a so-called spring in two-quart tin pails. The spring was a well made of a couple of hogsheads sunk in a muddy slough of despond half a mile off. So far from being a spring it was surface drainage. Its water seldom failed to yield small swimming things, which had to be fished out. As for the rest, I hate to reflect on all its invisible inhabitants. But none of us died of typhoid and all of us children are here to tell the tale. How could one have a bathroom on that basis? There were, instead, the whole Atlantic Ocean out front and the "shed" out back. It was some years before a town water system was put in, an artesian well driven by a chugging steam engine, which pumped its yield into an aerial standpipe that simmered in the sun. The whole system of piping lay naked and unashamed on the surface of the ground, whether mains or private lines. When the water reached you it was as lukewarm as the church of Laodicea, fit only to be spewed out. But over at the pumping station, where old Mr. Hutchins shoveled equal amounts of coal into his wheezy engine and tobacco into his burbling pipe—each yielding a dubious fire—the water came out of a tap at the pump head cold as ice. On a hot day it was worth going over there just to get a drink, to talk a while to Mr. Hutchins, and then to get a second drink. Not that there wasn't ice at the cottage, because there was. But the water from the pitcher that was put in the ice chest always had a dubious flavor of cantaloupes or lobsters, and often of both. For some reason best known to my mother, we didn't chip off ice and put it in the pitcher. Her rule on the matter may have had something to do with the necessary economies of the household. There was always a running feud between ourselves and the iceman as to the size of the block to be had for a quarter. As a silent protest against his niggardliness my mother one day cut out of some newspaper, and pasted on the lid of the icebox, a bit of doggerel that seemed to her relevant:

> Have you ever noticed,
>> When the summer days are cold,
> The iceman leaves a larger chunk
>> Than what your box will hold.
>
> But when the days are scorching hot,
>> And nearly fry your fat,
> He leaves the merest trifle.
>> Have you ever noticed that?

Let us never say that there is no justice in the universe. It is on such icemen that the moral order in due time revenged itself through the precise and passionless coolth of a Kelvinator. Moreover the ice we did get was cut in a shallow and muddy pond, and its underparts were not reassuring. That may have been another reason why the pitcher was put in the chest, but no ice in the pitcher. In any case the drink at the pumping station was better. In due time a more adequate supply from a lake in the hinterland made possible a tap in the kitchen and the ultimate amenities of a bathroom.

When we first got it, the cottage was finished in rough pine boards. Upstairs there was no ceiling to the bedrooms, only the rafters and the sloping roof overhead. The pine partitions went up far enough to insure privacy for the purposes of dressing and undressing, but there they stopped. Any given board in the partition ended where it ended without too much reference to the height of the boards either side. Across this serrated divide family small talk went on in the dark, after we had gone to bed, until silence was ordered by my mother. Eventually, in the interests of a little more seemliness the downstairs was sheathed in whitewood and shellacked, while the upstairs was given a ceiling over the rooms, and its walls were finished off with a more genteel pine, painted to yield a blue room, a gray room, a green room and a white room. The single board partitions survived unchanged, and even though their summits were now permanently cloud-capped by the floor of the overhead attic, they were never soundproof. To the last, one or two knotholes remained in these partition walls. They lingered on as a survival of the earlier days when sleepers had all things in common, and served as room telephones after we were boxed in. . . .

As the years passed and we made one move after another, the cottage became the depository of excess chairs, tables, pictures and the like, even a Chickering piano which was not bettered by nine or ten months of absentee landlordism. It was eventually "winterkilled," giving up its tuneful soul to salt rust. On the other hand the piazza chairs, and two or three rockers for the living room, were bought on the spot, one or two a year, off a peddler who came by with a vast apparatus like a fire truck, bristling with ladders, benches, buckets and the like. I wonder, does he still survive somewhere. He was a fellow of infinite variety, and the clean white wood of his wares a homely joy.

Not to mention other articles at length, there was an austere horsehair sofa, with mahogany legs, arm rests, and sinuous moldings on the back. Its contours were as majestic as the moral law, and its surface as slippery as sin. This sofa was a bequest from "Aunty Robbins," an old parishioner in my father's first church in Peabody, Mass. Whether it was accepted in the first instance as a welcome addition to our share of what Saint Augustine calls "the baggage of this world," or whether my father dared not offend the shade of the dear old lady by refusing it, I do not know. Of its kind it was undoubtedly a period piece, and age could not wither nor custom stale its grim severity.

It was, however, one of those pieces of furniture which live a secret double life. Its back was hinged to let down and rest on legs swung out from the frame, to make thus a full width bed. The result would have done credit to Procrustes in his more inventive moods. To begin with, the body of the sofa was just not long enough even for a growing boy to stretch out full length. Either your head or your feet hit the implacable arm rests, at the ends. The seat itself was overstuffed with horsehair which was supported by coil springs of varying degrees of conviction. Some of them had given up the struggle and collapsed. The back, on the other hand, also covered with horsehair, was thinly upholstered and tufted against a wooden frame. This sofa back perpetuated the most exacting New England traditions as to any and all chair backs, which were never intended to promote physical and moral collapse. When this back was let down, we had in front of it a gentle mountain range of authentic seat, with its uplands and lowlands. Next there was a dividing valley where for two or three inches there was nothing save the framework of the entire structure, with the unfolded hinges showing. And then against the wall there was the cobblestone plateau of the lowered back at a level well below that of the seat in front. No mattresses, pillows, folded comforters ever smoothed out that topography. When there were visitors in excess of our limited space upstairs, one of us children had to come down and sleep on this monstrosity, to learn thus the dark mystery of "white nights.". . .

We were summoned to meals by a brazen cowbell which was as indubitably handmade as the iron nail from the *Hattie J. Averill*. It is strange how far the sound of that cowbell carried, when it was so lacking in overtones. It could be heard for half a mile and never failed to call us back from our absorptions along the shore. We still have it and use it. It has vied with rivals by way of Chinese gongs, brazen platters beaten with a hammer, Westminster chimes, tinkling silver cymbals, and all the rest of the known devices for getting people to table. It has outlived them all—worn them down and out by its single insistent and unresonant note. It is of its kind the one man-made sound in the world that I have heard longest in my lifetime. And though it does not now always mean fried cunners and blueberry muffins it still helps to keep body and soul together.

If Aunty Robbins' sofa survived from year to year and decade to decade, not as much can be said for the succession of hammocks that hung on the front piazza. The earliest of them were of the fish-net type, now wholly obsolete. The first that I remember were made of hemp and were uncommon harsh on the human frame. They had, however, one advantage—they could be "invisibly" and very successfully mended with cod line when and where they broke. Those hemp hammocks were followed by a wave of cotton thread glories with fringes and furbelows, as many colored in their weaves as Joseph's coat. Reds and yellows predominated, but the dyes were fugitive and after a few days of rain and sun the whole affair lapsed into a nondescript orange.

These hammocks were intended for single occupancy, whether lengthwise or crosswise. If lengthwise, you were more or less bowed like a new moon. Theoretically you ought to have been able, by bracing your legs, to get your head well above the level of your feet; practically you weren't—the law of gravity worked while you idled and you came to rest with your feet at the level of your head and the bulk of you sagging between. Such hammocks were even less adapted for being sat in. The main supporting side ropes which carried from one eye bolt to the other, between which the net was woven, cut into the middle of your back, and coming under your knees in front hoisted them up under your chin. The resultant position was a good deal like that which seems to have been generally used in prehistoric burial. Psychology coming to the aid of archaeology suggests that this posture was chosen because it is that of the fetus in the womb. If so, let it be said at once that the nascent human being refuses to stay in this position indefinitely and insists on getting out and stretching. In defense of those net hammocks, it must in all fairness be said that they pitched youthful lovers into each others' arms and laps with erotic vengeance. They served as a kind of chastened setting for "bundling." It was impossible for any two occupants to get and to keep a quarter of an inch apart. But since my present memories antedate all such maturer adventures, the story of those hammocks is that of a battlefield where I and my sisters each fought for sole occupancy. Once in, and rolled up like a cocoon, the occupant could refuse to be ousted. Of the subsequent and still extant type of Gloucester hammock with its flat upholstered seat and its vertical canvas back and sides, I say nothing. When these symbols of a tamer civilization arrived, they became the preserve of my mother or my Aunt Annie. They never interested us children. They were too civilized, too spacious, too peaceful. It was useless to fight for their sole occupancy because you could not defend their length and breadth. But a hammock was only a stopping place, a nomad's tent for those in transit from the house inside to the world outside.

Two girls share a pensive moment at the seashore. From *A Message Through Time: The Photographs of Emma D. Sewall, 1836–1919*, by Abbie Sewall. *Courtesy of Tilbury House Publishers.*

Mary Ellen Chase
1887–1973

Mary Ellen Chase's childhood in the coastal village of Blue Hill was a comfortable one. Her father was a lawyer and legislator, and the large Chase family had deep roots in the area. Her great-great-grandmother, Edith Ward, was the first white child born on the shores of Blue Hill Bay. There were schoolteachers on her mother's side of the family and seafaring men on her father's. Young Mary Ellen, the second in a family of eight children, was a voracious reader and such a good observer of her times and society that her later novels and biographies have a strong foundation in the seagoing life of the 1890s.

Maine had long been a leader in the building of ships and in the commercial shipping trade. The Maine woods provided lumber suitable not only for building ships but also as cargo for export to other regions at home and abroad in need of masts, barrel staves, ship timber, or shingles. In the West Indies trade of the eighteenth century, Maine ships brought lumber, ice, and granite to the Caribbean and returned with molasses and sugar and rum. The coastal town of Blue Hill was a commercial shipping port, and 1768 saw the first vessel sail out of Blue Hill Harbor for the West Indies. The shipping trade subsequently took Maine men, and often their wives and young children, to ports around the world.

By the time Mary Ellen Chase was born, inroads had been made into Maine's dominance of the coastal freight business by the depredations of the Civil War, the opening of the forests of the Northwest, the spread of railroads, and the use of iron in shipbuilding. Nevertheless, the coastal shipping trade had a brief revival in the 1890s, the time of which Chase writes, and the ships, their cargos, and their fortunes were the social and economic center of village life. Most of the townspeople worked in some part of the *shipping business. Some owned shares in the ships that provided a market for local goods and farm produce such as butter and cheese, potatoes, dried fish, lumber, and cordwood and brought staples, household items, and special treats to the villagers. It was a high point of the week to see a Downeaster sail into Blue Hill Harbor with a load of "general cargo" for the townspeople.*

Mary Ellen Chase left Blue Hill to attend the University of Maine at Orono, one of its first women students, and then went on to the University of Minnesota to do graduate work. Like her mother and grandfather before her, Mary Ellen Chase chose a career of teaching, and after a few years at Minnesota returned east to Smith College, where she taught for forty years. She had, in addition, been writing since she was twelve years old and managed to combine these two careers, along with a third one of public lecturing, with admirable success. Her Maine novels, Silas Crockett, Windswept, *and others, made her famous. Her autobiographies, including* A Goodly Heritage, *from which the following excerpt is taken, allowed her to reflect upon her childhood and on the lasting impact of growing up in a Maine coastal village in the nineties:*

I write, then, of a scene which can rightly be termed a native American one, and I write not to draw a moral but to paint a picture . . . [to] seize upon what made an age distinctive. . . . I write alike of the comic and serious aspects of adolescence under a waning yet still vigorous Puritanism; of the lively effects of a seafaring tradition. . . .

Coast Children of the Nineties

(1)

The heavy toll which change and progress inevitably take as they make their inroads is today nowhere more evident than along the coast of Maine. In the smaller town and villages even the grass-grown ruins of docks have been destroyed; in the larger, shipbuilding except for the construction of pleasure craft or of an occasional steamship, has virtually ceased. The five- and six-masted schooners, which add a touch of romance to populous harbours like Portland, have floated, rotting, untenanted, and useless, for more than several years. Square-riggers are no more. The lithe and beautiful yachts, which cruise idly from Kittery to Eastport or catch the sun on their brass and mahogany as they lie at anchor about Mount Desert or in Camden harbour, speak all too eloquently of the new industry which feeds and clothes the coast. Maine, once secure in her integrity, depends largely for her livelihood, at least as far as her coast life is concerned, upon the capital of those who seek her shores during the summer months.

In the nineties this was not yet so. True, the tide of the new prosperity had already crept into the spacious harbours about Mount Desert and Casco. Bar Harbor already knew its millionaires and Old Orchard its many sojourners. But the smaller, more land-locked villages still kept much to themselves, their carpenters building only an occasional cottage for strangers, their small hotels, boarding-houses and homes entertaining only a few "rusticators." Blue Hill, now deservedly one of the most notable resorts of the coast, knew then neither golf-links nor club-house, neither estates whose clipped lawns sloped to the shore nor Chicago and Cleveland financiers who had money in plenty to spend. And Blue Hill children, although they were occasionally shy before city boys and girls with more stylish clothes and more urbane speech, had the village and the coast for their own.

We knew the manifold excitements of coast life, major and minor. We knew even then the drama of incoming vessels, waiting beyond the

Mary Ellen Chase 1887–1973 **151**

Narrows in the outer bay for the tides, tacking up the snug inner channel to anchor just off the harbour island or to tie up at the wharf to unload their provisions for the village stores and to load the staves and larger lumber for their outgoing. The names and the rigging of these craft were as familiar as the words in our spelling-books and far more welcome: *The Gold Hunter*, the *Mildred May*, the *John W. Stetson*. We knew, occasionally, the inexpressible excitement of the arrival of a "foreign ship" from Barbados, manned by strange, swarthy men with bright handkerchiefs around their necks, and in their mouths unintelligible sounds. Once, indeed, as we of our family sat one September evening with our lessons around the dining-room table, such a dark face above such a handkerchief appeared in our open window, its owner muttering outlandish words and gesticulating with tattooed arms and hands. My mother in her perturbation and terror well-nigh threw the lighted lamp at our caller, who, as we discovered upon the hurried arrival of my father, wanted only to know the way to the "medicine house." It was days before we recovered from our fright and more days before we ceased to be the centre of an envious group at school.

We knew and cherished with no little covetousness the stories of the "traders," which had gladdened the hearts of children of an earlier generation. A trader was a vessel from Boston or New York which earned the livelihood of its captain, or perchance of its owner, by carrying annually into the smaller harbours of the coast every kind of ware imaginable and selling its multifarious cargo at prices which the village stores could not meet. Blue Hill children of the sixties and seventies had waited months for the arrival of this floating junk-shop, scanning the sea from every hill and headland for an unfamiliar sail. According to the older people among us, its captain was invariably an accommodating soul, who was not in the least averse to interpreting as coin of the realm any stray bits of old iron, in exchange for which he would proffer oranges and great Boston apples, gorgeously striped candies, dates, figs, and nuts. Moreover, he carried in his hold, for those who had been most thrifty and parsimonious of their small savings, doll buggies and pop-guns, and for the despair of fathers and mothers, who could be lured to the wharf, bolts of cloth and shiny new shoes with voluptuous and alluring tassels.

Sometimes in those days, we understood, still with envy that progress had cheated us of so much greater excitement, Blue Hill had supplied her own traders. An obliging captain, with a weather eye out for his own pocket, sailing light from Boston or New York, Philadelphia or Norfolk, would gladly undertake the filling of commissions in those centres and bring home a sundry cargo. My aunt, a child of the sixties, told us on her infrequent visits the engrossing tale of a new bureau which she procured in this romantic fashion. At the age of six she had pieced together a bed-quilt by the "over and over" method, sewing together innumerable squares and triangles of calico, keeping as she did so the reward for her enterprise and perseverance ever before her eyes. Scanning critically for weeks each distant sail, she at last espied the *Merchant* ploughing through the waters of the outer bay. For hours she waited at the wharf until the tide should be sufficiently favourable for a landing and saw at last her bureau ready for unloading on the quarter-deck. Once again as a reward for industry or virtue (perhaps both, for in those days, as in our own, they were well-nigh inseparable) she was allowed the fulfilment of great longing. This time, impelled no doubt by her seafaring heritage, she made the choice of a trunk which came after long weeks of waiting by way of another ship, *The Python*.

These shopping sea-captains must, indeed, have been men of gregarious instincts and of great good nature. A slip of paper much torn and obviously incomplete, dated in 1859, gives a partial list of commissions to be fulfilled and suggests the arduous undertaking of the purchaser:

> For J. Candage, a hoss harness
> For Messrs. Holt, Horton, Candage, and 3 Hinckleys tobaco,
>   both chewing & smoking
> For J.C.—a new hat, my own size with 2 cravats & ties
> For the minister, one cane, snake's head prefered, not to
>   cost over $1
> For Silvester C., a good quantity nails, all sizes, & 12 brass
>   handles
> For Coggin family, to invest $20 in white flour & raisins, also

nuts of sorts, also toys such as marbles, tops, & a book of
    pictures
For Miss Clara Wood, stuff for weding dress with threads &
    silks for sewing same & white lace for triming
For Mrs. Duffy, 1 bolt flowered calico at lowest price, blue &
    white prefered, also buttons, also wools for kniting socks in
    bright shades, also pink roses for bonet brims
For Horton boys, 2 large pocket knives
For H. Henderson, 6 steel traps suitable for rabits or foxes
For little Osgood girl, a doll with black hair, blue eyes, big as
    possible for $1
For Mrs. Grindle, one singing bird in cage, for the church gift

Even we in the nineties knew at first hand something of this sort of
supply and demand. When I was in the neighbourhood of twelve, my
father, together with three other men of the village, bought a quarter
share in a two-masted schooner called *The Gold Hunter*. Rumour had
it that their act was largely one of charity since the captain and owner
had fallen on evil days by the decline of the coast trade. But whatever
its cause, the effect brought delighted satisfaction to four large families.
The Gold Hunter was summarily dispatched to Boston with divers
commissions to be accomplished by her relieved captain, and we
waited with atavistic feverishness for her return.

Perhaps her cargo, when after a fortnight she again drew to the
wharf, was less romantic than those of former days. I am sure, however,
that it gave no less thrill. We children of the four families concerned,
and we were many, watched with fascination the unloading of barrels
of flour, sacks of grain, kegs of molasses and vinegar, cans of pilot bread
(that invincible cracker!), bags of oatmeal—all the manifold sorts of
provender which were to prove the staples for the men and beasts of
our large and respective households during a long winter. We watched
too, the wet line on the black hull of *The Gold Hunter* as it increased in
width from her steady rising out of the water during the steady
disembowelling of her dark, musty hold.

Most remarkable of all her goods in those relatively fruitless days
were crates of oranges, two kegs of white grapes, packed in sawdust,

and most wonderful to relate!—a huge bunch of bananas in a long, slatted frame. It may seem impossible today to wax romantic over a bunch of bananas! But in that huge frame standing on *The Gold Hunter's* deck, behind those masses of brown, tropical grass, were concealed far more than bananas, delectable and desirable as they were in themselves. Therein among those unripe, green protuberances, of whose snug members we caught now and then a baffling glimpse, lay a prestige and a pre-eminence among our fellows which in all the years that have passed I have never been able to recapture. My father had bought the bananas as a surprise. We were all excessively fond of them, but since they were tacitly recognized as an indulgence and since the price of them in the village store, at least of enough to supply our family, was prohibitive, we never completely satisfied our desire.

The acknowledgment of our supremacy over all the other children in town began as soon as the bananas had been lifted from their frame, cleared of their wiry grass, and hung from a beam in our cellar. Visible from the entrance of our bulkhead, they immediately attracted a crowd of spectators. There was hardly a school-less hour, indeed, for a space of three days, when half a dozen pairs of eyes were not gazing in wonder and envy down those stone stairs. We children meanwhile managed our exhibition by sitting on the open bulkhead doors, swinging our legs and dilating upon our possession with suitable and, I fear, complacent comments.

The culminating moment in this daily-enacted drama occurred one noon when my father, upon inspection of the great ungainly bunch, suggested that we cut the yellowest. That he contemplated any distribution never once occurred to any of us, neither to exhibitors nor to spectators. We watched him procure a box, mount it, and draw his jack-knife from his pocket. I can yet feel the stilling of my heart when he handed down to me, who waited below with outstretched apron, five, six, eight, twelve bananas, when he proposed that we should treat our friends. From that day to this I have never been able to regard a banana with the supercilious stare of the cultivated mind and eye. The munificence and magnanimity of my father, the opulence and distinction of us as a family, remain, always to be evoked by any chance sight of that humblest and ugliest of fruits.

The minor and usual excitements of coast life were legion. In the nineties there were still among us old sea-captains, barometers of sky and sea, who, in addition to telling us chimerical tales, instructed us in the mysterious ways of weather. We learned to predict the ominous secrets of winds that backed, of restless gulls flying inland, of mare's-tails swishing their milky white across the heavens, of still, cloudless days. We knew what to expect of spring tides, always cherishing the hope that on a March full moon boats would be torn from moorings and lumber floated from the town wharves. We knew when smelts were most likely to "run," coming in great shoals from the outer ocean on night tides in April and May and seeking the tidal streams for spawning. On such nights we went to bed at sundown to be called at three o'clock by my father. Armed with all the pails and baskets of the house, we walked a mile through the darkness to the most favoured brook. The tide was out, and the smelts were foiled and trapped in their tardy return to wider water. Their silver backs and white bellies, as in thousands they hurried pell-mell down the shallow stream, gleamed in the light of our lanterns; and we gathered them in our cold hands by hundreds, filling great baskets full and perhaps, when the miracle was accomplished and we gazed upon our catch, feeling a surprise and exhilaration not unlike that of the boy of the Galilean picnic who began his exciting day with but three small fishes.

The offerings of the sea in the ebb of springs were always more momentous than those of ordinary tides. Shells were more plentiful and often more rare. Wreckage strewed the shores of the outer bay, logs and beams which not infrequently held within their golden brown sides bolts of iron caked with salt. These meant inimitable driftwood fires and were always carried high up the beach and left to dry among the vetches and the lavender. After a spring tide there was also much high talk of treasure and no little search for it. We lived, indeed, on a coast that at once invited and nurtured such fancies. Not far from us lay the very island which was rumoured to hide within its sands the bulk of Captain Kidd's ill-gotten gains. Moreover, not so many years past, two boys who lived near us had been granted an experience, the equal of which few boys of any time or place could boast. Following an old foot-path through the woods during a storm, they had rested against a small boulder beneath a pine tree. One of them, idly kicking the soft mould at the base of the rock, caught the glint of metal, tarnished yet still bright enough to be distinguished against the black earth. They dug farther, with feet and with hands alike, to discover at last an iron pot half filled with gold coins—coins marked by strange designs and a stranger language. They proved to be French pieces of the seventeenth century, probably buried there, so the learned of our coast surmised, by escaping French traders and settlers of the nearby town of Castine when their fort was surprised and captured by the Dutch. What wonder that we scrutinized the wreckage of spring tides and dug now and again in likely coves or beneath giant boulders!

Yet another tale encouraged us to hope for dramatic possibilities even in the ploughing of a spring field. A fisherman not many miles distant had unearthed one May morning, while attempting to cultivate a hitherto barren half-acre, a large piece of copper, marked with unintelligible characters. Seeing in it a remedy for a leaking boat, he tacked it securely to the hull, to be told a few weeks later by summer visitors whom he took out for mackerel, that he had utilized for most practical purposes the corner-stone of a Jesuit chapel, dedicated to Our Lady of Holy Hope in the year 1609!

There was hardly a winter in the nineties when the ocean remained open. By January, sometimes even by Christmas, a great steel-like sheet of ice began to creep farther and farther out toward open sea. Then one cold morning we woke to find no water at all between our shores and those of Long Island, seven miles distant. This meant skating in plenty on the inner bay, and on the outer, once the cold had continued a full week, the laying out of a great track and horse-racing in open sleighs. Not even a launching, which we alas! had been born just too late to see from our own shores, could have been much more thrilling than these village gatherings on certain clear cold afternoons, the participants drawn from village barns, the bells jingling, a blazing fire at the starting-point by which we could warm ourselves with much laughter and many wagers on the horses of our choice.

Those long stretches of ice meant, too, the cutting and hauling of island wood. Oxen drew the creaking sledges which smelled of pine and fir, and obliging farmers encouraged us, once we had obtained our parents' consent, to ride out empty and to return on the top of the load or clinging to the broad runners. The white expanse stretched far and wide beneath a clear, cold sky. The islands were surrounded by rough, uneven boundaries where the tide had cracked and broken the ice, throwing up jagged slabs and cakes around their edges. Wraiths of blue mist rose from the muzzles of the oxen above the icicles clinging to their hairy throats; the creaking of the sledges was now and then supplemented by the booming of the ice as the moving water far beneath it raised or lowered the great solid mass. The climatic changes, even of thirty years, have robbed the coast children of today of no higher adventure.

More suddenly even than it had come, the great sheet of ice broke up and moved seaward. Suspicious gleams of pale blue appeared here and there on a warm, windy morning in March or early April; sullen and explosive muttering punctuated the air. Then with the full outgoing tide the cakes of ice began to move, jamming and hurtling one another, sometimes being thrown into the air by the pressure beneath. Adventuresome boys of parents more careless than our own occasionally tried the risky experiment of crossing the inner bay by jumping from one to another if perchance the break-up occurred on a Saturday. If it happened on ordinary days, it must be intermittently watched from the schoolhouse windows, which on one side faced the sea, but which were placed so high in the wall as to be barely accessible even to the most ambitious vision. The difficulty of keeping one's mind and eyes upon one's books on such a morning was intense.

Tuesdays, Thursdays, and Saturdays in spring and summer were fish-boat mornings. By seven o'clock on days when the tide served, Captain Andrew Cole had sailed from the outer bay, having far earlier hauled his trawl. The young representatives of each family table gathered at the wharf, not reluctant to wait their turn while the green water slapped at the piers and the gulls were certain of full stomachs. A five-pound haddock, cleaned and scraped, could be bought for fifteen cents, the black stripe down his silvery sides guaranteeing wary purchasers against the despised hake, which no Maine connoisseur of fish could tolerate. There were clams, too, dipped from a sodden tub at ten cents a quart measure and, upon occasion, tinker mackerel in ravishing shades of blue and green, so cheap that two dozen might be bought without greatly diminishing the family pocket-book.

There were clams to be dug from the mud flats, many bare feet spotting them by the tiny jets of water which they spouted from their hiding-places. The backaches produced by heavy clam-hoes in tough mud were always less painful than those engendered by piling wood or cultivating garden rows of potatoes or beans! We baked them by building fires of driftwood beneath flat rocks and laying the clams between layers of wet seaweed. Nearly every summer these clambakes took on a co-operative character participated in by the village at large. On these occasions our elders chartered a schooner in the harbour large enough to consider a hundred persons a mere handful. We sailed then to Long Island, laden with foodstuffs sufficient for any ordinary siege, and spent the day on wider, sandier shores. The dinner served on such village picnics tested the gastronomic capacities of the community and could hardly be excelled by any eighteenth century repast. Lobsters and clams, broiled and baked, fish in chowders, hard-boiled eggs, sandwiches and doughnuts, fresh cakes, turnovers, and tarts, blueberry and apple pies, root beer, lemonade and coffee! What wonder that the sail homeward before a southeast wind was silent and that we trudged in families, still silent, up the village street, filled, among other things, with a sleepy content!

(3)

Beyond all these tangible influences, the coast itself, and the very fact that we lived upon it, placed its intangible mark upon our minds. Secure though we were in our safe haven, we knew full well that the sea was treacherous and insecure. Something of the same shrewd, patient wisdom must be the heritage of prairie children or of those dwelling by great rivers, who are born to scent disaster in rising winds and waters. Few of us of my generation will ever forget that tragic November night when the Boston boat went down with all on board. Reared on tales of shipwreck and suffering upon oceans near and far, we were not surprised by the hardships which every winter brought within our knowledge. We read or were told of lighthouse children drowned by falling into fissures of the rock, of a woman who tended a great lamp through a three days' storm while the body of her husband lay in the lighthouse sitting-room. We knew of outlying islands beset with starvation in an especially bitter winter, of mailboats foundered in high seas. Is it too much then to believe that there crept into our minds earlier than into the minds of most children a sense of the inevitability, not only of suffering but of endurance as well, that we grew, perhaps unconsciously and insensibly, to look upon sorrow not as an individual, concrete matter but rather as a mighty abstraction, necessary and common to all human life? An easier, more fortified age may well question such an assumption; but few who were born to a seafaring heritage and few who knew coast life even a quarter of a century ago will doubt it.

Charlie York
1887–1962

Charlie York's boyhood in Harpswell at the end of the nineteenth century was a typical Maine-coast fisherman's start. The waters off the islands and peninsulas of Casco Bay have provided good fishing grounds for centuries and have been the major source of livelihood for those who live there. Small wonder that Charlie York's early life was shaped by this environment. It was a given that, like his father and grandfathers before him, young Charlie would become a fisherman and, as it turned out, an exceptionally versatile and industrious one.

Bailey and Orr's islands were busy places when Charlie York was a boy. They were self-contained, as bridges to the mainland had not yet been built. Most of the large extended families were fisherfolk. Prince's store on Orr's Island served the industry by buying fish, selling provisions, and occasionally investing in the fishing boats. A sizable summer population of "rusticators" enlivened life on the islands and provided odd jobs for the year-round fishermen and their families. Steamboats connected the islands to Portland and took the islanders into the city for a change of pace. Industry was valued, and young Charlie was soon earning his own money from the sea, eeling, clamming, and looking forward to the day when he could own his own boat. His father helped arrange this for him and started him on what was to be more than fifty years of commercial fishing. York knew that "no fisherman could make a livin' from just one kind of fishing." He had to take into consideration that some kinds of fish is with us only a few months of the year and that sometimes prices is high and other times they's a glut. . . ."

He harpooned swordfish, trawled for groundfish, seined, drag-netted and gill-netted, set weirs and fish traps, fished for sardines and tuna and

Coastal boys would be expected to help with the lobstering. From *A Message Through Time: The Photographs of Emma D. Sewall, 1836–1919,* by Abbie Sewall. *Courtesy of Tilbury House Publishers.*

mackerel, and hauled lobster traps. He saw fishing boats evolve from sailing ships to power boats with sophisticated electronic gear, with similar changes in marketing techniques. He accepted with equanimity such diverse social phenomena as a thriving Ku Klux Klan on Orr's Island, a busy market in illegal offshore liquor sales during Prohibition, a conversion to the Methodist Church and born-again Christianity, and the loss to the sea of his father and some forty of his friends. He was an innovative and hardworking fisherman, and he loved and respected the sea. His childhood had prepared him well for this life.

My Boyhood in Harpswell

I wish I could make you see Casco Bay, from Cape Elizabeth to Small Point, with its 365 islands and hundreds of half-tide ledges, like it was sixty years ago. They was three fishin' schooners from Cundy's Harbor on Great Island, two from Lowell's Cove on Orr's, three from Water Cove on the north end of Bailey's, and several from Mackerel Cove on the southern end, one from South Harpswell, and two from Chebeague. They all worked under sail with no auxiliary power, and the skippers depended on the imperfect charts of the day and their soundin' leads. After the island fleet had sold their catch in Portland, Gloucester, or Boston, one by one they made their way no'theast to their permanent moorin's in their home harbors. Time and again you could find as many as a score of fishin' vessels with a dozen nested dories on deck, anchored or layin' to their moorin's in cove or harbor. From the hill on Bailey's you might see the smoke of half a dozen steambo'ts at once, and some rich man's schooner yacht makin' for Bar Harbor, or even a steam yacht.

Schooners, and even Friendship sloops, when in need of work, was sailed to a marine railway at Portland or Boothbay, to be hauled out. But the local fisherman, with some help from his neighbors, tended to his own smaller Hampton bo't. If all he planned to do was scrape and paint, he might pull her ashore at high tide beside a wharf, where a rope would hold her upright. He could fix up the bow half between tides over a period of two, three days. Then he'd bring her in stern first and go to work on that end. Copper paint can go on a moist surface all right, and it don't do no harm if it's wet soon after, but the owner would plan to do his paintin' on a dry day.

Sometimes a group of neighbors would pull the bo't out on the bank; I've helped and been helped many times. We'd lay a pair of plank down into the water, three feet apart, to make a smooth path for five foot rollers. We'd plant a crowbar on the bank and rig a block and tayckle to it. We'd bring the bo't in on a high tide and git her onto rollers when she grounded out. We'd make the tayckle fast to her and with men to hold her upright, a bunch of us would man the rope and roust her up the slope while others fed the rollers under her keel and moved a pair of planks ahead. Any good carpenter on Bailey's in them days could replace a broken or rotten piece of plankin' and we was all painters.

When I was a kid, everything and everybody come to Bailey's by water. Before the bridge was built, my Grandfather Burnham used to set people across the narrow channel to Orr's in his dory, ten cents a person, three or four for a quarter, or bring 'em on when he heard 'em shoutin' for the ferry.

The Harpswell Steambo't Company run year-round service to Portland. The steamer would leave Orr's Island at 7:00, put into York's Landing on Bailey's, then across to South Harpswell and on to Cliff Island, Chebeague, Long, Peaks, and dock at Custom House Wharf about 10:30. She left on the return trip with passengers, mail, express, and freight at 2:00. We young ones knowed the names of every bo't and we could tell which was which as fur as we could see 'em or hear the whistle: *Merriconeag, Sebascodegan, Aucocisco, Machigonne.* Indian names, probly.

The most excitin' time of day was when we'd hear the steambo't blow about 4:00 P.M. All the local people that could spare the time went to the wharf and, as it was summertime, the rusticators flocked down. The steamer's sides would be lined with men, women, and children as she come near, and the cap'n would bring her in at a smart clip. Then he'd give the engineer two bells and the jingler and fetch her right on a dime. I can see the mate now, standin' with the forrard spring line, and how easy he'd flip that hawser over the pilin' just right as the bow come by the dock. He'd hold a strain and she'd come against the wharf with hardly a jar; then he'd snub her tight. . . .

They was lots of tourists by 1900, only we called 'em rusticators. They'd been comin' to Harpswell long before my time. In them days they brought their trunks and stayed a month or all summer. Just on Bailey's they was Robinhood Inn, The Homestead, The Johnson House, Ocean View, and The Woodbine. They'd take care of twenty to sixty people each. Cottages was goin' up here and there; a thousand or fifteen hundred dollars would build a nice little summer place. Some years later the summer business got so heavy that a steamer run daily excursions to the Harpswell area, with a shore dinner at one of the hotels.

Heavy stuff like lumber, brick and cement, coal and cordwood, come on scows towed by small tugbo'ts. For fuel at our house we burned the spruce that growed on the island for our summer cookin'; but it's soft wood and don't hold the heat. As a boy one of my jobs was to pick up driftwood and take it home in a wheelbarrer. But our good, dry hardwood, the maple, beech and yaller birch, come by scow. Them that has never burned anything but oil don't know what they've missed!

It was cheaper in them days to send heavy seacoast freight by water. Outside Half-way Rock you might see coasters with barrels of lime from Thomaston, granite or pavin' stone from Vinalhaven, ice from the Kennebec, lumber and laths or Aroostook potatoes from Bangor, Stark and Baldwin apples from saltwater farms, cordwood from little villages along the shore. It was a pretty sight after a storm, when the schooners had been layin' up in some safe harbor. After the weather cleared, they'd git up sail and take off together. I've seen thirty or forty of them vessels within an area of a square mile, white sails spread to the wind, standin' out across Casco Bay.

Our ro'd wa'n't much, just a three-way track along the middle of the island, two for the wheels and one between, where the horse walked. Some places it went over bare ledges, and then through mudholes after a rain. I can faintly remember a big snowstorm and everyone turnin' out with shovels to clear the ro'd. They didn't need no orders from a town manager. One neighbor had a pair of oxen and he yoked 'em to a wedge of oak planks, with a cross-bar to support 'em. The men stood on the cross-plank to hold the plow into the snow; when they come to a big drift, the men went ahead and shoveled till the oxen could get through.

When I was a kid, they wa'n't no fellers my age at the upper end of the island and my special pal was Lula Doughty. She seemed almost as good as a boy to me. When the daisies and buttercups was in bloom we used to pick wild strawberries by the pailful on the west side of Bailey's. Our mothers would help us hull 'em and the rusticators bought 'em for twenty-five cents a quart. In August blueberries was ripe, and me and Lu found 'em in the fields where the juniper grew; we got ten cents a quart for 'em. They was raspberries and blackberries for home preserves.

Me and Lu had a regular partnership in the clam business from early spring till it got too cold in December. We went clammin' in vacation time, holidays, weekends, and sometimes after school if the tide served right. We dug the flats near home; if the weather was good, we rowed across the Sound to Stover's Cove. The diggin' was wonderful. Many a time us two youngsters dug three bushels on a low dreen tide. I remember how heavy they was to sack; we took 'em home in a wheelbarrer, or dragged 'em on a sled if they was snow on the ground. Our mothers and anybody else that had the time would help us shock 'em. In summer, the rusticators paid us twenty-five cents a quart, blacks removed. At other times, dealers give us fifty cents a bucket for clams or mussels for bait; the mussels was used fresh but the clams was salted by the barrel. Canners paid twenty-five cents a bushel in the shell. We split our money half and half. Years later, Lu married Elbro Cushing, a Cliff Islander, raised a nice family, and had a good life. She died a few years ago. . . .

They's nothing I remember better than clambakes on Cedar Island. At half tide you can walk across to it, and they's a pool there that stays about two feet deep after the tide has dropped. It was a favorite place for lobsters to stay durin' July and August, waitin' for their new shell to get hard.

We young ones always went barefoot, but for the job of huntin' lobsters we put boots on. If you see a furrow under the side of a rock, it meant a lobster had dug in, to be safe while his shell was soft. We would flip the rock over and then grab for the lobster; we didn't take no chances with the claws of the big ones, but they would be plenty that was small. What yellin' and splashin' as the lobsters backed away, tryin' to escape, and us kids after 'em. With a driftwood stick we could easy dig enough clams to go with 'em.

They was an old iron kettle on the bank and somebody had rocked up a small fireplace. Storms had piled plenty of wood above high-tide mark for our fire. We'd put a quart or two of sea water in the kettle and heat it, then in would go the lobsters, follered by the clams, and seaweed on top. We didn't need no melted butter nor other fixin's to make 'em perfect. They was seagulls all around, waitin' for whatever we might leave, herons stalkin' the flats on their long legs, fish hawks treadin' the air over a likely spot, and sandpeeps skitterin' here and there along the shore. Before the tide covered the walkway, we was back safe on the main island.

In my youth eels was considered a very choice dish and my Grandfather Burnham was fond of 'em. I went eelin' with him more than sixty years ago. He always had time and patience to teach me things. He showed me where eels was most likely to be found, how to stick 'em, and how to git 'em into the bo't before they squirmed off the spear. Come November, eels go into the mud and lay there till spring. Saturdays and Sundays, with the tide more than half out, grandfather would take me out in the dory and row away to some muddy bottom four to six feet deep at low tide, where the eelgrass growed. I was just a little shaver, but I could pick up the oars, about as big as I could handle, and move the bo't forrard or back as he told me, while he punched for eels. When he begun to find some, we'd put our rock anchor overboard and let the dory swing in an arc while he'd spear the eels and bring 'em up.

I liked it. Many a time I teased my grandfather into goin' when he didn't have no idea of it. I asked my father time after time to let me take his big eel spear, but he said not till I come ten years old, and then he would only let me have it when I was with grandfather.

I'll never fergit a November day the fall I was comin' on eleven, must of been 1898. It was a Saturday, one of them days you git in the late fall, sky covered with soft gray clouds, not a breath of wind, a wet chill in the air. Gulls was turnin' over little rocks, grabbin' clams by the neck, flyin' up, and droppin' 'em to break the shells so they could git at the meat. Now and then a crow, too lazy to fly south, was huntin' seaworms along the flats. I had the little square-sterned punt that had belonged to my Grandfather York. I asked Granpa Burnham to go eelin' with me, and he said he couldn't, so I told him I thought I'd go alone. He made me ask my mother and she put up quite a fuss because I'd have to stand up in the punt, but I told her how shallow it would be and at last she give in.

The punt was high up on the bank, out of reach of the tide. Garrison Cove, where we lived, is shallow, and I had a hard drag of most a hundred feet across sand and gravel. When I got her afloat and stood up, pushin' her along, with my father's spear at hand, I was a proud kid and I hoped people was watchin' from the shore. The tide was maybe two thirds out. Near the mouth of the cove some eelgrass was growin' in the mud. I'd never seen anybody spearin' eels there but I thought I'd try. The punt drifted along very slow and after three or four spears I hauled up a nice eel. On the next punch I got two at once, and I put over the rock that was tied to my painter.

I poked and poked with my spear and when I felt an eel on it, I would roust him in as quick as I could; I lost some, of course, I got so excited and worked so hard and fast that once in a while I'd have to sit down and rest. I'd started about two hours before low water and I never quit till two hours after the turn. Dinnertime had gone by but I didn't care. When I did head for shore, they was eels all over the bottom of the punt, ankle deep, squirmin' around my boots and up my legs. I'd brought a crocus bag to take my eels home in, but they was too many. I carried my rock and the painter high up onto the bank, picked up father's spear, and set out for the house.

Grandfather was settin' in the kitchen mendin' a net and mother was puttin' yeast bread to rise.

"How'd you do, Charlie?" asked Grandpa. I went to the stove and got some hot water to wash in.

"I got a puntful," I answered.

Mother spoke up quick and sharp. "Don't you lie to your grandfather, Charlie!" He looked up at me and grinned.

"Where be they?" he asked.

"In the punt," I said, "they was too many to lug."

I et some dinner and then me and grandfather put one of mother's wooden washtubs on the wheelbarrer and went to the shore. We come back with the tub full; he figgered about 100 pounds, maybe 200 eels. We dressed eels till suppertime at 4:30, takin' out their insides, skinnin' 'em, and cuttin' off their heads. After supper grandpa took his pail and went to milk the cow. I lugged in my usual four pails of water from the well, a hod of coal for the livin' room, and another for the kitchen stove. I carried out the orts from the table and some corn to the hens, and picked up the eggs. Then we went at them eels agin and finished late in the evenin'.

"Here's more eels than we know what to do with," said my grandfather. "Whyn't you go up to Clary's store in the morning, ask to use his scales, make up five-pound packages and see if you can sell 'em?" Which I done. Sunday mornin' I carried a nice mess to Mr. Clary and he helped me tie the eels into five-pound lots. I peddled 'em from house to house at twenty-five cents each and took in between two and three dollars; it seemed like a wonderful lot of money to me. . . .

In them days every boy wanted his own bo't, just like today every high school boy wants a car. I kep' after my father all the time and the spring I was comin' on twelve years old, he give in. He agreed to pay for half of the bo't if I would pay for the other half; father had ideas about bringin' up kids and one was that they needed to learn the value of money.

In March we took our dory and rowed over to Orr's Island to see Herbert Wilson who was a bo't builder. My father explained that we wanted a fifteen-foot sailin' peapod, double-ender some folks call' em, with centerboard, outboard rudder, small mast, regular rowlocks, and them raised oarlocks so a man can stand up and push. I got a lesson in dickerin'. Mr. Wilson admitted he wa'n't pressed for work just then and thought he could do the job for twenty-five dollars. Such a bo't would cost two hundred and fifty dollars today. But father wouldn't agree. Mr. Wilson hung on and the price was finally set at twenty-two dollars and fifty cents.

Grandfather Burnham helped me make some lobster traps and mother knit the potheads; I had twenty-five all ready when school closed. The day the bo't was delivered I thought I was made. I don't believe a boy today can love a car the way I loved that peapod. She was painted green with red copper bottom. She rowed easy. Father let me have a small spritsail and when I dropped the centerboard, she would beat to wind'ard like a regular vessel. All them peapods is good in a seaway.

My grandfather made me a flounder spear and at low tide I'd drift over shallow bottom and spear flounders and sculpins to use for lobster bait. When the tide didn't serve, I put a line over the side and caught cunners and harbor pollock. I run my gang of traps just like a man would, hauled 'em every day, throwed out the shorts unless we needed a mess at home, kept the counters, re-baited the trap and sot it out agin. In them days legal-size lobsters had to measure ten and a half inches or more from nose to tip of tail. They wa'n't sold by the pound; every hard-shelled lobster brought ten cents no matter what he weighed and a shedder was worth only seven cents.

Father was away fishin' and at the end of the summer we settled up. I paid him for my half of the peapod and handed over the rest of my money for him to put in the bank, but he placed the whole twenty-two dollars and fifty cents in my name and started a savin's account. I kep' addin' to it, and when I was twenty-two, got married, and built my own house, I had in the bank every cent I needed to pay for it with. People was savin' in them days.

From: Harold Clifford, ed., *Charlie York, Maine Coast Fisherman*. Camden, Maine: International Marine Publishing Co., 1974. Reprinted with permission of International Marine Publishing, Camden, Maine, an imprint of TAB Books/McGraw-Hill.

Robert P. Tristram Coffin
1892–1955

Robert P. Tristram Coffin was a virtually nonstop chronicler of his Maine. He wrote about his parents, Portrait of an American; *his ancestors,* Captain Abby and Captain John; *the history of Maine,* Kennebec, Cradle of Americans; *and about his own life. His fictionalized autobiography,* Lost Paradise, *and other autobiographical works tell about his youth. His love for his state and his pride in it ring loud and clear in his many novels, essays, biographies, and poems.* Strange Holiness, *a book of poetry, won a Pulitzer Prize in 1935.*

Coffin was born in Brunswick in 1892 and raised on a saltwater farm in nearby Pennellville. He graduated from Bowdoin College, was a Rhodes Scholar, taught at Wells College, and then returned to Brunswick to teach at Bowdoin until his death in 1955.

His strong sense of family pervades his writings, and his delight in telling of the people and events that shaped his life helps us to share them. The excerpts from Lost Paradise *and* Saltwater Farm *that follow give us a clear picture of the closeness to nature and the variety of experiences that made up a boyhood on a saltwater farm at the turn of the century.*

Chores on a Saltwater Farm

The game Peter was playing now was trying to think of the hardest work he had to do on the farm. He was doing his best to wean himself of thinking of it as a place that was all apple pie and huckleberry jam.

R.P.T. Coffin became one of Maine's best-known authors. *Courtesy of the Pejepscot Historical Society.*

This Thursday morning, he ran over the unpleasant jobs he had sweated at.

He dismissed sawing wood at once, for he was always able to prop a book up on the jaws of the sawhorse and read between sticks. His mother caught him at it once. She thought it was funny there were such long and regular pauses between saws. She knew something was up. She went out. She had put Peter to sawing for a whole day because he had had his corduroy trousers dusted by the schoolteacher the day before, for putting frogs in the school water bucket. A punishment at school was always repeated at home. It was the rule. A teacher, like a parent, was always right. It was Ansel who had told on Peter. Not meaning to, of course, but just because he couldn't hold in his curiosity as to how long Peter's bottom had stung after the strap. His mother might never have known about the frogs. When his mother came out to see just why each cordwood length took so long, Peter did not have time to slide *The Water Babies* under the pile of sticks. His mother took the book away. After that, that stent at the bucksaw *had* been hard work, with nothing but wasp nests to look at between times. But it wasn't usually. Peter had read half of *The Leatherstocking Tales* in the dim light of the shed and in the aroma of sawdust. When he was really resting, between every twenty sticks, there was the mowing machine seat to sit on. But the width and the heart-shaped intersticcs in the iron seat of the old New Warrior machine had been planned for a bigger pair of back cushions than Peter had to sit on, so it wasn't a place to rest on long. No, he couldn't put down sawing wood as the worst the farm had to offer.

It wasn't cleaning out the tieups in the morning, either. That was hard work while it lasted, but it smelled no worse than when tripe was being cleaned in the steaming kitchen. And there were gray spiders on the panes to fool by shaking their webs with the shovel handle, and wasp chambers to open up and see how the preserved spiders there were turning pink and blue pastel colors and getting tender for the infant wasps to make a meal of when they grew bigger.

There was a lot to be said for pounding up crabs for the hens, too. It got to be a science. You could open all five legs on a side if you hit the right kind of a blow. You had to be careful not to give a hen or two a crack as you did it, though. And you ate all the tomally in each crab yourself. That was too good to waste on hens. It was fun to play favorites among the fowls, too, and see to it that Dusty Gold or Sleepy Sue got all the nicest tidbits you shelled out. You tempted the wilder ones close and caught them and let them squawk their squawking out, or tried to pet them and tame them and got well bitten for your trouble. You let the rooster severely alone, though. He had male ways, like yourself, and you respected them. And, anyway, he always kept on the outer fringe of things and eyed you with a malevolent yellow eye. He was assuring the hens that he was the one responsible for this whole feast. But, all the same, he didn't trust you to keep up the illusion. No, you couldn't call that hard work, either. You learned too much about how people acted when you watched those hens.

There was digging clams, of course, on the still days when the midges were thick as fiddlers in Tophet and stung your eyes till they looked like two burnt holes in a blanket. But that was really fishing, and fun. And you got money for doing it—fifty cents a bushel, and that meant two more books for your own library, *Black Beauty*, perhaps, or *Heroes of the War of 1812*. You picked up all kinds of shells and odds and ends for your collection. A razorback clam and one of those shells that had a real stern seat in it, or a baby horseshoe crab, all dried out nicely for you, no longer than your finger. You saw infant fish with glass bodies and only their eyes and their backbones showing. You looked into jellyfish that were Winter moons. You surprised the hermit crabs and snaked them out of their shells before they knew what you were up to. Maybe, you put them into new houses too small for them. You matched them up for a bout, without their houses on their backs to run away into. They bit each other like good fellows. The biggest ones could even make an impression on you. You held your hand still till they thought the coast was clear, and put out their eyes on their little sticks and then their big-claws, and then you grabbed and had them. You turned up clamworms with live silk fringes all along them, and you manufactured them up into five or six new ones. They didn't seem to mind much, but went right on wriggling away. You had standing orders to tear up all the starfish you found. Edward and your father both said that they played the dickens with their lobster bait.

But you didn't like to destroy them, they were so pretty colored. You let them suck on to your fingers with their forests of soft legs. You got squirt on by a clam who thought your coming was the returning tide and so got rid of his shellful of old water in hopes to get a new. . . .

Turning the grindstone came pretty close to being what you might call plain hard work and nothing else. But then, it wasn't so bad, when you came to think it over. Except when it was Edward you were turning for, and he slapped you across the buttocks with the flat of the scythe if you turned unsteadily and tripped the blade and put a nick in it. The other people you turned for took you into their confidence. They were that close to you, you could see what made up a man's face and how it was different from a boy's. You could see how a man used his hands and legs. Quiet and sure, not quick and nervous as a boy did. And a man spoke to you here at the grindstone just as if you were no whit different from him, as if you were grown up and thought of women a lot and could mow hay or put a good edge on a scythe as well as he could.

"See! That's a pretty fine edge now, don't you think?—Wouldn't you call that sharp enough?—Perhaps a little more on the heel here. . . ."

Peter thought harder still. Water fences. There was a thing, now, that didn't seem to be very promising, no matter what way you looked at it. It was dirty and heavy work. You and Ansel had to carry the heavy flat stones to weight down the three-cornered fence posts your father had run up, to keep your fence from coming up the bay to meet you when next you rowed home. You might have to lug the big stones for hours and not get enough to hold the fence down. And as they came from the tide's way, they were bound to be good and muddy. Ansel and you carried the spool of barbed wire on a pole, and your father unwound the wire and made it fast to the posts. Sometimes, if you didn't step spry, you might get unwound, too. Your father had to carry the staples in his mouth, in tight places. The mud was deep and black and got all over you and finally into your eyes, if there were black flies around. And there always were. The job was a low-tide job, and low tide was their refreshment hour. You slipped on the rockweed and bruised yourself. You tore your fingers on the barbs. Ansel was an artist at walking so you did all the carrying. He was an inch taller, and that was easy. Once, you let go of your end of the pole and let the whole thing run through Ansel's hands and gash them. You didn't mean to, but you couldn't convince Ansel. Another time, the whole rigging got away from you and your brother and rolled down over a steep ledge towards deep water. Your father swore one of his very rare oaths and tried to tackle the spool, and only tore his whole trouser leg open for his pains. The wire plunged in and was lost in seven fathoms of water. You all fished for it, but you never got it up.

After the thing was done, the first high water brought the whole business to shore, if it hadn't been done right. You hadn't put on enough stones to keep it down. Anyway, even if it stayed, you had to make two or three trips more, and take up the slack in the wires, which kelp and eel-grass had sagged down so the cows got over. Just when you sat back and thought it was done for good till the Winter's ice would take it out, you looked up, and there were all twenty cows in the sweet-apple orchard, or knee-deep in the beans. They had got over the fence, or walked or swum around. The cows your father owned were the kind that could burrow under three stiff strands of barbed wire. Or swim around the whole blessed works, if there were no other way. It wasn't so much that they wanted the grass in the hayfields to eat. Their pasture was full of the finest pasture grass a cow ever tied up into cud bundles. It had pennyroyal and sage in it to make it spicy. It was long and juicy. It was just that the cows had a nose for adventure. It went with the kind of farm they lived on. They felt that the fence was a challenge to them.

And there were four of those fences. Peter's father had a farm which was not only hard to reach by road from town, . . . [it] was also on a point. The cows held the middle section, and so had four directions to get away in. The east or west side to get into the island farms and cornfields to the south, and an east and west way into their master's apples and hay to the north. They used all four. One of the upper fences, where the channel ran close to the opposite shore and under Misery Hill, had to be about half a mile long. There were terrific honeypots there. But those didn't stump the cows. They ran blithely into them to the tips of their silky ears. Twice Peter's father had to get all hands out, man the scow, and tie ropes to the cows' necks and pull them out as the tide lifted the scow. The cows enjoyed it. . . .

Salt hay grew on the Mash—that was the way Peter had always heard it pronounced and the way he pronounced the place himself. The Mash had come along with the farm when his father bought it, though it was two miles farther up Doughty's Cove. The man who sold Peter's father the farm had thrown it in extra. . . .

At the bottom of the Mash, a dyke bridge which dyked no longer was a marvellous place to explore. You could jump from beam to beam through a green twilight studded with blue and brown jewels of baby mussels. On each side of the bridge, even at dead low tide, there was a swimming pool twelve feet deep. Baby smelts, transparent except for their sad little eyes, bumped into you as you swam. You could open your eyes down under the water and be in a new world where nothing moved fast and everything had plush on it. When the tide roared through, you could swim in yeast and be turned under like so much eel-grass and rolled over and over down into green gloom. Or you sat with your feet dangling over the bridge and watched the swift water flash all into a sheet of liquid silver as the school of young herring tipped up sidewise all at the same time.

On still afternoons thrushes sang in the high oak-woods above the grassland until the world echoed with them. Wild strawberries hung as big as a man's thumb among the long grasses there. Black-velvet spiders splashed over with gold walked on the air between the plume-grass, and when you came near, they shook their shadowless house till you couldn't see it any more and the spider was a vibrating drop of fire alone on a blue sky. Ghosts of dead trees stood like skeletons as far as you could see. It was a lovely, lonely place. When you looked down into the salt pools, you could look deeper than you looked when you stared into the sky. Everything was very wild and very still. Raccoon tracks laced the mud around the ponds with fleur-de-lis. The mysterious arrows of great bird tracks went pointing off along the dark shoals. You might come upon a heron, looking lonely as the world was before there were any boys or men around, dozing at noonday over a sheet of salty silver. You did not make a sound, but all at once he was off. He flashed blue fire as he let go with the triggers of both wings, and sailed off with his crest back on his shoulders like a king's crown and his long legs trailing.

It was on the Mash that Peter had joined the brotherhood of Nimrod and Daniel Boone. He bagged his first game there. He had seen a spoon-bill plover teetering along a pool, and unbeknown to his brothers had got Long Tom, the family muzzle-loader that had been a rifle and shot Mexicans in the '40's before it had been bored out for a shotgun. Peter had watched his brothers load the gun. He put in three fingers of powder, and then two of shot. He rammed it all down and wadded it with chewed-up newspaper. He was only eight years old at the time, and the gun was two feet longer than he was. But he crept up on that bird and drew his bead. The muzzle went round and round. Then Peter pulled the trigger, and the world flew up behind him, hit the back of his head, and turned it into showers of shooting stars. The high woods echoed for miles around, and the sky was full of falling sounds as Peter lay on his back and quieted down. But when he got to his hands and knees, the plover lay there with its head couched on the open fan of its slender wings. Peter ran and picked it up. It stirred once in his hands, opened its eyes, and died. Peter stood there with it and burst into tears.

From: Robert P. Tristram Coffin, *Lost Paradise: A Boyhood on a Maine Coast Farm.* New York: Macmillan, 1934. Reprinted by permission of Mrs. Robert P.T. Coffin, Jr.

Going after the Cows in a Fog

The day was over, but there was no night
To take its place yet. All the trees were gone
Except the few that loomed beside the way,
And they were larger than beech trees should be,

They towered topless by the boy as he
Went up the path the many tracks of cows,
Hoof to hoof's end, and forty years of them,
Had cut ten inches wide through pennyroyal
And hardhack with its silver, hugged-up leaves.
The path went where the huckleberry bushes
And bayberry were, to brush off stinging flies,
It did not go the way a man would go.
It was not wide enough for even a boy
Ten-years-wide to keep his trousers dry.
The cobwebs were as solid as bead bags
Until the boy had passed, and then they were
Thin thread and dry and all their bright beads gone.
Although he could not see the woods, the boy
Could hear woods dripping busily each side.

"Coo-boss! coo-boss!"—His voice came back on him
And did not get past trees or up the hill.
It was lonesome, shut in with his voice,
Whistling did not help. The night was nigh.
It might be miles to go. The boy stopped still.
There was a muffled tinkling of a bronze
Bell somewhere or other, every side.
And then a wide white face built up itself
Out of the fog and stopped with startled eyes,
Warm in the mist, less than ten feet away.
"Soo-boss! so-boss!" The small boy stepped aside,
The eyes grew friendly, the curled horns shook once,
The mild head lowered, and the cow went by.
The boy stayed still, head after head came on,
Swinging, friendly, and sleek bodies after
Lurched by in peace. The boy turned his bare toes
And followed the swinging line off into night.

From: Robert P. Tristram Coffin, *Saltwater Farm*. New York: Macmillan, 1937. Reprinted by permission of Mrs. Robert P.T. Coffin, Jr.

Ardelle "Ida" Allen
1894–1984

The Maine woods have provided the state with its greatest commercial resource and one of its most enduring tourist attractions. The lumber industry—90 percent of the state is forested—has dominated Maine's economy since the early seventeenth century when the first sawmills were built in Berwick and York in 1634; and sportsmen have been hunting and fishing Maine's woods, lakes, and streams since well before Henry David Thoreau ventured north and wrote The Maine Woods *in 1846. Ida Allen's memories of her childhood in Moxie Gore, some fifteen miles southwest of Moosehead Lake, tells us much of the life of people who made their living in logging. In her later life she and her husband ran a sporting camp business, and so she knew both worlds.*

The transition from logging for lumber—for ship timbers and construction materials, for barrel staves and shingles—to the use of Maine trees for pulp and paper was underway in the late 1890s, but the logs were still brought out of the woods to the streams, Moxie Stream in this case, and driven down the rivers, over the falls, and into the ponds and lakes where they were rafted up prior to their final trip to the mills. Ida's father, brothers, and husband all worked in the woods, and while she was well aware of the hardships and dangers involved, she delighted in woods life.

Ida was the eleventh child in a family of thirteen. Like other woods families, hers was, of necessity, a close one. Their isolation meant that they made their own entertainment; grew their own food; made their own clothes, houses, and furniture; and hired a schoolteacher to come to live with them and educate the children. The world of the woods was Ida's idea of paradise, and she felt very close to the birds and animals whose woods

they were; an "animal queer" she described herself, an enthusiastic observer
and sometimes caretaker of the wildlife around her.

Despite her parents' hopes for a nursing career and a better life for her,
Ida was married young to Sam Allen, a woodsman friend of her brothers'.
Their marriage had a luckless start. The first house they built was struck by
lightning, which ran down the kitchen stovepipe, killed the cat asleep un-
derneath the stove, and badly cut and burned Ida's feet. Their second house
burned to the ground a few years later. Sam Allen gradually took to
working as a guide for visiting sportsmen; and after the death of Ida's
parents, the young couple moved into their house, built several cabins, and
embarked on a career of running camps for hunters and fishermen from all
over the country. Ida never lost her cheerful enthusiasm and her curiosity
about the wild world around her.

Born in a Logging Camp

In this story of my life in the back woods of Maine, I will do my best
to tell the true story of my happy life spent in the forests and hills of
Maine. I was born in a log camp built by my Father about sixty-five
years ago on an eighty acre lot of timber land on Moxie Gore. The
camp was built of logs and the roof was of pole rafters covered with
shingles, or what then were called cedar splits. These were made by
cutting straight grain cedar in four or five feet lengths, then with a
throw and a mall, splitting these shingles or splits about one inch thick
on one edge and one half inch on the other, reversing every other one.
These he put on the rafters in the same way they now put on clap-
boards, the inch thick side over the half inch, with about two inches of
overlap. The floor was made of logs smoothed off with an axe.

This camp he had built around twelve years before I was born. I
was the seventh child born in this camp, and I was the eleventh child in
a family of thirteen children. Twelve were born without a doctor in attendance—just a woman called a mid-wife whose name was Huldah B.

Young. She would be brought to our wilderness home on an old wooden tote sled, as that was the only conveyance that could get over the rough tote road used mostly by the lumbermen. Huldah would stay until the baby was born and then be obliged to go back home, for she had a family herself.

My first memories of our home were of Father cutting down trees and cutting up the largest ones. The small ones were piled up to dry along with the limbs. From time to time in the late evening, all the family would gather out in the clearing. Us small children would sit on a blanket, and Mother and Dad and some of the older boys, with buckets of water and spruce boughs handy, would light the brush piles of small trees and limbs. How they would burn! If the fire started to spread, they would wet the spruce boughs in a bucket of water and beat the fire at that point. That was the way the farm was cleared.

Dad always called me his girl. And many happy childhood days I spent with him in the woods and on the shore of Moxie Stream. He used to tend out on the stream in the Summer when the logs were sluiced through the gates and sent down Moxie Stream on what was called a head of water. "Tending out" meant watching along the river bank to see that the logs did not "jam," that is, pile up together and stop in the stream. On Moxie Stream is Moxie Falls, where the water drops ninety feet from top to bottom. These falls are sometimes called the Niagra of the north.

Ever since I can remember, I have loved to watch the giant spruce and pine logs as they were carried over these falls by the head of water. The falls were one and a quarter mile from our camp. Dad would come from the driver's camp which was one mile further up the river, and say: "Mother, they are going to sluice this afternoon," and he would say to me, "do you want to go, my girl?" Did I want to go? Oh, that would be a very happy afternoon. We would walk that mile and a quarter through the green forest on an old road and would most always see partridges, deer, squirrels, and other forest creatures, which to me made life beautiful. I would stop to watch these birds and animals, and Dad would say: "My girl, we must hurry, for the logs will be coming soon."

When we would get to the falls, the logs would not be in sight up the stream. I would always want Dad to take me out where I could look from the top of the falls down to the bottom. There was a large flat rock at the top on the bank, and a tree near it. He would hold me by the hand and let me stand on the rock and look over. Then he would go down the river bank a short way to a place where we could look directly at the falls and see the logs as they came to the top and went over. Anyone who has ever seen this sight will never forget it.

Sometimes, we would sit on an old log, watching up the river; soon we would see the white water tumbling and foaming, filled with the giant logs—some eighteen inches and more on the butt, and forty feet or more long. The logs rushed to the top of the falls, then seemed to stop for a second or two before going over the falls. They would disappear for a few seconds, then reappear, bark stripped from their sides and sometimes split by another log that had hit them as they were going down. Not often, but sometimes, I have seen one of these giant logs swing sideways and it would cause other logs to pile up against it just at the top of the falls. But this jam would not hold, for the pressure of water was too strong, and the logs would swing and I would see twenty feet or more of these logs straighten out over the falls before they would plunge down.

If the logs were slow in coming down the stream or stopped, Dad would say: "My girl, there is something wrong—the logs may be jamming up. I will have to go and see. Do you want to come?" Sometimes I would go, but other times I wanted to wait. If it seemed at all cold to Dad, he would take his coat off and put it around me and say: "Now you set right here until I get back—I won't be long." He would then hurry up the stream bank. I would watch him until he was lost from sight at a bend in the river. But I would keep watching, for he would soon return.

If everything was all right, I would know for he would be taking his time; but if a jam was in the making up river, he would be coming fast and I would know we had to hasten home. He would have to go the other mile to where the men were sluicing, a place called the *lower dam*. There, the sluice gates must be shut as soon as possible, because all the logs that went through them would then go down Moxie Stream and all would pile up on the jam. The gates would be closed as quickly as possible, and all the river drivers would take pick poles and cantdogs and go down the stream to the jam, and then would have to pick and strate out the logs and get them straightened out. When the sluice gates were opened again, and the water filled the stream, the logs would be carried out to the main river where the east branch of Moosehead Lake, Dead River and Moxie Stream all joined and the millions of feet of lumber were then driven down to the mills.

However, first these logs must be brought down Moxie Pond, now called Lake Moxie. This pond, or lake, is nine miles long, and the logs had to be brought down in raffs (in large quantities). To do this the lumbermen built a very long raft and on this was built a boat camp, thirty or thirty-five feet long, which was also called the head works, and was attached to the raft. This building was closed in on the two sides and had a roof. It was something like the dingle (cellar) of a woods camp at these times, and was the same width as a camp.

In this head works was what was called the capstan, which was made of wood and was two feet or more in width in which were twelve six-inch holes. These holes were lined with steel. The bars were made of wood around 16 inches through, flat on the sides and twelve feet long. The capstan and bars were used in towing the rafts which would be from eight hundred thousand to a million feet of giant spruce, fir, and pine logs brought together by the drivers and held together by what is called a boom.

The boom was made by boring large holes near each end of a long log and the logs fastened together by a chain, and then the boom was strung around the raft so as to hold it close together. This job being completed, the crew of twenty-four men, with the head works and raft, would secure the boom and come down the pond. An anchor would be taken out from the head works in a boat and shoved into the pond. The anchor weighed five hundred pounds or more and was attached to one end of a large-size rope five or six hundred feet in length. The other end of this rope was attached to the capstan in such a manner that it would turn around. Then the twelve capstan bars were placed in the twelve holes in the capstan, and with two men on each bar, the capstan would be slowly turned, and as it turned the rope would be drawn up around the bottom of the capstan and if the anchor held the head works and the raft of logs would be drawn down the pond until they reached the anchor. Then the anchor had to be lifted again. It would be placed on the bow of the boat and taken out again and shoved over. In this way, the rafts were brought down the pond. This was a hard job for those twenty-four men, as they had to work when the wind was favorable, and sometimes they would work night and day. Then if the wind blew wrong they had to fasten the head works securely at some island and get into some cove or the wind would take them back up the pond. For days, sometimes, the men had nothing to do but sing songs, fish in the pond, play cards and dance or play games. They had to furnish their own entertainment.

It would take twenty to thirty days to bring the logs all down to the end of the lake, depending on the wind. Here they would be held by a boom and were sluiced through a gate into Moxie Stream and then into the main river. After the logs had been brought to the lower end of the pond, the head works were secured and left until the next year.

Near the shore where the men left the head works, we children would sometimes coax mother until she would take a lunch and come with us up to the pond, which was three miles from our camp. We would all go aboard the head works to have our lunch in the camp and look in the bunks and around for anything we could see. We would spend an hour or two on board, then walk the three miles back home after having spent a wonderful day. There is something about a lumber camp that has always been an attraction to me, and I always feel I must go inside and explore.

Childhood Activities

There were six of us children that kept together as we grew up. Our names were: Joseph (who we called Joe), Georgie, Bunnie (whose right name was Alfred), Roy, Leroy (whose right name is Albert), myself (who everyone called Ida but my name is Ardelle), and Jennie. There was one younger boy named Stephen (who we called the baby), but he was too young for a while to be in our play. There was just our family around, so we had to plan our own games in the summer. We played a game called "tag and goalie." Tag was an old boot placed on a rock with one of the six of us to watch it, and the goal was the place where the other five would stand, with five rocks of whatever size we liked the best. The game was to knock the boot from the rock. The one who knocked it off must run from goal, get his rock, and get back to goal without being caught by tag, who must always place the boot back on the rock before he could try to catch goalie. If the boot was not hit by the rock, another could throw his rock and continue until all five rocks had been thrown, and then we would have to dash from goalie and try to get the rocks, even tho the boot had not been knocked off. Someone was sure to be caught, for tag did not have to bother about the boot and could easily get one of the five, and then that one must be tag. But this game very often ended in disaster, for frequently one of these five rocks would come in contact with the ankle of tag and the game would end in a crying quarrel which my mother would settle.

In Winter, we used for sliding on the snow barrel staves, shovels or whatever we could find. Another sport was to see who could run the greatest distance in our bare feet. We each would get a large chip of wood from the dooryard and warm it up in the oven. Carrying this chip, we would run till it seemed our feet would be frozen, they we would lay the chip down and stand upon it till our feet would get warm. Then we would run back to the house. Today, I wonder how we did those things without freezing our feet.

Time went by fast, and soon we were old enough for school—but there was no way for us to get to school. Arrangements were made by Father and Mother to have a teacher stay with the family. They were to give the teacher her board, and her pay was to come from the State. It was always a woman teacher, as a woman did not charge as much as a man.

We children thought the teacher was something wonderful, and she would play games and tell us stories about the outside world which we had never seen. I liked the school books, and I learned very fast. The teacher would always help me, and after school she was always willing to explain any subject that I could not understand. Mother and Dad were glad that I took so much interest in my studies, and they began to plan that I should go to high school and then be trained to be a nurse.

Dad would say to me: "You, my girl, you know that if you had been a boy, you were to be a doctor." They knew how great the need was for more doctors. But I was a girl, so the next best was to have me train to be a nurse. They were planning a long way ahead, but for something that would never be.

Also about this same time they began to plan to build a new home in the clearing which had expanded now to twelve acres. This was to be a frame building, twenty-four by thirty feet. As the older boys were now working and earning money, it would be possible to buy the boards, windows, doors and such. The frames, sills, beams and rafters they would make by taking logs of the right length and, with large rip saws, which they had also made, saw these logs lengthwise and then into whatever widths were needed. In order to do this, a framework was built on a hill. A log was dragged on to the framework; one of the boys would stand under the framework while another would stand on the top, and with the long rip saw they would saw these rafters, sills and beams. I am describing this so you can have some idea of the many hard days of work that were needed to saw the framework of a house thirty by twenty-four feet.

Finally the lumber was ready, and with Dad as carpenter the frame work of the house was started. With good luck in four or five years we would have a new home, even with four boys and father to work and earn money. Their pay was not a very large amount: Father got a dollar a day, and the older boys earned less. The youngest, George, worked for a farmer. He stayed with the farm family and helped at the farm chores and such. For this work he received just five dollars a month. He was five months with one family, for which he received twenty five dollars, and he brought this home to Mother. He had not spent one cent of his pay. I now don't see how it was possible for a boy to go five months without spending a cent, but he knew the need of saving money. The other boys—Charlie, Johnnie and Joseph—received twelve to fifteen dollars a month doing woods work, and what they earned they brought home. They would always give their money to Mother, for she saw to it that they had what clothes and things they needed.

I was seven or eight years old at this time, and mother had taught me how to knit. I could knit men's woolen mittens. I liked to knit, and the boys would take these mittens into the woods where they would sell them to the woodsmen at fifty cents per pair. These mittens were what was called "double mittens," made with two strands of yarn. After the yarn was paid for, I would have fifteen cents for my work on each pair, and this I could have for my very own. Some weeks I could knit two pair, which would give me thirty cents. The boys would always come home from the lumber camp each Saturday night, if possible, having to walk ten or more miles. Be it ever so humble, there was no place like home. And they would also want to have clean clothes, for in those days the lumber camps were not kept as they are now. Very often they would have "cooties" on their bodies, which they had gotten from the woods. When this happened, all the clothes they wore had to be scalded to kill the bugs.

My Favorite Brother

When I was around nine years old, out of all my brothers the one we called Joe seemed to be my favorite. That winter he was in the woods as "cookee," and at that time was around eighteen years old. The cookee is the one who helps the cook, washes dishes, sweeps floors of camp, cuts the wood, and such—which is quite a job. The cook in this camp was a woman. Joe called her Mrs. Sterling and he liked her very much. She was very good to him, and he would tell us each time he came home how she would make a pie, sometimes, just for him.

In these lumber camps in those days the men had to make their own amusements. They would play games, dance and sing—sometimes one would have a fiddle or a harmonica or some other musical instrument. Joe came home one Saturday night, and he was all excited. He said to me: "I have a husband for you when you are old enough to marry. There is the most wonderful man I ever saw in camp. He can sing, dance, play the harmonica—and he is a fighter. He is training me and has promised that he will come home with me some Saturday. His name is Sam Allen, and I want you to see him. I have told him all about you." But the winter came and went, and Sam Allen did not come to our camp. Joe was disappointed, but he said Sam *had* promised.

The Spring came and went, and then in August the four brothers one day planned to go blueberrying. Mother put up a lunch for them, and they started with packs and a rifle. To get where the blueberries were, they had to go through seven or more miles of deep woods, and there could be bear and other animals along the way. When the boys went into the woods, they nearly always took the old gun along. They had to go almost a mile to Moxie Stream, which they had to cross, and then go another six or more miles to Black Brook where the berries were. They had crossed the stream and gone a short distance on the other side when Joe stopped and said: "I am not going any further." He had been carrying the gun and was standing with the muzzle of the rifle on his foot. The other boys began to coax him to go along with them and as they talked the gun suddenly went off. The bullet passed through Joe's foot; he had accidentally pulled on the trigger. The other three frightened brothers carried him back to the camp, and one was sent to The Forks to get to a doctor, the nearest being in Bingham. How frightened we all were! This was the first accident that had ever happened. Joe was in terrible pain, and it would take a doctor three or more hours to reach our camp. Mother could do nothing to ease the pain, for we had never had medicine of any kind in the house.

Finally, after what seemed ages, the doctor came. He examined the wound, which did not look so terrible after being washed. However, the doctor said he would give Joe ether and clean out the wound. The bullet had gone straight through near the toes. Mother told the doctor she did not want Joe to take ether, and she wanted to know if there was some other way he could fix it, so it would be alright. The doctor said he thought that if he washed it out and did it up, it would heal alright—and that was all he did.

As our new house was finished downstairs, Mother said we would move in. It would cheer us up, including Joe. So a worried family moved from a camp to a new home. For a few days the wound in Joe's foot seemed to heal and looked better. But he would complain that it pained him terrible and would want one of the pills that the doctor had left for Mother to give him when the pain was bad. On the eighth or ninth day Joe had a terrible bad spell, and one of the boys was sent to The Forks to get a doctor as soon as possible. A new doctor had come to the town of Bingham, and he would come as soon as he could get a team. In around three hours he arrived. He looked at Joe and shook his head, and said: "I will do what I can." He gave him ether and opened up the wound in his foot, which seemed to be healing fine. But when he cleaned and put a swab through the wound, he brought out a small piece of the woolen sock. This had been carried into the foot by the bullet and had caused blood poisoning. We all blamed the first doctor, but he had been too kind hearted, I think, and did not want to hurt Mother. The second doctor said he could not understand how a doctor could do such a thing. There is no need to tell of the suffering endured by Joe. Before he died the doctor came every day and did what he could. But it was too late, and so the first awful tragedy came to our backwoods home. This was in 1904.

Enter Sam

Among the drivers that were to bring the rafts of logs down Moxie Pond with the head works the next spring, was Sam Allen. He stopped at our home, and when mother went to the door he asked if Joe was home. Sadly, he had not heard that Joe had died. And so I first saw Sam Allen, the most wonderful man in the world, but at the time of no interest to me. . . .

Also at that time at The Forks was The Forks Hotel, of one hundred rooms, where the woodsmen would stay after coming out of the lumber camps in the spring. Before they could go on the drive, the snow must be gone and the rivers and ponds filled with water. This might mean three or four weeks and sometimes longer that these woodsmen must stay and wait. If they had no home near, The Forks Hotel was the place many would stay.

The older boys in the family would walk to The Forks and sometimes spend a day at the Hotel with the boys they worked in the woods with. Sometimes they would bring their friends to visit with us, for everyone had always been welcome at our house. Mother and Dad always did their best to make the boys' friends feel at home. And one day, who should they bring home but Sam Allen. Mother and Dad were very glad that Sam had come to see them, for Joe had thought so much of him. I remembered what Joe had said about Sam making me a wonderful husband, kept at a distance, as I was at this time around thirteen years old. Sam was asked to stay a few days with the boys. He would play the harmonica and sing and dance and tell some of the most wonderful stories about old sea captains and fiery dragons.

Stevie, as we called him, was seven years old and the thirteenth and youngest of our family. He would sit on Sam's lap and listen to the stories. The first visit of Sam Allen was a pleasure to all. Mother and Dad told the boys they would be glad to have them bring Sam home as often as he cared to come. And so before long, Sam was spending most of his time, when not working, with the boys at our house, and we all had a wonderful time. . . .

Sometimes we would talk of Joe. He would tell me how Joe had talked of me so many times and how proud he was of me. One day he said: "You are too young to understand, but I am going away for a year." From his finger he took a band ring and broke it into two pieces. One he gave to me and the other he put in his wallet saying: "When I return, if you still have your half of this ring, I will know you are waiting for me. I will not write, but I will return. So be sure to keep your half of the ring." I promised I would, and Sam left. I very carefully added the ring to my treasure box and thought it my dearest possession. . . .

Soon the year had passed, and I was looking forward to Sam's return. Would he come? Around this same time, plans had been completed to take us to The Forks to school. I had been through one year of high school in our little school house, and now I could join the second year high school at The Forks. Great plans were made, and if I studied hard I would graduate from high school. In two years, then, I would go away to train for the nurse I was to be. This would cost Dad and the boys quite a sum of money, but they were sure they could earn and spare enough. When it was nearly time for the opening of school at The Forks, the boys bought a horse and a wagon. One of the older boys was to drive the school hack, as it was called. We scholars were looking foreward to this school year, for we would be in town and could have a good time.

One day, who should walk in but Sam Allen. Was I glad to see him! He was very nicely dressed and to me very good looking. He shook hands with Mother and Dad. He had always called them Mr. and Mrs. Crotto. And to me he said: "How is my little pal?" And soon he was telling us all about his year away. When we were alone together for a few minutes, he took from his wallet half of the band ring, and said: "Do you still have your half?" I sure did, and so a wonderful friendship began.

From: Ardelle Allen, *Ida: A Happy Life in the Maine Backwoods*. Thorndike, Maine: Thorndike Press, 1979.

Virginia Chase Perkins
1902–1987

Virginia Chase Perkins was born in Blue Hill in 1902. Her father was a lawyer, her mother a former school teacher, and her older (by fifteen years) sister was the writer Mary Ellen Chase. The Chase family was a large one; nearly thirty years elapsed between the birth of the first child and that of the eighth and last, and their village changed considerably during that period. They were well-to-do and respected in the community, and learning was highly prized. Virginia graduated from the University of Minnesota and did graduate work at the University of Michigan and Wayne State University.

Before her marriage she taught school in Maine towns. Subsequently she taught English at several colleges, ending up as a visiting lecturer at Smith College, where her sister had retired after a forty-year teaching career. Virginia Chase Perkins wrote four novels, works on Maine history, short stories, and the autobiographical and historical collection, Speaking of Maine, *from which this excerpt is taken.*

Her Blue Hill was a small village, subject to the sometimes cantankerous relationships found among small-town neighbors everywhere. Her family, as the episodes in the book demonstrate, was patriarchal. Edward Everett Chase, a descendant of seafarers, was confident of himself, his family, and his place in the community. Blue Hill had been settled by strong men. In 1762 Joseph Wood and John Roundy sailed up to Blue Hill Bay from Beverly, Massachusetts, and presumably found the wilderness countryside aesthetically pleasing and the generous supply of timber commercially attractive. They spent a summer clearing land and building log cabins on Mill Island. The next summer they returned with their families

The Chase family, c. 1910. Virginia is second from right. Her older sister (and fellow writer) Mary Ellen is third from left. *Courtesy of Virginia Halonen.*

as the first settlers in what would eventually become a small industrial and shipbuilding community.

An early priority of these Massachusetts Puritans, after voting to clear and establish a burying ground, was the hiring of a preacher and the building of a meeting house. At a town meeting in 1792 it was voted "that the Selectmen be empowered to procure one barrel of rum, also molasses and sugar sufficient for framing and raising the meeting house." Following a rapid succession of twelve ministers, the Reverend Jonathan Fisher became the pastor of the Blue Hill Congregational Church in 1796. A remarkable man, whose influence on the town was great—he helped form Blue Hill Academy—Fisher is the subject of a biography by Mary Ellen Chase.

Blue Hill, for which the town was named in 1788 after having initially been incorporated as "Newport," rises some five hundred feet out of the countryside to the north of the town. It is a commanding presence as seen from the waters of Penobscot and Blue Hill bays. Its name derives from the bluish tint of the evergreens that covered the hill in earlier days. It has served the town as a copper mine and a blueberry barren (Virginia Perkins and her husband were in the blueberry business for a while) and remains a sentinel marking the location of this sturdy Maine village of which Virginia Chase Perkins wrote with clarity and humor.

The Extraordinary Spring

Located on an old Indian campsite not far from the center of Blue Hill, it was, indeed, an extraordinary spring. People who had springs of their own—some of more than passing quality—came from miles around in carriages and jiggers bringing buckets to be filled. It was said that no horse in town would willingly have passed the trough supplied by its overflow.

In the lawsuit it was ultimately to provoke, witness after witness gave testimony to its excellence. Mr. Eben Mayo swore it to be "one of the best." Mr. George Morse, who had recently sold his house, asserted that in moving he "didn't calculate to get more than a mile and a half from it." Mrs. Abby Fulton, an early owner of the property, declared that it was the chief inducement for her husband, the village doctor, to choose the place in spite of her objections that it was too far (actually less than a quarter of a mile) from the post office.

It is odd that it should have sustained such appeal, for only a few yards separated it from the old village graveyard. Even in the late 1800s, when this story begins, such a circumstance might have raised questions, especially since in 1865 a cloudburst of historic proportions had hit Blue Hill, washing out bridges and so enlarging the gully between the graveyard and the spring that two coffins had been exposed not far from the spring itself.

Nevertheless its reputation had remained, even increased with time. So great was its popularity that Mr. Thomas Hinckley, who owned or was believed to own the property on which it flowed, began to lose his patience. Wanting to wash his carriages at the trough at his own convenience, he often found himself frustrated by long lines of thirsty horses and bucket-laden men. Finally, exasperated, he covered and padlocked the spring. The lock was promptly broken. The lines resumed. Essentially a philosophical man, he gave up completely.

His heirs were equally philosophical. They must have been generous, too, for they allowed my father who, after tasting the water from the spring, had become disenchanted with that from our own quite adequate well, to dig another spring beside it. Fed from the same source, it was easily piped into our house, which was separated from the Hinckley's only by the house of Captain Spencer Treworgy. All was tranquil until the arrival of Reverend C.M.G. Harwood.

Just when he came or where he came from is not clear. We knew only that, as a retired minister of great dignity and presence, he had preached mostly in the West (which to us meant anywhere beyond Massachusetts). Where he and Miss Treworgy met remains a complete mystery. It is possible he had first come to Blue Hill as one of the long line of substitute preachers who had occupied the pulpit for a Sunday or two, as indistinguishable one from another as a single crow in a flock. Or it is possible that she met him in either Skowhegan or Eastport where he held brief pastorates, though the county paper makes no mention of her having visited either town. The place of the marriage is also unknown, but the time must have been around 1880, for she was not listed as a resident of Blue Hill in the census of that year. Her age was then forty-one.

Miss Treworgy had long been known to the genteel of the village as a "maiden lady." To the unmannered young, she was simply an "old maid." The idea that she had a husband, any husband at all, seemed preposterous, even indecent. Indeed, many did not believe it until she returned with him in or about 1895.

To the astonishment of the village, the Reverend Harwood was a fine figure of a man. Clearly younger than his wife, he was tall with broad shoulders, heavy white hair, and a neat mustache. His clothes were always pressed, his collar spotless, his shoes well-shined. No matter what he was doing, feeding the pig or substituting in the pulpit, where his deep, bass voice was equally melodious in hymn or prayer, his appearance was impeccable.

The few who scoffed (mostly the barbershop loafers) focused on his name, insisting that the initials C.M.G. stood for Clement Marmeduke Gabriel. Clement was undoubtedly correct, for it appears on his burial certificate. There are some who still believe in the authenticity of Marmeduke and Gabriel. The Reverend Harwood himself gave no clue. Nor does his tombstone.

He must soon have found time hanging heavy on his hands, for he was often seen wandering out-of-doors, especially in the Treworgy pasture which lay across the street from their house and adjacent to the spring. On these occasions he always carried a yardstick. Obviously he was investigating their boundaries. He soon announced that the spring was not on the Hinckley property at all, but on land belonging to the town. That being true, he was as free as my father, he claimed, to profit from it. The Treworgys already had a spring in their own pasture, a spring as good as most, but he presumably had tasted the magic water and coveted more.

When his argument fell on deaf ears, trouble began between our two families. Up to this time the Harwoods had spoken to us, albeit coolly, in passing. They now passed in silence. The shades in the windows facing our house were drawn. But it was early in the 1900s, when our family put in a bathroom, that the real trouble began. Our water supply diminished, presumably by nightly bailings; a cover which my father placed on the spring was broken and the water routinely riled. The Reverend Harwood and my father, both speakers of local renown, refused to appear on the same platform together.

This turn of events was source of great concern to my mother. She tried to keep the particulars from the older children—this was before my birth—but, very conscious of the breach, they welcomed the excitement it brought. A neighbor tells how, on one of the guided tours to our bathroom—so frequent as to preclude its usefulness to the family—one of my sisters, eight years old at the time, pointed to the hot-water faucet closest to the Harwoods and whispered solemnly, "H is for Harwood." Then indicating the other on the opposite side of the bowl, she added, "And C is for Chase."

But as the older children's understanding increased, so did their fervor. Familiar with Mary Lamb's tales from Shakespeare, they saw themselves in the tradition of the Montagues and the Capulets; and, while careful to keep out of our mother's hearing, they stood just inside the kitchen windows, shouting, with appropriate gesture, the words of the feuding servants in the story: "I bite my thumb at you!"

In 1904 my father, taking an early morning stroll, apprehended Brooks Gray, a laborer hired by the Harwoods, in the act of digging a trench to deflect our water's flow. Indignant, he argued the Hinckley heirs, themselves indifferent to the situation and by this time widely scattered, into taking the case to court, with him as their attorney, in an attempt to establish forever the family claim, but principally, of course, his own.

The case was heard in 1905. During its procedure my father, agitated, inadvertently revealed what he was up to, and the judge, annoyed with both parties, dismissed the case. "Settle it between yourselves," he said.

After the trial things quieted down considerably. It was a time of watchful waiting. The Reverend Harwood placed an enormous "No Trespassing" sign in his pasture, set directly to face our house. (This seemed unnecessary since we had never felt inclined to go there.) My father put a heavy metal cover with padlock on our spring. My mother, fearful of some new provocation, began secretly to draw, except for drinking, our water from the well again. Things seemed almost normal.

Then one Sunday in the early fall of 1909 while we were eating dinner we heard a loud knock on the window facing the Treworgy house. Looking up, we saw the Reverend Harwood's white face peering in and heard his deep voice intone one word: "Fire!"

Now in our village we dreaded no disaster so much as fire. Storms, even hurricanes, we could handily weather. Blizzards did not faze us, nor did drought, though it took patience sometimes to wait one out. Sickness we took for granted. But fire was another matter. Our only method of fighting it was a village bucket brigade, summoned by the ringing of the church bell. This had limited success, especially during the hunting season or when fish were running in the bay.

My father, who believed in being prepared for anything, had organized the entire family into our own fire brigade and given each of us specific instructions for procedure. He and my brother would rush for the ladder kept against the wall just inside the barn door; my mother would seize the big bag of salt, used to douse chimney fires, that hung by the grain bin; each sister would steadily grasp one of the buckets of well water, always filled and set handily in an empty stall; I, the youngest, and in all practical matters retarded, would be best kept out of the way by bringing two heavy bath towels soaked at the kitchen sink, in case someone should require resuscitation. Thus equipped, we would fall into a procession led by my father and immediately begin action. So when we heard the dreaded word we responded instantly.

But things did not go quite the way my father had planned. A carriage left too close to the door impeded agility with the ladder. The twine suspending the bag of salt had rotted, breaking under the force of my mother's hand; fortunately the bag itself remained intact. One bucket, almost empty, suggested that a thirsty cow had paused to refresh herself as she passed. Only I, perhaps seven at the time, had met no obstacle and stood smugly, shamelessly enjoying it all. What would be the appropriate words to speak as I revived a half-conscious victim, especially a mortal enemy? Would it be "Fear not! I shall save you"? Or perhaps "Behold, we have come in your hour of need"? It was hard to decide.

By the time we were finally off, the smell of smoke was already in the air. Our progress was slow, hampered by the shrubbery and the necessity to skirt my mother's jealously guarded petunias. The smoke grew heavy.

The Treworgy house was a hundred feet above our own on the crest of a steep banking. Still in formation, we slipped and stumbled to the top. The Reverend Harwood had disappeared. Though the smoke was darkening steadily, we could not see its source. My mother set down the bag of salt and rang the bell. There was no answer. She rang again. No sound anywhere.

They were all overcome, I told myself, delighted. All, all lying unconscious. The Reverend Harwood had gone back in to rescue the others and had himself fallen. There would be a medal in it for me. Gold, of course, and since three would have been rescued, no doubt a diamond.

Getting no response to the bell, my mother had begun desperately to pound on the door. "Come out," she called. Still no response. She turned the knob, or tried to, but the door was locked from the inside. She pounded harder. "Come out. Come out," she kept repeating.

"Come out, come out," I echoed, extending the dripping towels. "Come out before it is too late!" Hearing the commotion, my father descended the ladder from which he had been inspecting the roof. It was then that he saw, through the steadily thickening smoke, flames spurting high from our *own* chimney.

For the first time in my life I heard him swear. Then, recovering, he picked up one end of the ladder. My brother seized the other and we dashed, formation forgotten, down the banking and through the shrubbery, trampling heedlessly on the cherished garden. My father and brother set up the ladder. My mother readied the salt. My sisters rushed to the well to refill the almost empty buckets. Drenched and disconsolate, a heroine no longer, I soberly laid the soggy, grimy towels over the mangled petunias.

The damage to the house was inconsequential, and for a time things went on as before, the same drawn shades, the same public snubbings from the Harwoods. There was, however, a change in Blue Hill itself. Grown soft or more fastidious, more people began to demand bathrooms. This meant artesian wells, abundance of water seeming more desirable than quality. As a result, there was a gradual drop in the water level of the village. Springs lowered precariously, sometimes dried up. Daily we could watch the Reverend Harwood cross his pasture, presumably to inspect theirs. Our own remained remarkably stable.

It may have been for this reason alone that around 1912 tension again mounted. Though there was nothing you could put your finger on, you could feel it in the air. "Look out and see what's going on," my father would say to one of us, meaning, of course, look in the direction of the Treworgys. Sometimes in looking we could detect a movement of a shade, indicating that one of them was spying too. This generated considerable excitement. When a day was particularly dull, we would take a drink of water from the faucet, loudly pronounce ourselves poisoned and writhe, groaning, upon the kitchen floor until my mother came to put a stop to it.

But it was not until 1914, six weeks before my father's death, that a crisis—the real crisis—came. The Hinckley heirs finally got together and decided to sell their property, quietly offering it to my mother. Distraught as she was by my father's illness, she decided to buy, knowing it was something he himself would have done to better establish his claim to the spring.

The results were almost immediate. My brother, by this time a sturdy young man in his early twenties, looked out very early one morning to see a large pile of gravel beside the spring, with Mrs. Harwood, then seventy-five and very frail, busily shoveling from it into what appeared to be a large hole in the well's metal cover. He hurried to the scene. Arrived, he bent to examine the hole, allowing Mrs. Harwood a fine opportunity to hit him on his head with her shovel. He turned, seized her lightly around the waist (she was so small his fingers met) and set her neatly on the edge of the watering trough. Then as he bent to pick up the crowbar with which she had made the hole, a gesture which she interpreted as threatening, she broke the long silence with a shrill, continuous scream. He headed home. Before night he was served a subpoena, charged with assault and battery.

The hearing, for such it turned out to be, was public, with most of the town present, while our family, except for the accused, remained at home, sitting discreetly in the parlor. The Harwoods were represented by a lawyer "from away." My brother handled his own case, his plea being self-defense. He was a young man of keen wit who had long since seen the absurdity of the entire situation. No records exist, but those who were present tell me there was never a funnier show in town. Once again there was no verdict, and it broke up in general laughter.

According to the undertaker's records, the Reverend Harwood died on Christmas Day, 1916, though the inscription on his stone reads a year later. He and my father lie in the graveyard by the shore, the same distance apart as in life, while the extraordinary spring, supplanted, diminished, half-hidden by weeds and bushes, flows on.

From, Margaret Shea, ed., *Speaking of Maine, Selections from the Writings of Virginia Chase.* Camden, Maine: Down East Books, 1983. Reprinted by permission of Virginia S. Halonen.

Hazel V. Hall
1902–1988

Hazel Hall's short book—No, we weren't poor, we just didn't have any money—*is a hymn of praise and a return of thanks for her perfect childhood on her grandfather's farm near Sebec. (Unlike most reminiscences of this kind it also contains recipes, for crisp molasses cookies and apple cake.) Looking back from an advanced age, she remembers years that were "very secure . . . problems seemed very far away." When the whole family rode to the county fair, "it was usually a bright sunny day." Never was such a delightful grandfather as hers, and as we read her charming pages, we do not disagree.*

Only once, and for a comparatively short time, did Hazel Hall leave a life centered on the land. But her grandfather's farm has suffered changes in modern times. A main highway now runs in front of the house, and the new owners no longer farm the land. Hazel married at eighteen, and she and her husband bought a hundred and twenty acres in East New Portland along the Carrabassett River. They raised beef cattle and sold meat in the surrounding area. During the Second World War her husband worked as a carpenter at the Portsmouth Naval Shipyard in Kittery, but that was their only absence from the farm. She continued to write and left three children's stories in manuscript. Her only book, when it was advertised in the grocery-store magazine Family Circle, *brought her admiring letters from all over America.* No, we weren't poor, we just didn't have any money *was dedicated to her nine grandchildren. Her daughter plans to reprint her book with additional family history and more from Hazel's pen. Hazel died at the age of eighty-five, her husband at ninety.*

Eight-year-old Hazel Hall (left) and her sisters Myrtle (center) and Jennie.
Courtesy of Laura Dunham.

Life on Grandfather's Farm

The generation of today may wonder what the girls did to pass the time away on a farm without electricity, radio, movies, television, or automobiles. I recall that there were very few lonesome hours because we kept busy helping with the many chores that were numerous on a farm and found out at an early age that we would have to find ways of entertaining ourselves, and this we did.

Our family of six consisted of our father, mother, grandfather, two sisters—one older and one younger, and myself. We were a very close family, one of the reasons being the self-invented entertainment that we enjoyed.

My Grandfather's farm was a very delightful place to live. Its many acres provided several ways to entertain us girls.

The large two and a half story house was built by my Grandfather, and all the lumber was taken from the farm. He cut the lumber and hauled it (with a small horse) twelve miles to a sawmill to be sawed at the specified dimensions. He then hauled it home, dried the lumber, and framed the house. He stored the remaining lumber in the roof of the barn; when he was ready, he put up the house. . . .

The house that Grandfather built was not a little Ranch House, it was a large house lathed and plastered from cellar to attic. It consisted of a large kitchen, dining room, buttery, front hall, living room, and spare bedroom downstairs, four large bedrooms and a hall upstairs, with two very large rooms in the attic. Every spring and fall it was cleaned and at least two rooms were papered and painted.

The buttery always was a very important place for my sister and I because it always contained a big pail of molasses cookies and a jar of mother's biscuits. In the dish cupboard was a pitcher of molasses that we spread on the biscuits and if we were really lucky, we might be able to snitch a couple of slices of salt pork that mother had fried for dinner that always sat on top of the old iron teakettle on the back of the old wood stove. It sure tasted good to a couple of very young, active girls.

The Bangor and Aroostook Railroad ran through our farm at the back, and the Piscataquis River at the front. When I was a child, the Bangor and Aroostook Railway was a very busy line. There were two passenger trains that went from Greenville to Bangor every day—one was the Flying Yankee and the other one was a mail train. In the middle of the day several freight trains shuttled back and forth carrying pulp, potatoes, live stock, and apples to Boston; most all farm produce and, in fact, most everything that people ate, wore, and used were shipped by train. The train was a friendly thing in some ways; my sister and I liked to watch it. We would put horseshoe nails and safety pins on the rail, after the train had gone by, we would rush out of our hiding place and pick up our flattened prizes, but in another way it was a nuisance. The north field of Grandfather's farm was across the tracks, so when my father was hauling lumber or hay across them we had to be sure it was between train time as it was a long down grade across our farm and the trains always traveled at a high rate of speed.

As my sister and I grew older, we would hear two little toots; and the fireman and the engineer would wave their hands to us. We thought this was very nice of them to bother to help make our days a little more pleasant. In those days, there weren't many earth shaking things that happened so we had to be satisfied with the small ones. All of the produce that was shipped into these small towns came by rail to the freight or express office. Then the farmers with their two and sometimes four-horse teams, with a long sled in the winter and wagon in the spring and summer, would haul the freight to the stores. These were known as a tote team. It was a very hard job, especially in the Spring—in mud time when the roads were just about impossible to travel over—but it was like show business; the work had to go on. Then, in the early 20's the men began to buy trucks to haul their freight. The first one in our neighborhood was an International truck with hard rubber tires; it was used to advantage in the summer when the roads were dry, but in the spring it was stuck in the mud most of the time, so it had to be hauled out by the farmers' horses. Today there isn't a passenger train in Maine and very few freight trains because everything is shipped by truck or plane. . . .

In the winter when darkness came early, we always had our supper at five o'clock. While my sister and I were doing the supper dishes we would sing for our Grandfather. Although at times it was probably not very melodious, he seemed to enjoy it. We would sing all of the old songs, then all of the new ones that were popular at that time. On moonlit evenings we would put on our heavy clothes and play out-of-doors until bedtime, which was usually eight o'clock. We played fox and geese, slid off the barn roof into the big snow banks when the snow was soft; we would make snow forts and snowmen. Many of them looked quite real.

About seven o'clock, my father would ask if it wasn't time that we had some apples to eat. So my sister and I would light the kerosene lantern, take an old wooden bowl from the kitchen table and go to the cellar. Here we would always find barrels of Blue Pearmaines, Tolman Sweets, Russets, and Spys, also Peewalkies.

Father finished reading his weekly Commercial. Mother was tired of knitting and we girls had played our games until we were getting sleepy so we would be glad of a few apples before we went to bed. Dad always peeled the apples with his jackknife and passed the quarters to each of us on the point of the blade. The apples had a different flavor in those days.

Mother would bring in a big plate of her crisp molasses cookies and a pitcher of cold, creamy milk to go with the apples that Dad had prepared for us. This was nothing very exciting, but life was very secure and problems seemed very far away.

(One cup molasses, one cup of sugar, one cup of melted lard, one cup of hot water, four teaspoons of soda, two teaspoons of tartar, salt and spice of all kinds and a good dose of vanilla. Add enough flour to roll soft.) This is my mother's favorite molasses cookie recipe. I can never recall a time that she didn't have a twenty-five pound lard pail full of cookies to help yourself to whenever you wished.

One spring, I remember very well my father wanted me to help him plant by hand some beans. He passed me a big ten-pound lard pail of beans to plant. I was to put five or six beans in a hill and kick a little dirt over them. Well, of course, that pail of beans looked awfully large to a child of eight or nine. I planted for awhile and it was hot and the flies were thick, so I happened to think that I wanted to go swimming. I took about half of the beans over to a big rock pile and dumped them down into a hole. I put a big rock on them and then went swimming. A short time later the beans began to stick their heads up where I had planted them. All of a sudden they stopped and there wasn't any more that came up and none could be found in the ground.

My father was always puzzled about that as he couldn't understand why they came up so good on one side of the garden and none at all on the other side. In later years I told him the reason and he said that he thought there was something fishy about the whole thing.

There are not many different kinds of beans raised today in comparison to the amount grown in past years. The old time favorites were Jacobs Cattle, Goose Crop, Sulphur Beans, add a few cranberries along with the old stand-by, old fashioned yellow eye. Now in the stores one mostly finds Soldier beans, Yellow-eye, Pea beans and once in a while Red Kidneys.

There are a lot of people today, especially in the younger generation, that don't have the faintest idea how the beans that they purchase in the store in two pound bags got that way.

First, they have to be planted, then in the fall they are pulled and stacked so as to dry before the heavy frosts come. My Dad would haul them into the barn and store them on an open scaffold where the breeze could blow through them. This dried them thoroughly so that they would not mildew. Then some good, cold Saturday in December, my father would say to us girls, "We are going to flail beans today." We would sweep the barn floor clean, lay down a big canvas and pile the beans onto it. The tool that my father used to flail the beans was a very odd looking gadget. It was composed of three parts, a long handle with a shorter handle attached to the long one by a piece of raw hide leather. It was made so that when you lifted it up high, the shorter piece would swing and come down hard upon the beans. The one thing that you had to watch out for was, unless you were very skillful in handling this great invention, you would get the short stick on the back of your head instead of on the beans. So the one who did the thrashing usually had learned how to handle the flail the hard way and was very careful just how he manipulated it.

Back and forth, over and over he worked, and with each hard blow of the flail the dried beans would pop high in the air. Then the layer was stirred up two or three times with the pitchfork. When all of the beans were flailed, the pods and vines were forked off the beans and the dirt and a few nanny plums were swept into a pile. Then they were run through a winnow machine that removed everything except the bright shiny morsels that would be our Saturday night supper for the next year.

When I was about eight, my father brought home a beautiful shiny new surrey. It was black with a red stripe on it and upholstered in a dark green wool cloth. It had a silk fringe around the top and two little kerosene lamps on each side of the front seat. Now that was considered a Cadillac in those days to be sure. When you started out in your linen dusters and veil, with your horse all shiny and polished, and a silver trimmed harness, you thought you were something. Even they were only owned by the upper class.

It was in that surrey that I first remember going to our County Fair. Now that was a day we girls looked forward to for a whole year. The day would finally arrive which was around the fifteenth of September and as I remember, it was usually a bright sunny day. My younger sister and I would awaken long before daybreak in anticipation of the wonderful day ahead. Dad would have the chores done early, and the horse and surrey just shining. Mother, poor Mother, would have the most wonderful and delicious lunch packed. It contained fried chicken, done to a beautiful golden brown; home-made yeast rolls that would melt in your mouth; a large dish of potato salad that was not mixed with the home-made salad dressing until we were ready to eat; home-made dairy butter; filled cookies and apple cake that was covered with a beautiful yellow frosting made from boiled icing colored with the yolk of an egg as there was not any food coloring in those days.

The apple cake was made as follows: stew two cups of diced apples in two cups of molasses until clear. Remove apples from molasses and add one cup of butter, two eggs, one cup of sour milk, two teaspoons of soda, three and two-thirds cup of flour, spice of all kinds. Add the apples last; this makes two loaves.

Then Mother would get us girls ready with our starched home-made gingham dresses which were both just alike and long black cotton stockings.

My sister Jennie was always made to sit in a chair until we all were ready because she had the habit of always getting wheel grease or something worse on her clothes at the last minute. We always kept a few hens and they ran loose; so to be on the safe side, Jennie was made to stay in one place.

At last we were ready to start; we had the lunch basket in the surrey and off we went for the trip of five miles to the fairgrounds. All through the year Jennie and I had saved our Lincoln pennies for this great day. Perhaps we would have fifty cents apiece and sometimes only twenty-five. All we could see was the Merry-go-round and that was where we spent all of our money at five cents a ride.

About four o'clock Dad would round up us girls, or at least try; we did not want to go home so early. So when he had found one of us, the other would disappear. We worked that for awhile, then finally he would make one of us hold his hand while he found the other. Then, we would start our long drive home satisfied and tired but planning how we would go again another year. . . .

Grandfather's farm was three miles from the Post Office and in the winter time we got our mail only on Saturday. What an armful father would bring home. There would be something for each of us. Among the mail would be found the Bangor Weekly Commercial, the Maine Farmer, Comfort Magazine, Youth Companion, and several letters from our aunts—Melissa, Lucindy, and Sophronia. My father would hitch up one of the work horses and start for town. My sister and me knew that he would be gone for more than two hours because he would have to stop and talk with all the neighbors on his way home. Thus we took advantage of this situation—when the cat is away, the mice will play. We would hitch strings on the cows' horns, get on their backs, and play we were cowgirls. We also had two large and very ugly rams, Sam and Elijah. We would get on their backs out in the barnyard and go around and around until they were exhausted. Even the biggest dare-devil of today would not think of such things. Our father was a very strict man so we had to get the most out of a short time. All I can say is that it was a good thing for us that he did not catch us doing those things.

I remember distinctly one winter my father and I were out in the woods hauling up our next winter's wood. We had to cross the railroad tracks and we knew that it was almost train time, but decided that we would have time to cross, so we started. One of our horses caught his toe behind one of the spikes that holds the rails in place. It threw him and there we were; just about that time we heard a train whistle in the distance, my father took a red handkerchief from his pocket and told me to run up the track and around the bend to try to stop the train. Now that was quite an order for a ten year old child, but I was in the habit of doing what I was told with no back talk so I started. As I was nearing the curve, I heard the whistle for the crossing. I was walking right in the middle of the tracks, waving my red signal frantically. It happened that they were driving slowly, they saw me, stopped and the fireman got down and helped me up into the cab of the locomotive. We all went down to where my father was, and they had to use a pinch bar to pull the spike before Prince could get up on his feet. I called that a rather thrilling experience. . . .

On Grandfather's farm, my Dad always kept six Jersey cows and every Tuesday was the day to churn the cream into butter. First the cows were milked by hand. There were no electric milking machines in those days. The milk was strained into large pans and set in the cupboard in the cellar overnight. In the morning Mother would take her skimmer and skim the cream that had risen to the top of the milk. It usually was very thick and yellow. Mother would then put it in a big jar and stir it (the cream). The next morning she would do the same until the jar was full, then she got out the churn. First she washed this in hot, soapy water and then rinsed it in ice cold water. Now it was ready for the cream. My Grandfather would bring up his chair and sit turning the crank until he heard "plop", "plop", "plop". This sound meant that the cream had turned to golden nuggets of butter. We then drained off the buttermilk which we kept to cook with or to drink. Mother would then wash the butter and work it with her hands until the water was all clean of milk. Next she would get her big wooden bowl and put the butter into that and mix it with one tablespoon of pure salt for each pound until thoroughly mixed. Then the butter was put into the butter mold, which was a square hinged box with a removable bottom on which four different designs had been carved by hand in the wood.

There was usually a design in each corner, sometimes a sheaf of wheat, a clump of acorns, or roses, etc. Then the butter was placed into parchment paper and now it was ready to go to market or to be enjoyed at home on hot biscuits, pancakes, etc. by the family. This delicious home-made product was quite different in taste from the so-called butter squares of today.

In the spring after the snow had disappeared we would go looking for dandelions. This was our annual spring tonic. We would go armed with butcher knives and dish pans to gather the tender morsels of which grandfather's farm yielded aplenty. After they were dug and carefully cleaned and washed, we would serve them in several different ways. For instance we would put a big piece of salt pork on to cook about one hour before we wanted to start the greens. Then when the greens were all ready we would cook them in the broth of the pork and water until done, with potatoes added for the last half hour of cooking. We always served a mustard sauce on the pork. This was made with dry mustard mixed with vinegar plus a little sugar and salt. This was most certainly a dinner fit for the gods. Other times we would fry out several strips of bacon, mix a little vinegar, sugar, salt, and raw onion in some of the fat and pour over the greens and stir until wilted. On Saturday night we would make a salad of the little tender leaves by mixing them with vinegar, salt, sugar and pepper to go with the delicious, golden baked beans. By then we had about gotten our fill of the vitamin filled food in the various forms.

Then we began to dig and clean and salt the greens for our winter's use. We would fill our jars full of greens and then wait a day or two and repeat this process as the greens had shrunk. Finally the day came when they were all filled. We would cover each jar with a plate with a good sized field rock on it and wait until winter to sample the wonderful flavor of salted greens. . . .

On Grandfather's farm we had what was called a well room where we also hung our harnesses both double and single. It was there that we always harness and unharness our horses. There was a very deep rocked up well that we drew water from in an old oaken bucket with a chain on it that was attached to a windlass with a crank and turned the water into a large tub made from a molasses barrel that had been sawed in half, for the horses, cattle and sheep in the winter time.

After offering water to the animals for a day or so and they not accepting it, my father began to wonder what had happened to the well, so he lighted the old-fashioned kerosene lantern, tied a rope onto it and lowered it into the well. What do you know, there sitting on a projecting rock was a good sized skunk. Dad pulled the lantern up as carefully as possible in order not to disturb him. The next thing was to find a way to get him out. We all thought of different ways that didn't turn out to be of much help until my father thought of a big fish hook he had. He tied this onto a stout string with a good size piece of beef on it and lowered it into the well and what do you know, the skunk grabbed the meat and hung on and he lifted him out. I guess he was glad to be out of that dark hole and to get something to eat. We took him into the woods and let him go. After a short time the horses drank the water the same as usual and that was the end of our skunk.

It wasn't as easy for two girls to go to High School then as it is now and I feel quite sure that if my granddaughters had to go through the performance we had to go through in order to go they would decide it wasn't worth it.

We lived five miles from the Academy. The only way to get there was with a horse and wagon in the fall and spring. In the winter we roomed in town and boarded ourselves. This involved a lot of work over the weekend. We had two rooms on the second floor of a ladies' house, one we used for a bedroom and the other was our kitchen. Friday around 3:00 our Dad would drive up to town to pick us up as soon as school was out. In the winter it was a cold ride home but we had big buffalo coats. Mother was always home when we got there and had a nice hot supper ready. Saturday we had to start to get ready for the next week. First we had to wash our clothes and get them out to dry. Then we had to cook enough to last two girls a week. We would bake a big pot of beans, roast a big loin of pork, make a brown bread, bake two big tins of biscuits, two cakes, a batch of cookies, plus pickles, jelly, sauce, and apples. It would usually last most of the week if we didn't invite too many of our school mates. We also had to take two gallons of milk and a pint of thick cream that we could reduce with some of the milk.

Then we also had to haul wood for a week, we had one stove to cook on and one to heat our rooms. Sunday we had to haul in the old wooden wash tub, take a bath and shampoo our hair, then do the ironing and press our skirts. We didn't have the clothes that children do today. I remember I had a yellow blouse and brown skirt and a white blouse, and a wine colored skirt. We wore high laced pointed toe shoes. The top was cloth and the bottoms were leather. And that was my wardrobe the first year I went to high school. So you can see we had to go through quite a lot to go to high school in my time; quite a lot different than what my grandchildren have to do. . . .

When our mother and father had to go away on business or to town for groceries or grain, my sister and I always stayed with our grandfather. He was a delightful grandfather, indeed, to stay with. He would amuse us royally; he taught us our alphabet frontwards and backwards; he taught us time by drawing a clock face on a cedar shingle until we could tell all the different times; he taught us to count in French, although he was not French—he had picked it up someplace where he worked. He would tell us tales about the ships he helped build at Bath when he was a young man and about the deer that would come from the woods and eat with his sheep when he first moved from Bath onto the farm, where I was later born. He also would tell my sister and me about his family that lived in Mercer and about his mother's death when he was young and how mean his step-mother was to his brothers and sisters. Some of his brothers ran away from home and the others married and settled in other towns and cities. One brother that kept in contact with my grandfather decided to go West during the Gold Rush. We would hear from him every so often and he would tell us about the great wild West. Finally he wrote that he had gone in partnership with another miner in Cripple Creek, Colorado and that he had struck a very large vein of gold. He expected to get some machinery to open up this vein. The next thing we heard was via a telegram for Grandfather delivered to our door which said your brother had been murdered and his partner had disappeared. So we never did hear what became of the mine or whether his partner was ever found and tried for murder.

He would tell us girls about the Civil War. He had enlisted in the

22nd Regiment of Maine Volunteers Co. He fought in several of the big battles and was very lucky he escaped unhurt. He told us at night it was impossible to lie down on the battle grounds without getting into both human and horse blood.

He belonged to the Grand Army of the Republic and every Memorial Day he would march to the cemeteries with his comrades to put the flags on the graves of the fallen ones who weren't as lucky as he was. One of his neighbors was a war prisoner and was used rather rough as when he got home after being away for more than two years he had to crawl on his hands and knees to get up to his home. After some good food and care he lived for more than fifty years in fairly good health.

Grandfather always smoked Lady Grey Cigars which he bought by the hundred. He would smoke half of one one evening, so after supper he would take down the half left from the night before, stick a toothpick through it then smoke it.

He also was a man that never drank although he would send to Boston and get four quart bottles of whiskey at a time and keep it for special occasions. One special occasion was when one or more of his war comrades would call to spend the afternoon with him; he would get his little whiskey glasses out and serve his friends a little nip while they reminisced about the narrow escapes they had had and how thankful they were that they didn't get wounded. He also used the whiskey for sickness in the family.

In other words he was a wonderful Grandfather, a great carpenter, builder and farmer. He lived to be ninety-four years old and was always very much loved by his three grand-daughters and we also were very thankful to have been born on grandfather's farm. . . .

The first automobile I remember was a Stanley Steamer; it was designed and made in 1897 by twin brothers with the names of Francis E. and Freelan O. Stanley who were born in 1849 in Kingfield, Maine.

The Stanley brothers moved to Newton, Mass. where they made a fortune with their Maine designed vehicle.

The driving horses were very frightened by the sight and sound of the first horseless carriage. As time went on and they became more numerous, the horses became used to them and now it is hard to find one that pays the least attention to it.

The steamer was very small and had wheels that looked almost like bicycle wheels and instead of a steering wheel it had a stick to steer it with; it would travel about 25 miles an hour which would be rather slow today with all the high powered cars but that was fast enough on the roads they had then. I can vouch for that. It was something like riding a bucking bronco. . . .

Late in the fall, after all the crops had been gathered and taken care of, the men folks and neighbors would begin to talk about a big husking bee. The ears had been plucked from the stalk and hauled into the barn to dry; it was stored on barn floors. My sister and me thought these husking bees were planned well ahead of time (in the spring) because there must have been a large number of red ears of corn planted. It seemed that in every ten ears of yellow corn that were husked there would be a nice red one which meant a kiss from the boy that found it.

The women folk had been very busy for several weeks planning and getting the material ready to feed such a large crowd. Sometimes there would be thirty to forty men, women and children from all over the neighborhood. Sometimes we would have a wonderful fresh oyster stew, made in the big copper bottomed boiler that we heated water in to wash with. In the boiler my mother would fill it ⅔ full of milk, add a quart of cream, 1 lb. of nice dairy butter and one gallon of fresh oysters that had been cooked in their juice until they began to curl, salt and pepper to taste. We always served those large thick square soda crackers that Dad bought by the barrel, homemade cucumber pickles—the tiny ones, homemade pumpkin pie and also homemade doughnuts and a new cider. Then after the corn had been all husked and the supper was over one of the men would bring out his fiddle and we would have an old-fashioned dance.

We would dance the Lady of the Lake, Two step, and the waltz until about midnight when the mothers would bundle the sleeping children in the wagons and sometimes several people would put a lot of hay in the hayrack. Everybody seemed to enjoy the evening and talked about having another one next year and for that husking supper we probably would serve baked beans, brown bread, yeast rolls, cabbage salad, a dozen kinds of homemade pickels, baked Indian pudding with homemade ice cream on it and coffee. Then again we sometimes would have a Harvest supper with all the fall vegetables cooked with a home cured, smoked ham, hot mustard sauce, homemade apple pie, with homemade cheese that had been stored for six months in the oat bin to cure to just the right taste, and coffee. . . .

As they say all good things have to come to an end so I will try to finish this up by saying I hope my children, grandchildren, friends and neighbors will decide that my childhood on Grandfather's farm was anything but dull, and that we were never poor, we just didn't have any money.

From: Hazel V. Hall, *No, we weren't poor, we just didn't have any money.* New York: Carlton Press, 1970. Reprinted by permission of Laura Dunham.

Summer rusticators arrived at Squirrel Island by ferry. From nearby Damariscove Island, Alberta Poole Rowe's father provided them with fresh milk and farm produce. *Courtesy of the Maine State Museum.*

Alberta Poole Rowe
1910–?

Alberta Poole Rowe was an island child; her family moved to Damariscove Island when she was only one month old, and she spent the next twelve years there. Like most island children, she was a free spirit. These youngsters, whether the children of lighthouse keepers or island farmers or caretakers, usually had the run of the island on which they lived. It was their playground. They roamed unfettered over a kind of wild wonderland, very much aware of the natural world around them. They were a different breed from their land-bound counterparts. Alberta Poole was an especially independent child. A barefoot tomboy, she took full measure of the rocks and beaches and fields and farm animals and family members around her. She didn't miss a trick and was delighted with it all.

Damariscove Island, to which Alberta's father and his brother moved their families in 1910, lies in the waters off Boothbay Harbor, and because of its location and its deep harbor, it has been a part of the recorded history of Maine since the seventeenth century. Its name is said to derive from one Humphrey Damerill, a seaman from the Georges Colony who established a trading place on the island. "Damerill's Cove" became Damariscove. In 1622 Ferdinando Gorges hired thirteen fishermen to live on Damariscove Island and fish those waters year-round, and fifty years later fifteen men from Damariscove Island were among the signers of a petition requesting a greater show of concern and support from the Massachusetts general court. In response the County of Devon, encompassing Damariscove and the nearby islands, was formed, with Pemaquid as its county seat, but Damariscove Island was not to be a peaceful nor a permanent settlement for years to come.

Indians, of course, had been using the island as a fishing camp for years *prior to the arrival of the English and continued to be an influence on the life of the island. As relationships between the Indians and the white men deteriorated—French and Dutch as well as English were attempting to colonize the coast of Maine—tales of skirmishes with the Indians abounded. In 1676 some three hundred residents of Arrowsic, Woolwich, and several neighboring towns sought refuge on Damariscove Island when Indians burned their homes on the mainland.*

It wasn't until after the War of 1812 that Damariscove Island became a peaceful year-round farming and fishing community. The island Alberta Poole Rowe later knew was taking shape. The forests were cut; sheep were brought out to the island. Houses were built, and a schoolteacher was hired. A small granite-quarrying operation was developed. The United States Coast Guard built a rescue station at the entrance to the harbor in 1897. Alberta Poole Rowe can tell you the rest.

Today there are no houses inhabited on Damariscove Island. Most of the island is owned by The Nature Conservancy. The harbor, despite its ominous ledges, "the Motions," is still a haven for fishermen, yachtsmen, and picnickers. Alberta Poole Rowe now lives in Boothbay Harbor. The following represents a portion of her memories of her very special childhood.

An Island Childhood

It is necessary to stress the fact that this story is a child's view of Damariscove Island. This twelve-year period, from 1910 to 1922, marks the first twelve years of my life. Papa's perception of the island was not as fond as mine, as he pointed out in his eighties, when he did not share my urge to once again see Damariscove. . . .

Papa wanted to settle outside of Pemaquid. He married and enticed his quiet brother Chester to have a place of their own on an island. He knew that it could be done. So they decided at twenty-one and twenty-two to buy this island. He went to Bristol to find out more information. He got Damariscove for next to nothing from a person named Chamberlain, I think.

So Papa led the expedition out to Damariscove. I had been born on January 19, 1910 at Pemaquid Falls. We ventured off in a small lobsterboat around the first of February, 1910. Mother held the baby (me) surrounded by two other small sisters, as they made their way from the beach at Pemaquid. There were no wharves at Pemaquid then, and so Papa actually just pulled his boat up on the banking. As we got into the broad ocean there was a blinding snowstorm—and the boat had no compass as most do today. They found themselves right abreast of the Cuckolds Light. In spite of the weather, Papa made his way from the Cuckolds in that blinding snowstorm, past the Motions somehow, and into the fjord-like harbor of Damariscove. They tied up to the float and proceeded to wind their way up this grassy treeless slope up to the farmhouse. . . .

Damariscove is a rocky island, just rock, mostly granite. There are no white, sandy beaches down there. There are two or three little beaches of tough rock. There are no bricks of any kind, not even the chimneys.

Damariscove looks like one island, but it's really two, although no boats can get through. But, with a little of man's ingenuity in between, it became one! The big, wooden bridge connected the north end and the south end. It was put together with heavy bolts and nails. The bridge was about ten feet wide and eighteen feet long, with very sturdy railings on each side. Just before the bridge was massive boulders and quite a few rocks on the southern end of the bridge. These rocks were loose and dangerous to slip on between the treacherous rocks. We drove sheep through the sharp rocks. If a sheep's leg broke, it would never mend, and you'd have to kill it. Luckily, nothing happened.

I was hardly ever up at the north end, except to drive those sheep down. There was a beach up there at the very end of Wood End. This beach was used by boats in stormy weather when they couldn't make it around the Motions.

On the east side the height of the land was much higher. I never went to the east side, except when I was picking mushrooms. Everything was the west side for us, not east.

There was a wreck at the head of the harbor. It was probably a three-masted schooner, but only the rotten hull was left, sticking out of the harbor. There was another wreck below the station, on the Inner Motions. That was a dangerous spot—in rough weather the fishermen didn't go inside the Motions. They moored their boats in the harbor near the Stone Wharf, which had a ramp down to the float and pilings. . . . There weren't any hotels and motels—only the Farmhouse. Our part we called the "ell." Mama had only three rooms: the kitchen, dining room, and bedroom, as well as the attic. The attic was over the kitchen for the purpose of old clothes and so forth. That's where Father found the spinning wheel. We didn't use that up in the island; Papa later sold it or gave it away to a summer person.

We ate in the kitchen with all those people. The dining room, actually the parlor, was not used for dinners. Also in that ell was one bedroom. Mama and Papa were in the bed, and Josephine and I were in the crib. Susie must have had a bed in the other side, Uncle Chester's part.

We lived in the ell, three rooms. The other six to eight rooms were lived in by Uncle Chester and Aunt Alice and their six children. Downstairs was at least three bedrooms for the teacher and hired men. Later, we moved into Uncle Chester's part, and I had a bedroom all to myself. In it was a great, massive spool bedstead, bureau, a little rocking chair, a wickerback chair, and one straight-back chair. There was also a washstand with a beautiful porcelain washbowl and pitcher to match, with a washcloth and towel. Finally Uncle Chester's part had a cellar, like a feudal cellar, all dripping on the mud floor. . . .

The island was interesting, but the people were more interesting. If a person or family wishes to live out on that island, they need to be of a certain breed. You take the knocks and then forget it. If you live where you have to fight the elements, you have to be strong. On Damariscove were people from Bristol, Bailey's Island, Pemaquid, and Nova Scotia. So it was a mixture of people with different ideas. But we had a few down there of "the blind and the halt." There seemed to be a big distinction down there between the larger percentage of the population who were bright and intelligent and smart. You get the blind and the halt no matter where you are. These were the few who had to be dragged through life; they were the leaners rather than the lifters. They couldn't lift their own weight. . . .

I went with Papa on his boat when he towed his scow loaded with cows over to the pastures of Heron Island. When Papa and a hired man took a scowload of ten or twelve cows to Outer Heron Island, they turned left out of Damariscove Harbor and went around the southern end and past the east side of the island. Outer Heron looked funny as an isolated island. They had no gangplank to get those cows up into the rugged island. So they'd go into the sheltered cove, as near as they could to the rocks, and then push the cows overboard. All the cows would manage to climb up onto the island; none of those cows ever got drowned. This extra fodder and grass of Heron supplemented our limited supply on Damariscove. These cows were not milk cows, and so they were fattened up on Outer Heron for the summer, out of the way and where there was plenty of grass. In the fall the cows would be brought back to Damariscove to be slaughtered.

Father bought Fisherman's Island from Reverend Wilson when I was ten. He used to take scowloads of fifteen to twenty cattle over to Fisherman's. This entailed lots of hard work, but the added pasturage was worth the effort. . . .

Both Papa and Uncle Chester had bought a bull which had a ring in its nose. That bull didn't like the feeling of that ring. They attached a long wooden handle to its nose for taking him around with. The hired men were always leading this awesome bull in and out of the New Barn by that ring. But I didn't get very near it. One night lightning struck the New Barn, catching the hay on fire. Papa yelled, "Oh, Ella, the barn's on fire!" Papa and the rest of us dashed out to the barn and saw the $1000 bull lying on the barn floor with its fur singed by the lightning. That bull was deader than a doornail. Not one cow had been killed, only the prize bull. This loss was an awful adversity for Papa, his investment wasted, but as usual nothing was said. People out there rarely talked about their trials. But to me, a little kid, it was a traumatic experience. I had been scared to death of this powerful living creature just the day before. We had thought that bull was all-powerful. The next day we thought he was nothing. . . .

Cowflaps, or cow manure, was commonplace on Damariscove. There were many big, round puddles of it. Those cowflaps were very good, they fertilized the ground and went right back to nature.

Cowflaps, along with hen and sheep manure, was the best fertilizer. We didn't need any modern fertilizer. It was a cycle. . . .

The Milk Room had to be kept spotless. There was no running water, and they had to boil the water. That was Mama's job to take that separator and all those pails, not just washing them, but boiling them too. The milk could have been dangerous if they hadn't kept them sanitary. She'd be scrubbing and scrubbing and scrubbing. None of those Squirrel Island people got sick from drinking Papa's milk. He always said, "If you give them plenty of milk, they'll be all right."

We had no shortage of milk. Milk was a staple. Papa would often say, "If you have enough milk, you'll grow up." We didn't have an icebox in the house, and so we never kept any surplus of milk. We used ice all year long in the Milk Room for keeping the milk and cream from spoiling. We got just enough milk from the Milk Room to last us until the next day. There were so many kids, and everybody had all the milk we wanted.

Papa supplied Squirrel Island with milk as his first job on Damariscove. In addition, he did a little fishing and lobstering. He'd do anything to make a dollar. Papa supplied Squirrel from 1910 to 1918 with milk and other products.

In 1915 I was to go with Papa in his boat to Squirrel. Nobody else was allowed to go. Mama made two long braids in my curly dark brown hair and attached a handsome ribbon. She dressed me in a little yellow straw hat, a long white dress, funny stockings pulled over my knees with a garter, black patent leather pumps, and also an inexpensive blue coat. I didn't go too often with Father, but, as always, he was up at four. With the help of a hired man, he would put the ten or twelve five-gallon cans into Papa's Bailey Island boat. This was a very rugged boat with a broad stern, a spray hood, and a good engine. Papa's spray hood was made of canvas and tacked down on the sides of the boat near the bow. It acted like a tent and kept off the seas. I hated the smell of the engine exhaust on Papa's boat. So I'd get under the spray hood.

Papa landed on the float on the other side of Squirrel Island. It was someone's private float below the rich Davenports' cottage near the south end. He'd take one five-gallon can in each hand and head up the island along the boardwalks. He sold his milk to most of the people on the south end. I can remember Papa with those big milk cans approaching each of the cottages. At one house, an elderly woman came toddling out with a dish. Papa had a quart dipper, and so he would pour out as much as she wanted for cooking and drinking. He'd collect his money. Lord knows how much, probably ten cents a quart. In those days you could get a quart of milk for little or nothing. Funny that he was giving milk and receiving a little pittance for the milk that took so much work to produce. He didn't weigh over 150 pounds then, and his hard work is how he got the drop stomach that he carried all of his life. He needed an expensive bandage on his stomach for the rest of his life.

Squirrel Island was real wooded, but it had the same houses that still stand today. There was a beautiful hotel, the Squirrel Island Inn, that has since burned down.

I knew that Papa was a real busy man, but I was more interested in the store with five cent candy that I had passed earlier that morning. I weaseled five cents out of Papa. I'd only seen that store once, but it was especially attractive because we had no store on Damariscove at that time. So I started up the long gangplank from the float. Then I walked up that wooden boardwalk. Damariscove had no wooden boardwalks but Squirrel Island did. They were nice and dry, and I loved to walk on the boardwalks with those black shoes. It seemed like a long way to the store, but I didn't care because there was a rainbow at the other end! I'd run into several old women and some would talk. But I wasn't too polite, I had an errand to do with my nickel, and so I shied around and headed for the store. I knew I wasn't supposed to dawdle and make Father wait. So I hurried to the store, finding it with no difficulty, and ate my candy. But when I finally got back to the float, Papa and the boat were no longer there! I was in a world of my own. I had always had my father. I was alone on the wharf and didn't know anybody. But I really didn't get very upset. There was a man standing nearby, and I told him, "Well, my father was here and now he's gone." This friendly summer person said, "Gone, where's he gone?" I replied, "Well, he's Mr. Poole and he's gone to the Harbor." He helped me by taking me in his private speedboat. We headed in to Boothbay Harbor, and Papa was on the fish wharf right where Fisherman's Wharf is now. I don't remember what he said; he wasn't too surprised. But he wasn't too surprised at anything I did!

That night there was a fog bank that you could cut with your knife. People warned Ike Poole not to return to Damariscove. But we started back at four in the afternoon in the fog mow. We went around Squirrel Island and then approached the Motions in the fog mow at low tide. We went inside the Motions instead of the usual arrival outside. But when we got inside the Motions the engine went out! We could see the ledge and rocks and much seaweed. That day was calm. I was underneath the spray hood eating bananas while I watched Papa desperately pushing us off the Motions by means of a gaff. I didn't get excited as long as Papa was there. He shoved us off the Big Motion, and then Father started up the engine, easing her through the water around the Lifesaving Station and finally into the harbor. Everybody on Damariscove had gathered at the wharf, thinking that we were shipwrecked. My Grandfather Albert Sproul, who I'm named after, was down there on the wharf, and he scolded Father. "I thought you were drowned. You should never have left Boothbay Harbor with that little girl through this mess."

Every morning—rain, snow, or sleet—Papa never missed a day and never was sick. Papa would be in Squirrel at five or six in the morning, and after he had his business over by around noon, he'd get something to eat at Boothbay Harbor. Dinner we called it. So he'd shop for the Squirrel Island people in Boothbay. He was the only person to go off the island, picking up barrels of flour and some boots. He'd shop where Fisherman's Wharf parking lot now is: that is, at McKown's grocery market, Merrill and Fred Perkins grocery store, and Robert Boyd's fish market.

It was a dangerous business because the water could really get rough between Squirrel and Damariscove. He did freeze his nose and ears once in one of those awful cold gales that come down through there. He never wore hats in that cold weather. In the afternoon on the Flat Ledge my sister and I would watch his return from Squirrel Island. Sometimes the waves were so high that we couldn't see his boat in between the waves. We often sang, "Papa's coming, tra la la!" Then we'd run like the devil to the wharf and watch him round the station. We knew it was dangerous business—that's all the father we had. What faith we had in our father—we worshipped him! . . .

When the Poole brothers and the hired men plowed up the gardens, they unearthed some blue English dishes, called "Dresden china," which were quite thick. We also used to find old money, such as an old English penny. There were also white clay pipes, teeth, and arrowheads.

Potatoes were the real staple down there in that rocky soil. The ground was rocky, and some vegetables couldn't be grown. There was no corn, but we could grow potatoes in those vegetable gardens. The potato garden had eight long rows of potatoes. The cultivator was pulled by the horse between the rows.

One year the potatoes were loaded with potato bugs, and Papa told us kids to take these bottles, shaped like our coke bottles. He tempted me by saying "I'll give you, Alberta, one penny for each potato bug." So I went down my entire row of potatoes and then gave them to Papa. I asked for my money, but he told me, "You eat three meals a day, don't you?" No more was said of my great transaction with the bugs and potatoes. This shows that we were a poor family, all of whom should be content with bare survival; that is, with the privilege of staying healthy and eating three good meals a day and a place to sleep.

We also raised peas in our vegetable gardens. One year the peas blossomed so beautifully. I didn't know that the pea blossoms turned into a pea, at the age of six or seven. So I went out and picked every blasted blossom. I went into the Farmhouse as Betsey be damned and said, "I have flowers for you, Mama." All Papa could do was laugh and say, "There won't be any peas this summer, Ella!"

Most of the men on Damariscove were lobstermen and handliners. They weren't farmers because the rocky soil was not productive. Father and Uncle Chester were the only ones who had gardens and a dairy farm. . . .

The Grunter was the fog horn way out for fog mows. The Cuckolds fog horn flashed in my room every night. It also had an awful queer noise. Wasn't that some disturbing for a lonely girl. . . . Once in a while boats would pull in during storms for refuge. Damariscove's harbor was very protective. I certainly had a child's view of the harbor after a storm. The harbor seemed full of soap suds, actually sea foam resulting from the storms. The harbor was all white foam. . . .

There was a great massive mackerel trap on the west side of the island near the Flat Ledge where we had our picnics. The mackerel trap was daily pulled before dusk at around four o'clock and even later in the summer months. Mr. York,* Mr. Johnson, and Mr. Black would go out before supper. Occasionally I would go along with one or two of Uncle Chester's kids. Usually Merton York and Clayton and Florence Johnson would also come along, and the gang of us would go up in the bow of the boat. We would ride out around or through the Motions, depending on the weather. The trap consisted of corks holding the net up. Three or four men with York and Johnson would pull the net up by their hands with white mittens. It was cold work as they pulled it up onto the boat and dumped the fish on the bottom of the boat until they got the net emptied. We'd watch those gorgeous, great big, two foot long red salmon, the mackerel, great big ugly monkfish with big mouths and horns, and little fish called butterfish which tasted elegant. There were no squid and few groundfish because they were in deeper water. There might be a small cod or small pollock. No lobsters could crawl into that thing. Wasn't that fun to watch those fish from aboard the boat!. . .

Jellyfish were especially numerous after a storm. Damariscove Harbor would be filled the whole length with the poisonous reddish-pink jellyfish. They were funny things, but not as fun to play with as the crabs. They were pretty things, great big things and gorgeous, with curly edges. Because they were poisonous, I didn't touch them. They were just a nuisance.

Monkfish had a great big mouth and were funny looking. I didn't like them any more than the jellyfish. Like the jellyfish they also came in with the storms. They had horns all over them—scared you to death to look at them! They weren't any good for anything either.

I also recall the squid that squirted that black ink. We never ate squid.

---

* Charlie York, whose own reminiscences begin on page 161.

When I was with my father I used to see these big, massive whales come up and spout. Those whales looked like a great big fish spouting. Nobody went after whales. In addition, once in a while there would be a dead whale that would wash up on the flat ledge. They were terrible looking to us. They had either been sick or shot. They just rotted and decomposed because we had no use for the meat and other parts of the whale.

The seals were on the smaller, shallower islands. They'd sun themselves and then go overboard again. . . .

We were the hotel. If you went down to Damariscove and had no place to sleep, you could go to the Farmhouse with an extra room or two. It was not just a hotel because of the extra rooms, but because there were two good cooks—Mama and Aunt Alice. Mama boarded the schoolteacher and the hired men (they slept in Uncle Chester's part). They didn't pay Mama and Papa anything for room and board. It wasn't a money thing. The teacher may have gotten a little pittance of fifteen to eighteen dollars a week, and the hired men must have been on the same basis too, with free room and board.

We were quite conscious of what you should eat and what you shouldn't, especially with Father's delicate stomach. And we never had any shortage of food. About all Mama did was wash and cook. Mama's old flour board really went fast and furious! We never skipped a meal: we had breakfast at seven (four o'clock for Papa), dinner at noon, and supper at five, the same time every day. Berdine Webster years later told me a yarn: "I went down there to Damariscove when I was eighteen years old from Boothbay Harbor to teach this school with sixteen to eighteen children in it. I was like a 'picked crow.' Your father's and Uncle Chester's milk and cream saved my life. It was not just other good food, but I began to put some flesh on me because I had to drink so much milk and cream." She began to feel better and look better. . . .

Uncle Chester had a store in the big hallway between his part and Papa's part of the Farmhouse. It was their own store to sell to the other people on Damariscove, rather than making extra trips to Boothbay. This store had shelves of flour, sugar, biscuits, spices, fruit, and nuts.

There were also barrels of flour and sugar. The store lasted for an interval of two or three years from 1915 to 1917.

Papa got all their groceries and probably all the mail for Damariscove and possibly Squirrel. Papa would get barrels of flour and sugar, and then he used the barrels for storing the grain. We always had plenty of salt in big bags from McKown's or Perkins' market on Boothbay Harbor's waterfront. We used this salt for table salt, for preserving our meat and fish, and for the sheep—bags of salt were kept in the Yellow Building for the sheep—I often got some salt for my sheep and she loved it. It was just like sugar for children. Papa would sometimes put a big bag of those elegant candy kisses in five pound brown bags. We weren't allowed to go and grab anything in the store. If we asked, we might get it. There were no soft drinks in that store, just milk or water. My father would send me on an errand to Uncle Chester's part for tobacco or cigars. He'd tell me to repeat it and then he'd say, "Go!" I always ran both ways with no talking to anybody else, I'd just do it. There was no time for relaxing and dawdling in that house. . . .

I took the part of the boy, I was the tomboy. They put pants on me most of my life, knickers when I was ten or twelve. On Damariscove we kids went barefooted. It was not a lack of shoes and stockings, but convenience. We spent days wading through the water. But our parents made us wear shoes and stockings to Squirrel and Boothbay Harbor. They were proud people and dressers, we had to look just right. Put your hat on!

Papa was strict regarding the postures of both boats and people: "Look how she walks, her feet are going all ways. Look at how she walks, one foot's going out the wrong way. She isn't lined up right." You were supposed to walk straight. If you wore pants, they better not be dragging in the mud. Papa, Uncle Chester, and the hired men all wore blue overalls. Papa was handsome with his blue eyes, light blue overalls, and black hair. He was skinny and handsome. He only dressed up in his suit for funerals.

All the fishermen always wore boots up to their knees. When I was five or six, I wanted those boots because they seemed to symbolize maturity for a barefoot little girl. One day Papa pulled into the harbor with his boat and tossed me a pair of little black boots up to my knees. I was thrilled—it seems that everything I really wanted, I got. He was a lovely father, so poor then, but so good.

When I was four, Mama gave me a wide brimmed sunbonnet and a dress to match, probably from the Bellas and Hess catalogue. She put that on me in the morning. Nobody paid any attention to me, and I thought I was beautiful. So I decided to show the crabs and sea gulls in the cove at the head of the harbor. I walked right into the water with the jellyfish. I kept walking, and the water was coming up. Pretty soon it was under my arms, and then the salt water lifted me up and my toes went up off the sea bed. Before I was drowned, I made it back to shore. No one else was there, just me, a solitary little girl.

Out of our catalogue—that was our store—Mother bought me a pair of blue bloomers for $2.98. It had lots of cloth along with a sailor's blouse and a blue tie to go with it. I dressed up in this novel outfit when I was eight, and I thought that I was Katherine Hepburn in my bliss. So I went down to the Coast Guard Station in my new outfit, where I hoped that these eighteen-year-old young men would finally note my existence as a lady. But nobody paid any attention to me, and so my pride was dashed. I proceeded to go up to the roof and slide down it in my dismay, taking the whole seat out of those bloomers and thus ruining it. They had been worth $2.98, big money to us, especially at that time. Mother was very strict, but she never spanked us or hit us. . . .

We kids had no sleds; rather, we slid on our bottoms. There was a bit of an incline through the field from the Farmhouse down towards the shore. It was grassy in the summer and icy in the winter. We slid on what the Lord gave us to slide on. Sometimes we'd take an old barrel stave or cardboard from a surplus of heavy cardboard boxes in Uncle Chester's store. But usually we couldn't find anything. But we'd still go sliding for a while.

In the summer our playmates were the crabs and sea urchins and sea gulls and medricks and plovers and curlews. All the birds were our friends. We were wild creatures.

Mama would say to me, "Go play!" The little Johnson girl, Florence, Fern, and I would go over to the west side on the rocky cliffs. They looked like a great big mountain to a little girl. We'd go over these and make playhouses out of the mud and shells all through those big cliffs, which looked like a shelf.

One great big tall rock was shaped just like a chair. I'd sit down in that chair, hanging my legs down and looking down at the ocean and rocks below. We'd see the boats go through from up there. We watched the fishermen haul their lobster traps from their small lobster boats. We didn't seem to care much about time. We played an awful long time when nobody watched us. We could tell time by the sun or if it was high or low tide or by our stomachs growling. I had many good times on those cliffs. We were kind of like wild creatures, and we played anywhere on our part of the island.

Down by the beaches was some soft red rock. We used it almost as a crayon. It was fun to write with it on the rocks.

One day on the west side a lot of us kids were on the beach. Suddenly I looked and saw a man on that beach rolled up in a blanket! I shouted to the others, "We've got to get Uncle Chester!" We all ran on our sheep's legs back to the Farmhouse. Uncle Chester went back with us. We eight or ten kids didn't dare to go back down on the beach. We just stood and watched him from up on the rocks. But Uncle Chester came back laughing. It was only a log with a quilt that happened to be wrapped around it while thrashing around in the ocean. But it had looked just exactly like a body. Uncle Chester was awful good with us kids.

We kids were near the shore when we saw a perfectly round rock, and we were sure that we had found Captain Kidd's treasure. So we went back to tell Aunt Adelaide. She got a crowbar and we set out. Whether the tide was up or we had gotten too tired leaping over the rocks, we couldn't find it. It was right near where I picked those mushrooms, not the middle of the island but in the southern part of it. What I'm saying is not foolish and was not a hallucination or a child's fascination. . . .

On the southern part of Damariscove were formations like caves. If the tide went down, I could go barefooted and pick up the beautiful shells, not periwinkles or sand dollars. They were pretty colors and different kinds. I'd collect them and take them home just to play with. We'd play store a lot. We'd put a price on each shell with a piece of paper. We used my shells and some buttons as coins.

Besides playing house or making mudcakes, we'd go down in the seaweed and find the puddles where the water had been at high tide. We'd find sea urchins; the sea gulls would take the shells and eat the inside and leave the shell. So usually the shells we found were empty. We thought these shells were beautiful. The little crabs were always in the puddles along with the sea urchins, which were all over the place, even on high and low land. But the live ones were found quite often in the water.

We were often picking up crabs at the shore under the rocks and hoping that we wouldn't slide overboard. It was a pastime, we weren't after food. We didn't eat them, we didn't kill them; we just picked them up and put them in cans. We played with the crabs and counted them. Took them up to the house and Mama wouldn't want them. But they were our little friends. They were of different sizes, little teeny up to a baby's fist. We'd never hear tell of eating a crab. We liked seeing them crawl. They'd open their claws and nip us if they had a chance. They were alive and animated, like us. We'd have liked to play with the sea gulls, but we couldn't reach them. But we could touch those crabs and caress them.

We played on those wicked rocks. None of us could swim then, even when I was twelve. If we'd gone in, we would have drowned. We had no conception of fear of those rocks—I leaped just like a goat over the rocks. Damariscove had no sandy beaches, they were more like muddy beaches. When we went swimming, we went off the rocks. I never liked to swim too much. I had a fear of the water because when I was seven or eight I'd get into the deep water where I'd go down under the surface. When I came back up, Papa would push me under and I'd go back down with the bubbles going up. That scared me and so I still had that fear years later. . . .

Wasn't it peaceful on Damariscove! There was no kind of a car. Just a reaping or plowing machine way off in the field once in a while.

I only heard the chugging of a motorboat once in while as they'd go out to fish or come back. Music in the ell was only the children howling and the Cuckolds fog horn. You might hear sheep bleating, a cow moo, and the sea gulls squawking. The medricks might be making a funny noise. You might hear the wild birds go over. You wouldn't be hearing any human voices; they were milking the cows or doing other work. After the storms, the ocean hitting the rocks would be like a constant roar. . . .

The families out on Damariscove each had a place to live, clothes to wear, food to eat, and candy, whist, and dances for recreation. We had no enemies. There were no fights, everybody got along. If you needed help, all you had to do was ask for it. This was in part because there was no drinking. We enjoyed our food and drinking milk. There were no thieves on the island. No one had to worry that anyone was going to take anything. What a wonderful thing it was to live in peace down there with no fear of theft.

So Uncle Chester went back to Pemaquid after ten years on Damariscove. My father stayed ten more years alone. When he finally went off for good, he sold the island to Fred Higgins. Papa knew fish and he knew meat, and so he got into the fish market in Boothbay Harbor, when he and Fred Granger went into partnership by buying Albert McKown's meat market.

Those first twelve years on Damariscove made me strong and was the foundation of my life to hold me through the trials of my future. Not because it was difficult but because it was peaceful, with no fighting. We were free as the birds. That life makes you rugged of body and makes you help other people. . . . I was brought up on the water, and I was much happier there than on the land. I'm not afraid of it, I loved it. We were sea peoples, not landlubbers. I was raised with the sea gulls. How long do you think you can lock the sea gulls on the land? Not long! I still prefer an island to the mainland because this doesn't challenge me here. It's much more interesting down there to make your own way, and it's much more of a challenge to life.

From: Carl R. Griffin III and Alaric Faulkner, and including the reminiscences of Alberta Poole Rowe, *Coming of Age on Damariscove Island, Maine*. Orono, Maine: The Northeast Folklore Society, 1981. Reprinted courtesy of the Northeast Folklore Society.

John Gould
1908–

John Gould is the present dean of Maine humorists. His college, Bowdoin, celebrated his deanship by awarding him an honorary doctor of letters degree in 1968. The state university followed in 1976. Maine takes its humorists seriously. It has been one of the state's distinctions to provide the American people with a series of nationally recognized wags, usually in the person of a mild-mannered countryman who asks the right question at the right moment to deflate a pompous authority, or displays how one of our esteemed national institutions looks when reduced to the scale of the village green. In the 1830s Seba Smith invented a naive down-easter, Jack Downing of Downingville, to make fun of Maine's bumbling politicians and the overzealous office seekers in Andrew Jackson's Washington. Next came Artemus Ward—Charles Farrar Browne of Waterford, Lincoln's favorite, who, in interviewing Brigham Young and learning that he had eighty wives, asked Young in all innocence, "How do you like it as far as you hev got?"

John Gould, in twenty-two books written between the 1940s and 1980s and still coming, has not written on many national matters. He calls himself an amateur "researchist" of Maine's folklore, reporting from the inside. The subject, he says, affords endless material. "It's like dipping the ocean dry with a spoon. . . . The State of Maine . . . is busy twenty-four hours a day, the clock round, year in and year out, creating, refining, embellishing folklore. I, or any researchist, will never catch up." Gould's books contain his autobiography. He was raised in Freeport, and after his graduation from Bowdoin, took jobs in local newspapers, bought the Gould family farm near Lisbon Falls—said to be the oldest farm in Maine continuously in the same family—and lived there until he moved to

Friendship in 1973. His first columns, written over twenty-five years for the Christian Science Monitor, *tell the story of how he and his wife rebuilt the old farmhouse, lived off the farm and his journalism, and raised their children. When he became editor and co-owner of the* Lisbon Enterprise *in 1945, he transformed a sleepy four-page weekly with 286 subscribers into a paper with a subscription list of two thousand spread far and wide beyond Lisbon Falls. He had to buy a new press, which, he reported, was delivered by the strongest vehicle in the village, a manure spreader. John Gould never moves far from the Maine scene, but, as one admirer told him, "Your items are so local they're universal."*

The Three Birdies

No birdie with a yellow bill ever hopped upon my windowsill, cocked his shining eye and said, "Ain't you 'shamed, you sleepy-head!" Waking up, for me, in my down-Maine attic room with the faded, forlorn wallpaper roses, was Grampie Nugent, Secretary Potter and Whisperin' Gleason. We had birds, but those three got up before the birds.

Secretary Potter wasn't a secretary to anything. He got the title from John B. Manchester, who had inherited three seafaring fortunes which he invested wisely and consequently was not a man to clean out his own backhouse. Our Down East coastal community had no public sewers then, and a backhouse was an unfunny necessity that required occasional laundering. This wasn't a job people ran around looking for, and any useful citizen who would oblige was much in demand. Potter was available, although his major profession was housekeeping at Harry Dunbar's livery stable. Mr. Manchester had asked Potter to perform and he was now under the end of the barn performing. Mr. Manchester was at a discreet distance, sitting on the top strake of the white-washed barnyard fence, superintending the labor, when Mrs. Manchester stepped out of the house to toss a few table scraps to the

White Wyandottes. "Who's that?" she asked, with a natural interest in the identity of such a contractor, and Mr. Manchester said, "I'm giving a little dictation to my secretary." It stuck, and ever afterwards he was Secretary Potter.

About five-thirty every morning in summer, Secretary Potter would open the big rolling doors on the livery stable and sweep out with a rattan barn broom. The wheels on the doors had never tasted oil, so they set up a protest that cringed the whole village and fetched up against my faded wallpaper roses to bring an end to sleep. Morning, birds or not, had come.

My second alarm clock, had I needed one, was Grampie Nugent. He pushed a wheelbarrow to the village every morning and greeted everybody along the way with his high, squeaky voice—a voice tuned to the squeal of his ungreased wheelbarrow wheel. He never bought so much that he needed a wheelbarrow, but it went where he did. From my room I could hear him when he cleared the Baptist church on Main Street, where he said good morning to Jack Randall. Then he would say good morning to Guy Soule, to Fred Moulton, to Cap'n Jule Soule, to Edgar Conant, to Mrs. Luce—and at last to Whisperin' Gleason.

This took him almost to the village, and Whisperin' Gleason would fall into step beside Grampie Nugent and walk along as far as the livery stable, where he trained some broken-down trotting horses not yet written off. Whisperin' Gleason was called Whisperin' for the same reason we called bald-headed Joe Ramsay Curly, and six-foot-six Lester Glover Shorty. His good morning to Grampie Nugent was a burst of cannonade. Even when he imparted the most secret thing you could hear him all over town. For a hundred yards Grampie Nugent and Whisperin' Gleason would talk along—discussing such things as the prospect of showers, the shortage of good hay, and always the state of Grampie's health. He was having trouble holding his water, and the personal and intimate details of this distress came to me in my bedroom and were interesting. When I heard Whisperin' Gleason greet Secretary Potter I knew they had reached the livery stable, and the day had begun.

One day a year, at planting time, Grampie Nugent would leave his wheelbarrow home and take his garden hoe to town. Beginning at the Universalist church we had a cement sidewalk that ran all the way to the "corner," which is what we called the village. It was the only paving in town, and it offered Grampie a grindstone he didn't have to turn. He would drag the hoe along behind him and the concrete would hone it to a wonderful edge for murdering weeds. There is nothing a birdie on a windowsill could ever sing to equal a hoe dragged through town on a cement sidewalk. On the mornings he did this the racket drowned out his greetings to Jack Randall, Guy Soule, Fred Moulton, Cap'n Jule and Mrs. Luce.

But not Whisperin' Gleason. Nothing drowned him out.

Every morning of my growing up began in that attic bedroom. It had no heat in it, and I was mostly grown before we ran up a wire and had an electric light. I had a stand for my kerosene lamp, but mostly I would undress in the dark. I could see the lights of the village from my window, and millions of stars. The four-pane frame didn't go up or down, but it would lift out entirely and I usually slept with it out, winter and summer. I was taught to believe in fresh air. When the wind hauled southerly and we had a slashing warm rain, or when a bitter no'theast blizzard whipped biting snow, I left the window in. There were hot nights and cold nights and not much in between but mostly it was a wonderful place to sleep. The rain would slant against the roof faster than it would run off sometimes, and it was a lullaby kings couldn't hire. In winter driving snowflakes would seem to be wearing the crisp cedar shingles away, and the rafters would creak in the wind. Here I kept the private souvenirs of my youth, and good comforters for subzero nights. When it was cold I would jump up in the morning and dress fast, pulling on the clothing that had been cooling for me all night, and I would hurry down to the kitchen. I didn't hurry like that when it was summer time.

In summer time, when Secretary Potter opened the doors and made ready for the influx of horse-hiring drummers who would come on the 7:18 train, waking up in my room was joyful. I could tell exactly what time it was by looking to see which faded rose was fairest in the newborn sun. As the year revolved, the roses brightened and dimmed with the angle of the dawn. When I had the measles I counted the roses on my walls, and there were one thousand four hundred and eighty. I had to move the bureau to count behind it, and I was too weak to push it back—so Mother thought I must have been delirious. When the sun got over to the row of roses by the bookcase it was August, and that was the best time of all. The Minister Apples were ready, and those that fell during the night were mine. They were Strawberry St. Lawrence apples, really, but my father observed they were pretty to look at but mealy to take and he called them the Minister Apples. I never thought them mealy. I didn't wear much in August, so it didn't take long to dress and get out to pick up Minister Apples before the hens and birds got to them.

Through the house and the kitchen, through the shed and the barn, and out the back barn door I would run, and the dew on the grass was suddenly cool and beautiful on my bare feet. Dew on bare feet on a bright August morning is the greatest diuretic of all, so I would pause, feet wide apart, and my best shot was about eight feet, freehand. I killed all the grass outside the back barn door, until my father told me to find a new place or we'd be living in a desert.

In wintertime waking up was to the bells. Somebody would tingle a cutter down the main street with the little shaker bells ringle-jingling, or a heavy team would go by with the matched, mellowed, steel melody that muted itself in the frosty air. No two teams had the same bells, and I could tell from my bed if 'twere Merle Prout or Bess Means, or sometimes George Bartol bringing an early load of pressed hay to the team track for the police horses in Boston. He had that contract sewed up, and loaded cars off and on all winter, and his team had a peal of bells that was majestic. I was almost through high school when one morning was massacred by a new and hateful sound— George Bartol had bought a tractor! It snorted its way to the railroad, and he could make bigger loads and go faster. Whisperin' Gleason said, "B' Gawd, Bartol, when everybody has them things what's to haul hay to?"

If the night had snowed, the team bells in the morning would be Milt Dill's. Milt teamed for Edgar Conant, who had the town contract to break roads. In those days he who broke least broke best, because every farmer in town had sleds. Edgar just shoved a timber through the stays of his logging runners, and Milt would drive around. It packed the snow down some, and smoothed it a little. It would still be hip-deep to us short-legged youngsters when we wallowed to school, but we were thankful for Milt. Without him, the going would be tough.

Summertime was warmer, but it was no prettier. I used the backhouse in the barn in winter and didn't dally around. I could look out the back barn windows and see my Minister Apple tree dark against the snow, and beyond it the black spruce woods. No apples now, but under the spruces would be fat rabbits to make hot pies with crunchy crusts, and pa'tridges would be coming from under the new snow to sit on limbs and wait for me. Not on weekdays—after-school time was too short. But on Saturdays I would give things my attention. So when the morning brightened my attic window, summer or winter, a whole world was out there inviting my attention—to do with as I chose. I just had to get up first, and except for measles and mumps and things like that I did. I never missed much.

From: John Gould, *Last One In*. Boston: Little, Brown & Company, 1966. Reprinted by permission of John Gould.

Mary Gabriel
1908–

In 1982 a Passamaquoddy Indian woman, Mary Gabriel, told the story of her childhood to her daughter, Debbie Brooks. The two women were sitting in Mary's house near the Passamaquoddy Indian Reservation in Indian Township close to the Canadian border. Mary had been born in this Princeton area seventy-four years earlier. The interview begins as another sad-happy tale of the poor. Mary's mother worked and was unable to keep her baby daughter, so she gave Mary over to her own parents to raise. Years later, Mary could look back and say, "I had a happy life with my grandparents. They loved me and kept me living." But as Mary continues her description of the poverty of her grandparents and her mother's abandonment of her—she called her grandmother "Mother"—the story takes on another character. It begins to sum up the demoralizing human condition of an underclass of alienated Maine people, the reservation Indians. Behind Mary Gabriel's story lies the 150-year history of Maine's combination of neglect and exploitation of its Indian wards, the Passamaquoddies and the Penobscots. During Mary's lifetime the two tribes had reached their nadir in terms of both how Maine people viewed Indians and how Maine's Indians viewed themselves. In Indian Township in 1964 almost 75 percent of the Passamaquoddies able to work were unemployed, most families lived on welfare checks, and many adults were alcoholic. This oral history can be read as a daughter's protest that such a childhood as her mother's could ever have happened in Maine in the twentieth century. That Mary Gabriel's daughter chose to record her mother's history also suggests that for Debbie Brooks the Maine Indian world had begun to change.

In 1980 a Maine Indian leader made this statement about a new Indian identity and new Indian hopes for the world of their children:

We had been invisible for so long, you see, that the whites simply could not conceive that we had any rights except those they chose to confer on us. Well, we're not invisible any longer. We're in the process of establishing our own civil and criminal laws and our own tribal courts, and once the settlement is signed and sealed, we're going to take possession of our land and build upon its resources so that our children will have a better life. When that happens we will have witnessed something that no one around here thought possible when I was young—the rebirth of an Indian nation in the state of Maine.

The settlement that the leader referred to involved the celebrated Indian land claims case and how the two tribes found justice in the federal courts against Maine's earlier taking of tribal lands in disregard of Indian treaty rights. The whole story is too complex to be reviewed here. Historically it belongs to the 1960s, that decade of civil-rights agitation on behalf of America's minorities across the nation. It began in Maine with a protest action of a few Indians standing before a bulldozer near Princeton, defying the loss of a small piece of tribal land to a motel owner intent on building a few more cabins. After ten years in the courts, where the Indian rights were established and defended by a group of idealistic young non-Indian lawyers, the tribes agreed to a federally funded negotiated settlement. On December 12, 1980, 81.5 million dollars were deposited in the United States Treasury in the accounts of the Passamaquoddies and the Penobscots. The settlement called for twenty-five million of this award to set up a trust fund for members of the tribes; most of the rest was to purchase at fair market value three hundred thousand acres of Maine land, some from the state, some from large private landowners. Mary Gabriel's tribe bought in 1981 a five-thousand-acre blueberry barren near Machias and became the largest commercial grower in Maine. They bought back four thousand of the six thousand acres of Indian Township that had been illegally taken years before by the state. For some years before selling it to a foreign investor, the Passamaquoddies owned and operated the cement manufacturing plant near Thomaston. Mary Gabriel has lived long enough to be part of an economic, civil, and cultural revolution that brought her people into full status as citizens of the United States.

A Passamaquoddy Childhood

I was born right here on what they call Princeton strip—it's not up at the Point on the reservation. I think there is more people here now than at Peter Dana Point. I grew up with my grandmother. Yes, I was born at home—nobody used to go to the hospital. I had all my children at home and never went to the hospital. My mother was living here on the strip and had her own home. I was born in 1908—I'm 74 this year, on November 12th. I lived right here all the time after my grandmother died. I grew up with my grandmother and grandfather—my mother never brought me up at all. I guess my mother took me to my grandparents right way because I heard she worked and didn't have any time for me. I had a happy life with my grandparents. They loved me and kept me living.

After that, my grandfather got a job taking care of a place on Big Lake. Rich people owned it and as far as I can remember, their names were Goddards and they owned it jointly with another lady, not married, by the name of Mrs. Smith. One time she wanted to adopt me—she asked my mother if she could adopt me and my grandmother said no, and besides, they were not Catholic—she wouldn't let me go anywhere where they weren't Christians. My grandmother told my mother "you gave her to me—why should I let her go." After Mrs. Smith went away, she never came back—I guess she died. They never told me this but I gathered that much. The Goddards came back every year and my grandparents—my grandfather took care of that big house. There were about 10 or 15 bedrooms there. It's still there—they call it the Reed place, so evidently the first owner was a man named Reed. I lived there when I was growing up—I was all alone; there was no other children, so my grandfather would get some cats and kittens and he brought me a puppy one time.

I would always wait for him when he went down-town on the ice. It was two miles from there to Peter Dana Point and he used picks [pointed sticks used for propulsion?] on a little sled. He put a box on top of it so he wouldn't have to kneel down because he was old. I would always run out to meet him—maybe half a mile. I would see him coming, so I'd go out to meet him to give me a ride back. One day I ran out to meet him and heard a noise under that little box where he was sitting and he didn't tell me anything—he wanted me to guess. When we got to the house, he opened the box and there was this beautiful black puppy. He was always doing those things.

In the summer time he used to take me with him setting traps and then again in the morning when he went after them to see if he could get some muskrats. He'd bring them home and I'd ask him—I'd beg him when he was skinning them to let me do some of them. He would pick the smallest one, I think it was a female. He said he could not give me a male one. He was afraid of the smelly stuff—where the perfume comes from, the musk, and he wouldn't let me skin the males. I got pretty good at skinning the females. Then, he'd teach me how to spread them—he'd take some sticks, little twigs and round them up and put them inside the fur. The fur would be inside and the skin would be outside and then he would hang them up and dry them. Then he would go and sell them. He was a very smart man.

One time, he wanted to make money so much that one winter he took off alone—he wouldn't take me in the winter because it was too cold—and when he came home he could hardly walk because his clothes were all frozen. He had jumped in when he shot an otter. He shot an otter and the otter went into the ice in the hole. He jumped right in there after him and he got him. He brought him home but he was frozen. My grandmother was swearing at him in Indian. She couldn't talk English. My grandfather was half French—Joe Mell—and his mother was French from Aroostook County. But my grandmother, Julia, Joe Mell's wife, couldn't talk English. His mother was named Louise and she could talk Indian because she married an Indian. She could talk three languages: French, English and Indian. Sometimes she would mix it up. She was a dear lady. I used to stay with my great-grandmother Louise, when I went to school. She lived at Dana Point where the school is.

They used to transport me from the Reed Place to Dana Point either on the ice or in the canoe. That's how I went to school. Sometimes I went every day when my grandfather was not busy. He loved me so much that he wanted me there at school. It was two miles. When the ice was bad, we couldn't go—in the spring. In the summer when it was real windy, we couldn't go. So I didn't go to school as much as the rest of the children did. I stayed with my great-grandmother when the weather was bad, or sometimes she would want me to stay with her because she was alone. But I was hard to handle because I would run away from her and go to play with other kids and she didn't want me to. So she would tell on me and I would have to go home.

My grandfather, Joe Mell, had a hard time when he was growing up. His father died and Louise, his mother, married again and he abused my grandfather. He pounded him until my grandfather had to run outdoors barefooted. He ran from there—it was around the point or around the cove—so he ran from there to Dana Point all the way barefooted, and some people took him in. That was when he was younger, and after a while he met my grandmother and they got married. They had a lot of children, mostly girls and only one boy she used to tell me about named Clement. She talked about him all the time. They all died, one after another, from influenza or whatever they had there. There was no one left but my mother that survived. My grandmother used to call her the devil. She said she couldn't die because she was the devil. She never listened to my grandmother.

I never saw my mother too often. She was always away. One time, even though my grandmother could not talk English, we managed to go to Eastport to visit her where she was working in a hotel. I never called her my mother—I called her Margaret because I don't remember her as my mother. We managed to get to Eastport although she couldn't talk English and I couldn't either at that time because I was very young—I wasn't even in school then. That was where I had my first ice cream at that hotel. I loved it. I ate it and ate it until finally they stopped me.

I also remember the times we used to go to visit friends in Calais. There was some Indian land there—there still is, but there's no Indians living there now. A circus used to come there at a certain time in the summer by train. There was an Indian woman living there and the train would go by not too far from her place. They'd say, let's go see the train come in, and we'd see the animals go by. There would be a lot of them watching for the train to come by to see the animals, because a lot of people weren't able to go to see the circus—some were too poor. I don't remember that I ever went to see the circus, except to see them when they went by that place.

Every spring, she would go to buy some clothes for me—my grandmother, but I called her my mother. She saved her own money and would buy the clothes. She did a lot of things, making pies, cakes or bread. She used to make beautiful home-made bread. She sold it for 25 cents a big loaf. Everybody would come over to buy some. She couldn't make enough. Then she would make the Indian hulled corn. It used to come in bags and the corn was big. I've never seen any here lately. She'd take a great big black pot and put the corn in and boil it for so long. There was some stuff over it and she'd say she would have to take all of that off. So she took stove ashes and put it in the pot and that stuff would come out—it would just burst to make them clean. She'd take the whole thing and take it down to the lake and wash them all in the lake. When she got done with them you wouldn't think there was anything on them before. Then she would get some beans and cook them and then put them together with the corn. They call it corn soup; that's the Indian food. She put pork in it, salt and pepper. It took a long time to cook it in a great big pot. She would tell people she was going to make that, and everybody would bring their pots and pans and she'd put it into their pans and they would pay her for it. That was after we lived at the Reed place because I can remember it. I wouldn't try it because it's too much trouble. That's how she made her money. Then she would go with some other women and sometimes old men that weren't working up to Big Lake to get cranberries. Sometimes we'd fill up bags and bags there were so many cranberries. I used to do it with them. We'd stay right there on one of those islands for two or three days. I was still young. Then we'd bring it back and clean it and then go sell it downtown—or swap it for vegetables or anything edible. She made money all the time and she saved it. We didn't eat like rich people.

They saved apples. They saved everything. They used to have turnips. My grandfather would go out and get some turnips. When he came back, he'd cut one in half and scrape the turnips with a table knife and eat them. I got used to doing that myself. Every once in a while, I eat them raw like that now.

He used to make canoes—the very best canoes that anybody could make. He made ax handles and paddles. It used to make me mad when he'd make me sit down in one of the canoes he was making—the canoes would be hanging and he wanted the canvas to tighten, so he would make me sit there when I wanted to go out and play. While I was sitting there he would tell me a story so that I would stay. He used to have a wheel with a handle on it to sharpen his ax—that I didn't like to do either. I used to have to crank that wheel. I used to do a lot of things for him. When he got wood in the woods, I used to go with him.

In the spring, we used to go about a mile in the woods on a hill. There was a lot of maple trees. I used to help him. They used to have great big cans or pails and they'd bore a hole in the tree and put this can on and the sap would come out and go into the pail. Every morning we used to take all of them and put them in big barrels. They would make a fireplace 8 to 12 feet long and all the big pots would be hanging to make the syrup. I didn't like to stay there because it took so long and I was still a child. My grandmother would boil that herself. My grandfather would help her fill up those barrels, but then he would take off again. Just her and I were there outside. When my grandfather thought it was about time to be done, he'd come back with a big sled. Then, they'd talk and test the syrup to see if it's still too thin or just right and after a while they would get it right. Then they poured it into containers and we took it home. There was always a lot of porcupines there in the trees making noise at each other. Squirrels and rabbits were all over the place.

My grandmother would buy clothes for me in the spring and in the fall—just twice. We got them in Calais. An old man had a car—maybe he was the only one who had one and we'd go hire him to take us. Or, before that, the train used to come up here to Princeton from Calais. We'd get on the train and go. I often wondered how we ever made it back from Eastport—such a long way when you don't know how to talk English. She'd have her money separate from his because he had more. He used to work as a guide for William Lyman Underwood—the one that made the typewriters. I still have the first book that he wrote. He signed it and sent it to my grandfather. It says "to my faithful guide of the woods in Maine and companion to the big city of New York." When he died, my grandfather didn't want to guide any more. They were more than friends. They were together when they were here in the summer. He came to Maine every summer. He'd just bring his cameras—he wouldn't kill a deer—he'd just take a picture of them, even at night. That book I have has pictures of my grandfather catching fish at night with a spear.

I was a very happy person before my grandparents died, but after I got married I started having sad experiences. My grandfather died while I was carrying Sylvia and my grandmother died when I was carrying Clare and I don't know how old they were. I try to put that picture out of my mind—the time I was not happy when my husband, Simon, ran around with anyone. I was married when I was seventeen. We didn't have much to eat. I was living here on the reservation. He stayed five years and finally he ran off with a woman as old as my mother because she drank and had a little money so he didn't have to work. After he left, we didn't have much of anything. I had seven children. We'd fry potatoes in lard. This girl used to stay with me and helped me with the children. She loved to stay with me and I told her she could stay as long as she wanted as long as she didn't starve. I told her we didn't have anything, but she wanted to stay. At lunch time she'd say, "what are we going to have." I'd tell her that we'd have potatoes and lard. She'd say "what about supper time," and I'd tell her we'd have lard and potatoes.

Mary Gabriel Interviewed 11/20/82 by Debbie Brooks, Acc. #NA1621, Northeast Archives of Folklore and Oral History, Orono, Maine. Reprinted by permission of the Northeast Folklore Society.

Margaret Philbrook Smith
1913–

Margaret Philbrook, like Alberta Poole, was an island child. Her island was Hurricane, west of Vinalhaven in Penobscot Bay, and her reminiscences tell two stories: one of her carefree and unusual years on the island, and the other of the sad and sudden demise of the village of Hurricane.

Hurricane Island is a mile long, three-quarters of a mile wide, and solid granite. When General Davis Tillson bought the island, with two partners, for one thousand dollars in 1870, he had plans for a granite-quarrying operation there. A man of great organizational ability and energy, he built the Hurricane Island Granite Company into a notable success. After the Civil War, in which he served, granite was in great demand for public buildings and monuments as well as for such things as paving stones and breakwaters. Tillson imported stonecutters from Italy, Ireland, Scotland, and Wales, from Finland, Sweden, and Norway. He built a community on the island that could accommodate up to a thousand residents and that included six large boarding houses, private dwellings, a school, town hall, Catholic church, company store, and a dance pavillion.

The granite was easily accessible, the workers were skilled, and granite-carrying sloops and schooners tied up at the wharf to load cut and finished stone and to carry it off to ports to the south. Hurricane Island granite went to Washington, D.C., for the Washington Monument and the Library of Congress; to Saint Louis for the post office; to Boston for the courthouse; and to Chicago for paving blocks.

A lively international community lived on Hurricane. The Italians brought a version of bocce ball to supplement the baseball team, formed the Italian Socialist Club, and added their music to the songs of the British

The Philbrook children sailed their boats on a small pond at Hurricane Island.
Courtesy of Eleanor Motley Richardson.

Isles and Scandinavia. All was not serene, however; there were labor disputes. The granite cutters' unions resented the not so benevolent dictatorship of General Tillson and fought for the right to have their wages paid directly to them instead of to the company store. They reported the company's dishonest practices on government contracts to President Hayes. They very likely resented the ban on liquor. Visiting ships—floating bars—helped them to circumvent this Tillson tenet. When liquor finally was allowed on the island, a lock-up had to be built immediately.

Tillson's business interests expanded to include quarrying on other islands, a fish-packing plant on Hurricane, a whale-oil factory on Green's Island, and orange and vegetable groves in Florida. He gradually turned the Hurricane Island Granite Company over to his son-in-law, William S. White. Tillson died in 1895.

In 1914 two tragedies befell the Hurricane Island Granite Company, which was already in trouble because of the increased use of concrete in large construction projects. A granite scow captained by Ansel Philbrook, father of Margaret, foundered while under tow in a storm and sank. The men were rescued, but twelve hundred tons of granite were lost. Two weeks later, John Landers, the indispensable superintendent of the company, died suddenly of typhoid fever. Company officials immediately stopped drilling and blasting operations, and the workers all left the island during the next few days, looking for work and leaving their homes and many belongings behind them. Hurricane became a ghost town.

Three years later the Ansel Philbrook family moved out to the island. Philbrook's charge was to serve as caretaker and to demolish the abandoned houses and public buildings. His ten children were enlisted to help with this project, and so Margaret Philbrook, in the stories she related to Eleanor M. Richardson for the book Hurricane Island: The Town That Disappeared, *tells us of the eerie quality of life in a deserted town, of the grand fun of having a whole island to play on, and of the unusual experience of being part of a demolition team.*

Margaret Philbrook moved off Hurricane Island to go to high school, went to work, married, raised a family, and now lives in Eliot. The island, now owned by a physician from New York, is home to the Outward Bound School—a program designed to "conduct safe adventure-based courses structured to inspire self-esteem, self-reliance, concern for others and care for the environment." Margaret Philbrook knew about all of these things.

Childhood in a Ghost Town

I don't know how my father got the caretaker job on Hurricane, but when the superintendent died and the island went down in 1914, a lot of people moved off the very next day. They left everything—tables all set just as they was laid out. There was nothing for them to do but to go get a job somewhere else. . . . I was born on Vinalhaven in 1913. I think it was 1917 when we went out there. I remember my father packing up the town records and shipping them off to Augusta. That's when we first went to Hurricane. I don't remember what the box looked like. It didn't cost anything to ship anything hardly either. A few pennies.

My mother was born Nellie Raymond on Vinalhaven in 1885. My father, Ansel Philbrook, was born on North Haven in 1878. They lived on North Haven for a long time when they was first married. I think one of my brothers was born on North Haven in fact, two of them might have been—Charles and Ernest—I can't seem to remember where them two was born. But I know they must have had to live there before I was born because that's where they came from when they moved down to Hurricane. North Haven doesn't have a granite rock on it but Vinalhaven's full of rocks. North Haven's got just about enough to make a few stone walls.

My father and mother had lived out there on Hurricane before with their family—with the children that was born before I was born. . . . Willard, another brother, was just two years older than I was. We used to pal around together, Willard and I.

We had one brother that was born on Hurricane while the island was running. His name was Pearl R. Philbrook. He was born in 1912 just the year before I was born, April the 25th. Right after the *Titanic* sank. He lives in Springfield, Massachusetts now. I don't know why they named him Pearl. I guess our mother must have just liked the name Pearl or something. During the war he had trouble. They'd draft him and tell him where to go. And he'd get there and they'd be all women. It was a woman's name, Pearl. He said three times they got him down there, then they'd send him back home again. So he never did go to war. . . .

All of the time we were there, Hurricane was a plantation form of government. When Hurricane became part of Vinalhaven, they changed the name of Vinalhaven at the same time. The Haven used to be a capital "H." And then they made all one word out of it. Three or four years we didn't go to school at all because the state was dickering how or whether they was going to put a teacher on there to teach us children. Six of us that would have gone to school. But you had to have seven to make it compulsory for them to put a teacher on there. So then they decided that our father would have to take us to Vinalhaven. But he wasn't going to take us unless he was going to get paid for it. So they gave him $2 a day for landing us on Vinalhaven. And he used to land us at the shore in the Thoroughfare next to Green Island. And then we walked two miles to school and two back. He'd come and get us at night.

He had a sloop boat. It had a sail on it but usually he used the engine. And when it rained he'd take us way down to Carver's Harbor. And we'd walk from there. And then if it come up a storm, late in the fall, we'd go just as long as we dared to. My sister Dot got seasick every time. She never did get used to it. We had to stay over on Vinalhaven sometimes. We'd go along the road with our brothers and knock on the doors and ask the people if they'd take us in. The boys always found places for Dot and me first.

Sometimes we had to stay in the boat. As you look across Hurricane to Vinalhaven there's a place called Old Harbor. My father used to get up as far as there sometimes—it'd be an awful storm—and he'd drop anchor and we'd ride it out all night. And our mother used to say—I've heard her tell it so many times—she said she almost went crazy. She'd look out, you know, and she'd just see the end of the mast because it was rocking so. She was afraid we'd all get drowned before we ever got across. We laid there all night lots of times. So we went for seven years back and forth to Vinalhaven that way. But just in the spring and fall. Our older brothers taught us in the winter. We played school just about every day. We had the old school desks from the island and the school things in the top of the barn.

We lived in a house down near the island's steamboat landing. That big old barn was between our house and the road before you got to the cove. We walked up the hill a little ways to a well for our water. We were supposed to tear all those buildings down. Some people owned their buildings, but not too many. They were mostly all company houses. The ones that owned them, some of them wanted to tear them down and save the lumber and make a house somewhere else. Mr. White owned most of them. He'd sell a whole house, that's the way he'd do it, because when we tore them down, we tore them down in such a way that the lumber was all saved. The windows even. Everything was saved. And then, we used to put the lumber and everything down to the wharf and someone who bought it would come with boats and get it. Then they'd either build it somewhere else or make whatever they wanted out of it. A lot of houses have got Hurricane lumber in them.

I had eight brothers, six older and two younger. Me and my sister helped tear the buildings down, too. In the summer and winter we tore down buildings. And we'd slide the chimney bricks down to the wharf on our sleds during the winter.

One time my brothers, Ernest and William, took it into their heads to go around the island pushing over outhouses. Our father was in one.

I used to wear a sailor hat all the time. They couldn't keep that hat off me. And I was frozen all the time. I never got warm. It was my system, I guess. I had to have clothes, coats, long stockings and everything. Well, it's about 15 degrees colder than Vinalhaven. You get a rake of the wind right down through Hurricane Sound. . . .

When you came straight up the hill from the steamboat wharf, the church was on your left. I don't think the church was moved to North

Haven like you've heard. And I don't remember a Protestant church. Just the Catholic one. It had three beautiful leaded stained glass windows on each side. They each had a picture of a saint, or something, and on the bottom was a square with the name of the person who donated it. I went back once, after I grew up and we moved. I went back two or three times but the last time was in 1939, I guess. And the door was down then, and instead of going up the steps, people was walking on that door and going in. But someone had broken in and stole the carpet. There was no carpet on the floor any more. But the Catholic people came over and took all the artifacts and things out of there. They went to Rockland, I think. Over in the Catholic church. So as far as them moving the church, I never heard of them moving the church.

You know, I can't seem to remember what became of the town hall or where it even set. Unless it was called—they didn't say that it was a socialist hall did they? Because they had a lot of people on there that was, what do you call them—socialists or something? Yup, and that was their hall. The Italians built it. They used it for all kinds of things. . . .

The schoolhouse was a great big building all by itself. Do you know the old steamboat landing? Well, you go right straight up from there, that was a road at one time, and there was a sidewalk on the left. You went part way up the hill and turned right after the McCormack house and that was Broadway. But if you didn't turn, and you went up to the top of the hill, on your right there was a great big building and that was the school house. We tore that down and Roy Coombs bought it. He hired us to help him tear it down. I remember we pulled nails forever. I don't think he put the building up somewhere else but he used the lumber for something. Right beyond the school was what we called Ol' Lady Landers' house. It had the most beautiful apple tree in the yard—with sweet russet apples.

Did you ever hear of Broadway? It was nothing but one big ledge. It was beautiful, all white. It was white just like you'd scrubbed it. There were four or five houses on one side. There was two houses, the McCormack house on the right and the Shields house on the left. Then there was a space. You could keep on going up Broadway and there was four or five more houses. And then as you got up to the end of it there was three or four nice big houses up there.

We used to get a lot of snow in those winters. It was up to the cross bars of the telephone poles. It would come a hard crust. And we would climb up on top of the snow and we would slide down the snowbank and that's how we would get into a lot of them houses. The snow would go to the bottom of the windows. Then we would go up on that snow and climb in through the windows. But believe you me, we covered our tracks so our father wouldn't know we'd been in there. Our father wouldn't allow us to go in houses. Kid-fashion, the minute he was gone for one day off the island, why we'd go and have the greatest time going in the houses. But the doors was all locked, you see, and we couldn't get in, but sometimes there'd be a square of glass out and we were small enough that we could squeeze through that square of glass.

The furniture and everything was all in them. And the table was set just like they'd walked right away. In those days, you know, when they'd get up from the table and the women would do the dishes and put everything away, they'd set the table for the next meal. And, of course, there was tablecloths on every table. They never ate off a bare table. There was no plastic of course. There was oilcloth and cloth. . . .

Down at the southern end of the island is Barsugli's Cove and down there was Barsugli's boarding house, next to Barge's Head. There was another one set right next to it that was called the Block. And another next to that and that was Nichols'. Then across the way was the Patterson's boarding house. Then down beyond that there was another one. But as I remember, it was nothing but a cellar hole then. That may have been a place for the men to wash up when they come in from the quarry and took off their dirty workclothes. A kind of bath house. I don't know what the name of that one was. So there were five big boarding houses. The water would come almost right up to where they were built.

We used to have a lot of fun in them old boarding houses. We used to play all kinds of games in them. There were stoves, great big black iron stoves that burned wood. And they had a door on both sides. And you could crawl right through them. So we used to hide in there. We used to play hide and go seek. They had what they called a smoke room. In the evening, that's where the menfolks used to gather. There was a big old pot-bellied stove in there. But I don't think the big rooms where they slept had any heat in them at all.

In the smaller houses they had just the woodstove in the kitchen. Up in the top of the ceiling they'd have a thing they called a register. That was all the heat they had in the bedrooms. They must have had to bring a lot of the wood onto the island. The big old boats with firewood used to come to Vinalhaven, even. They used to burn everything in those days, even spruce. That's why they had so many fires.

Down on the western side was a great big building. It was a double tenement up in that little cove. That was Tom Sullivan's and Jerry Sullivan's. They were two brothers with their families. One lived in one half of the house and one lived in the other. Tom was the postmaster. Jerry drove the grocery wagon.

As you came up from the wharf was a big, drab building. That was the store and in the front corner, that was the post office. They had a big platform that was right across the end of the whole building. And they walked up on that and put their letters in the slot. They used to put money in if you didn't have a stamp. So when we tore that building down we got a lot of money out of that corner where it slipped through the crack. There might still be some there. The old Indian heads and the old "V" nickels had a Liberty on one side and a big "V" on the back instead of a buffalo. And there were some nickels with a big "5" on them. And right across from that store was a bowling alley. My mother used to keep one of them big old, bowling pins at the top of the stairs as a weapon when my father was away with the older boys and she was at home with the younger ones. One night my brother, Charlie, came home late. He'd got some new white gloves he hadn't told her about. When he put his hand around the door, she thought it was a prowler and he almost got it with the bowling pin.

With ten children, we didn't have any trouble finding things to do. In the winter time we played with our sleds and things. They were homemade, too. Mostly, we'd slide down Broadway because that was almost a glare of ice. We had the whole run of the island. We had beautiful places to play.

But I'll tell you what we used to do. I don't know if anybody in the world ever did it, but some apple trees on there had real beautiful apples. But they were so old that they didn't have too many apples on them. They wouldn't have a barrel on the whole tree. But we gathered up all there was. Each one of us kids would take a box and we would go into the woods someplace and dig a hole and bury them, way, way down where the frost couldn't get to them come wintertime. Then in the springtime, when our apples in the barrels that our father had bought was getting low, we'd go and dig up our apples. And we'd trade them with our brothers to get something they had.

If you went by the school house at the top of the hill and kept on going on a little bit of a slope, and you went for about, oh, maybe a quarter of a mile along there, on the left was the pond. We had our play boats in the pond. Our brothers and father made us the boats. We had an awful lot of them. And we had engines in them all. They were made from old clockworks.

The little quarry hole is the one we used to play in the most, even more than the pond. Not the quarry in the valley, but the little one next [to] the big quarry. There was only one place that was real deep. The big quarry had trout in it. When we tore down those boarding houses, they had wooden sinks in them. Father gave them to us kids. We stopped up the hole and they were our boats. We had canvas over the bottom and we painted them with three or four coats of paint. And then they were waterproof. They were big, five or six feet long by three feet wide. And there was two I think, in every one of them boarding houses. That's what we paddled around in. Our mother used to let us go down and play in them any time we wanted to.

People came out the year round while we were on the island. You'd be apt to see anybody anytime. Then there used to be a lot of those big yachts come down from North Haven, the Herzogs and people like that. There was no vandalism or anything. There was some people who came back and got their furniture. My mother bought some furniture out of some different houses. I don't remember what become of the rest of it. Maybe thrown away. Maybe they gave it away.

We used to play at J.T. Lander's house, across from the church. One time my mother went down to the barn in the summertime to pull some shingles out of the pile to build a fire. A big old frame was sitting on top of the pile of shingles. So I went down, kid-fashion, and I got to playing with that frame. And my mother said to leave that alone or you'll have that down on your head. Of course, I kept right on, kid-fashion. And bye and bye, it fell down, and there was a nail in it. It hit her right on her head. I was scairt to death. I thought she was going to give me a licking. So I ran out of there as fast as I could, and I ran up to Lander's house. They had a great big horse chestnut tree up there. And I went up that horse chestnut tree. I stayed there until dark because I was afraid she was going to give me a licking. I think I gave away about every toy that I owned to my brothers and my sister if they would just play around that tree so I wouldn't be up there all alone. Well, it came almost dark and my mother came up and says, "Well, you can come down now." So I come down. But I didn't get no licking. I don't think she ever licked us once.

You know, I've thought so many times, if it had been me on that island with ten kids, I would have been crazy. All them little kids running all over that island, they could have got drowned in those quarry holes. I don't know if she ever worried about us. But she must have. My brother Willard and I used to chum around together. And then Dot and Pearl was together a lot. We all played together. But if we went anyplace around the island it was always Willard and I that would go. So every morning at five o'clock, Willard and I'd get up, winter and summer, and go all the way around that island to see what had come ashore in the night. We could have slipped overboard with all of the ice in the dead of the winter.

We used to find a lot of weir poles. You probably don't know what a weir pole is. Well, they used to make weirs to catch herring in the coves. And these poles would come up out of the mud. They'd get loose and drift off and they'd have to replace them. They were nice poles and you could get quite a lot of money for them Maybe a dollar. That was a lot of money in those days. So we earned quite a lot of money by getting those. We bought a lot of our school clothes with the money.

My big brother, Smith, got a new hatchet one winter and he wanted all of us little kids to see him cut down a tree. That tree was frozen and bent down in the snow. When he hit it, up came the tree and broke his nose.

Then we used to have what we called a sling-shot. We all had one. We used to make ours out of the crotch of a tree. Then we'd take an old piece of rubber that was down around the works and tie it on. And then we'd take the tongue of our shoes for the thing to put the rock in. But we didn't have rocks too much. We had what you call the ends of plug drills. They'd drill a hole in the stone with a plug drill. They get dull and after a while they'd break off and they'd throw them away. Then they'd make a new end. When you hammer it, it comes down like a chisel. Then you hammer it once, then you have to turn it, then hammer it again and that makes the hole. That was all hand work. And when the hole was deep enough, they'd put two little things in there. Then they'd put a wedge down the middle and they'd hit that and that would break the stone along the grain of the rock. If you didn't go with the grain you'd break it and lose your stone. It wouldn't be no good.

We shot birds—them little sea birds—with our slingshots. We could hit them things as quick as could be. And then we'd take them home and cook them. We used to call them Jenny No-Tails. They were just about as big as a pigeon. They were winter birds. We'd have to fish them out of the water after we'd killed them. We'd take a pole or something and try to get them ashore. I don't know why we didn't fall overboard.

Besides birds, we ate a lot of fish, I know that. We caught them. Lobsters were always around the wharf. You could fish them up with a fish line. You could see them down there. You'd keep the hook going up and down until by and by it would catch on something and you'd pull the lobster up. There was much more lobsters then. Mother used to tell when she was little she'd go down on the shore and just pick them up. Doesn't seem possible. That would have been the early 1890s.

We used to eat a lot of salt fish. Salt fish was good. Our father had a business of salt fish while he lived there. He used to buy fish and salt them in big old hogsheads. Then he sold them. Codfish, hake. You had to freshen it out. I love salt fish. You soak it in water and let it come to a boil. Then change the water, then boil it again, then taste a little piece of it to see if it's freshened out enough. You still want some salt left in it. Making salt fish, first you catch the fish and split them down through the middle, then lay them out flat. Some people put them in pickle. But usually they plaster the salt all over them, rub it right in, and then put them out in the sun to dry and then turn 'em over to dry the other side. It takes three, four or five days to dry one fish. They get hard, not awfully hard, because they're too thick and there's too much salt in them. And that's a salt fish. And you don't have to refrigerate them.

Mother made two quarts of flour into biscuits three times a day. That's how much her sifter held. The thing we liked the best. We used to have it for supper on Sunday nights usually. We'd fry up some salt pork and put some molasses in your plate, put some salt pork fat in that and sop the biscuits in that. That was good. You could sprinkle the salt pork pieces over the top. You ate any kind of vegetable you could get. We had a garden. But our father used to buy a lot of vegetables. And he used to buy barrels of apples and eight barrels of flour every year, white flour. They used to buy sugar by the barrel in those days. I don't remember maple syrup, just molasses. We didn't have too many sweets. I suppose there was so many of us my mother couldn't make too many sweets. She used to make a great big one-layer cake. We used to love that. And she used to make johnny cake, like corn muffins only there isn't quite so much leavening in it. It's a little bit harder. It has a little bit of sugar like corn bread.

We loved mussels. We had lots of mussels and clams. There was one place when the tide would go out extra long up on the northern end of Hurricane that you could dig clams. You go by the valley and by the little quarry. And as you go north around the end, when there was an extra low tide. That's where we found them.

We had hens, a sow and a horse and a pig. There were berries, lots of raspberries. Not too many blueberries. We used to go across to Green's Island to get blueberries. And we used to go over there and get a lot of apples. There's a lot of nice apple trees on Hurricane, too. There was some blackberries and a lot of huckleberries, like blueberries, but on a high bush and black. And there were lots of wild strawberries. We could go over to Vinalhaven and get food. Our father went once a month in the winter to get supplies. They had so many things laid in that there wasn't too many things except the staples that you might have to get. We had milk from our cow and eggs from our chickens.

Sometimes we got sick. Once, all ten of us children caught the measles at the same time. Our mother's pig caught them, too. She doctored him along with the rest of us and he lived. My brother, Lyford, whatever he was playing with, he put it up his nose. One day he was helping my mother cut up beans so he put them up his nose and couldn't get them out. They tried everything, a button hook, a crochet hook. Finally they had to go over to the doctor in Vinalhaven to get the beans out.

The winter Hurricane Sound froze over we were on the island five days with nothing to eat. And Albert was a baby. Our father was going to kill the cow the next day if they couldn't get across to get any food at Vinalhaven. Well, they didn't get to Vinalhaven. Instead they took the town dory from the boathouse on the shore, and went to Heron Neck Light on Green's Island and they telephoned the order from there to Vinalhaven. The steamboat, when it came our way from Carver's Harbor on Vinalhaven, was supposed to stop when he could see Hurricane. Then the boys and my father was to row that dory over to the steamboat to get our groceries. But, it was all froze over. What father and the boys had to do was get out on the ice and they'd pull the boat and they'd get back in because the ice would break, and then they'd push with the oars until they'd get to another big ice cake. Then they'd get out and pull the boat again.

But the steamboat never stopped. It kept right on going. So the next day when the ice had kind of broke up they got to Heron Neck Light again. They telephoned again and the captain said that he would see to it that they stopped. So they went out the next day and they got the groceries off the steamboat that day—the same way—pulling the dory over the ice.

Us ten kids were all howling we were so hungry. Our mother sent the oldest boys around in the houses to see if they could find anything that the people had left that we could eat. Do you know what a firkin is? Well, they found one of those full of brown stuff that looked like graham flour. Mother had plenty of fat left from when they killed the pig, so she mixed that flour up with some of the milk from the cow and made doughnuts out of it. And we ate it. But we didn't know if it would kill us or not. Nobody knew what it was. We named it "Rough on Rats." That was a survival, all right. But father didn't have to kill the cow. They got across on the fifth day. Of course since Albert was a baby, he needed the milk from the cow. So they held off just as long as they dared. But they was going to kill it the next day.

We left the island because it was sold. So my father was no longer the caretaker. Anyway, we'd torn down most all the houses. My father and brothers went back a couple more winters to take down the rest. They moved to Vinalhaven and I finished out school there.

From: Eleanor Morley Richardson, *Hurricane Island: The Town That Disappeared*. Rockland, Maine: Island Institute, 1989. Reprinted by permission of Eleanor M. Richardson.

David Etnier

About the Editors

"Maine people, like people everywhere, organize themselves first and last as families. One way to understand how a family works is to see it through a young person's eyes," write Samuella and Charles Shain. They planned *Growing Up in Maine,* their second anthology, not only as a cross-section of Maine history but also as a record of how children's lives have changed over the generations. Their combined backgrounds—Charles's in American Literature and Samuella's in Library Science—make the Shains the ideal editorial team to compile this unusual collection.

The Shains both have longtime Maine connections. They presently live in Georgetown and have traveled widely across the state in the course of researching their books. Charles is now retired from teaching careers at Princeton University, Carleton College, and Connecticut College. Samuella uses her talents as a writer and researcher on behalf of a variety of philanthropic, educational, and environmental organizations. Their other co-edited book, *The Maine Reader,* was published by Houghton Mifflin in 1991.